Also by John O'Connor

Postgate: How the Washington Post Betrayed Deep Throat, Covered Up Watergate, and Began Today's Partisan Advocacy Journalism

THE MYSTERIES OF WATERGATE

What Really Happened

John O'Connor

A POST HILL PRESS BOOK
ISBN: 978-1-63758-613-6
ISBN (eBook): 978-1-63758-614-3

The Mysteries of Watergate:
What Really Happened
© 2022 by John O'Connor
All Rights Reserved

Cover design by John O'Connor and Allison Baltzersen

Post Hill Press
New York • Nashville
posthillpress.com

Published in the United States of America
1 2 3 4 5 6 7 8 9 10

This book is dedicated to my great family: my wife Jan and our children John W., Christine/Christy, and Caroline/Carly, and those they have brought into the fold, including grandson John Kawaja, son-in-law Evan Valle, and "adopted" son Ike Nwankwo.

TABLE OF CONTENTS

SECTION 1: WATERGATE MYSTERIES

SECTION 2: WATERGATE JOURNALISM

Image of President Richard Nixon, public domain.

PREFACE

FEW UNDERSTAND WHAT REALLY HAPPENED in the Watergate scandal. And even fewer comprehend that the cause of this opacity is the selective reporting of the *Washington Post*. This book is designed to correct this lack of clarity. For the first time in fifty years, the public can learn the true, highly intriguing story.

Until now, The *Washington Post*'s Watergate reporting has been hailed as the gold standard for all Western Hemisphere journalism. And I for decades was among its loudest fans. This felicitous combination of gold-plated source ("Deep Throat") and tireless young reporters (the *Post*'s Bob Woodward and Carl Bernstein) was, to my way of thinking and that of many others, journalism at its best.

This reporting changed the course of history. Richard Nixon had been overwhelmingly reelected in November 1972, five months after the Watergate Office Building burglary arrests, carrying forty-nine of fifty states. His popularity was still soaring in November 1972, while America enjoyed both great prosperity and hegemony over the free world.

But in the wake of the *Post*'s sensational, relentless, "investigative" journalism, Richard Nixon was back on his heels by the time the televised Ervin Committee hearings began in May 1973.

Eventually, forty Nixon administration officials were convicted of crimes. Richard Nixon became the only president in our history to resign from office, forced to do so by his imminent impeachment that was sure to succeed. Successor President Gerald Ford called the episode, appropriately, "our country's long national nightmare." A large factor in the election of Jimmy Carter was the country's disgust with Watergate, combined with the pious Carter's promise to have a government "as good as the American people." This, of course, was a direct slap at Nixon and all Republicans.

A well-meaning but weak liberal-leaning Carter begat strong conservative Ronald Reagan, seemingly far to the Right of the moderate Nixon, the beginning of the Left-Right seesaw that the country continues to ride. Watergate also enshrined a number of emerging legal and ethical norms such as "shield" laws for reporters, governmental respect for their sources, and "whistleblower" protections.

Not all outgrowths of Watergate resulted in sanguinary effects. As a result of the post-Watergate Senate Church Committee hearings on intelligence agency abuses in 1975, the FBI's decades-long program of warrantless counterintelligence surveillance came under intense scrutiny. The ultimate result was the conviction of the head of the FBI's Watergate investigation, W. Mark Felt Sr., for a legitimate counterintelligence operation to locate members of the violent Weather Underground Organization. The result of his conviction was the Foreign Intelligence Surveillance Act of 1978 (FISA), which allowed agents to be protected against charges for good faith, honestly predicated counterintelligence operations. The recent "Russiagate" fiasco, however, showed that what should have been unnecessary FISA legislation has the unintended consequence of enabling politicized surveillance to the harm of our country, both on the Right and the Left.

We come now to yet another unintended effect of Watergate's highly praised journalism. Many idealistic young people, inspired by the reformist effects of this reporting, eagerly oriented their careers toward the media. But in doing so, these aspiring journalists were necessarily seeking political *impact*. But if that is their goal, then the incentive exists to report only one side of the story, or to report that side in such a slanted fashion that it becomes untruthful. In short, Pulitzer Prizes and bestsellers, it was rationally concluded, come when "investigative" journalism yields scalps. Investigative journalism, then, necessarily morphs into prosecutorial journalism. But these unlicensed prosecutors do not have the same training and experience of law enforcement investigators, nor do they recognize the same ethical and prudential guardrails.

Accordingly, it is at least arguable that the slanted, partisan journalism that results from Watergate-style reporting is a major cause of the yawning divisions in our society. Extreme reporting in one direction usually causes an equal and opposite reaction in the other direction, perhaps through conventional media journalism, but often, more ominously, from social media association. There is no doubt but that our tribally riven society is to some degree the result of Watergate.

But one may ask, per our discussion here, wasn't Watergate the result of a felicitous combination of energetic young journalists and a highly knowledgeable, experienced source, Deep Throat? Yes, to some degree. But in this book, we will deeply analyze what really happened in Watergate and how it was described by the universally lauded journalism, that is, the gulf between the narrative and the facts.

How do we explain this divergence given the reliability of not only Deep Throat, but also a number of informed, non-partisan FBI agents, the true heroes of Watergate? Please recall that one development of the scandal was the widespread use of anonymous sources. While the question is often asked whether reporters should trust the credibility of anonymous sources, the better question is how does the public know that the reporter has reported the source's insights truthfully, or, more aptly, that he has reported *all* of the source's insights?

In this book, I will detail the extraordinarily interesting factual strands of Watergate, which, if woven together with skill and candor, would have made for a much more intriguing, disturbing and, yes, entertaining narrative than the single-strand story provided by the *Washington Post*. In short, Watergate should have been a three-ring circus, not a one ringer.

We noted above that the misunderstanding engendered by this reporting caused the societally harmful prosecution of the supremely capable head of the Watergate FBI investigation, Deputy Director Felt. Ironically, it was Felt, I had concluded in 1976, who was "Deep Throat" of Watergate notoriety and mystery. In 1974, Woodward and Bernstein's bestseller *All the Presidents Men* featured the highly mysterious character Deep Throat, an executive branch official who met Woodward in late-night garage conferences to guide the reporter in his investigation.

I was fascinated by the Deep Throat character and thought him highly important for reasons beyond Watergate. If Deep Throat was a one-off, a "unicorn" who, against self-interest and propelled by conscience, blew a whistle on his own political tribe, then this source was heroic but of no institutional moment.

But, on the other hand, if Deep Throat was a public servant talking to Woodward to keep the system free of corruption, then his cooperation was the residue of design, a self-curative bureaucracy helping to keep the ship sailing straight.

I spent the next two years as a compulsive hobbyist, trying to assess the identity of Deep Throat. In fact, I saw in Deep Throat's description the suggestion that his methods, which seemed inscrutable to Woodward, were in fact impelled by ethical concerns I understood as a Department of Justice prosecutor.

For instance, when Deep Throat told a beseeching Woodward that the reporter had to do it "his way," the reporter implored him not to continue to play this "chickenshit" game. As a prosecutor, I understood the distinction between giving a reporter confidential information from a case file, which is unethical, and telling him to go question the witness himself, which was perfectly proper. I saw Deep Throat's imposed limitations as the recognition of ethical guardrails.

In any case, there were far more clues than this pointing to a DOJ high official, which, by process of elimination, eventually led me to identify Felt, definitively, by late 1976.

This process left me with a bigger question. If Woodward was indeed a "friend" of Deep Throat, trying his best to protect his identity, why would he lard his book with abundant clues such that a young prosecutor could easily prove the identify of his source?

Indeed, why would the reporter tell anyone at all that he had a *secret* source? Shouldn't the fact that a source was *secret* actually be kept *secret*?

This apparent contradiction puzzled me profoundly. The only justification I inferred, perhaps speculated, is that Woodward had paid a portion of the book proceeds to Felt, retired at the time of the publication. This would make the outing of his secret source ethical. But not otherwise.

After identifying Felt to my satisfaction in 1976, I looked forward to my wedding in mid-1977, anticipating that I would soon be raising a family. With the expectation that I would need a job in the civil law sector of legal practice, I traded my criminal cases for civil cases then handled by a Civil Division lawyer champing at the bit to become a criminal prosecutor. His name was Robert Mueller, later a successful, well-regarded FBI director.

I, of course, did not think that anyone would be interested in who I had determined was Woodward's mysterious cohort known as Deep Throat, so I mentally closed the book on Watergate, went into private practice, and raised a family.

In 2002, by chance, I learned that my daughter's Stanford University chum, Nick Jones, was Mark Felt's grandson. When I found this out, I immediately said to Nick, "You know your granddad is Deep Throat, don't you?" Nick was stunned, noting that his grandfather had always denied it but that there had been hints here and there. I asked him if I could talk to Mark because I believed I understood why he was keeping mum and what buttons I needed to push, such that he would feel better about his role as a secret source. The rest, as they say, is history.

The method I used to coax Mark to come out, it turns out, had great significance for posterity's understanding of the scandal. Per my plan, I first qualified myself as a Justice Department lawman. I told Mark I was an assistant U.S. attorney during Watergate. He nodded approvingly. My father was an FBI agent. Mark liked that. My father's former law partner, for whom I worked one summer, was William Ruckelshaus. More approval. I worked with Bob Mueller. In Mark's eyes, I was qualified as a lawman. I knew Mark cared deeply about how Justice Department types would view his actions. Did he do the right thing or was he a rogue, scofflaw agent? So, I said to him, "All of the prosecutors thought this guy Deep Throat was a great guy..." As soon as I said "Deep Throat, his fingers gripped his chair tightly to the point of white knuckles. His jaw tightened.

Then I continued, "...because he saved our justice system. He ensured that it was incorruptible..." As I continued, I saw his grip loosen and his light blue eyes seemed to melt, as if I were giving him absolution. I had hit it on the head: he did not want to be identified because it would reflect badly on his beloved FBI. But if he thought that the law enforcement community would understand the morality of his actions, that would embolden him to reveal his identity.

His actions, as I had for years inferred, resulted not from a hatred of Nixon and a corresponding desire to bring him down. Instead, he wanted the Bureau to do its job without interference and not be artificially limited in scope, as Nixon's men had thus far achieved by October 1972 when he first met Woodward in a garage.

There is another implicit and important aspect to this inferred motive: the narrative Felt originally had spun for Woodward was a reasonable *investigative hypothesis*, not clearly certain fact. This concept would come into play strongly as Woodward and Bernstein ("Woodstein") engaged in their sensational reporting. If it turned out that this highly reasonable investigative hypothesis did not bear fruit, but that another narrative (less unfriendly to Nixon) did, would Woodstein have the intellectual honesty to discard the disproven narrative in favor of the subsequently proven one? What if Deep Throat later realized that a highly sinister force outside the Oval Office was deeply involved, to such an extent that it was threatening murder of witnesses? Stay tuned for the answers.

I then talked to Mark about "coming out," that is, telling his story to the public while he was still alive rather than letting Woodward define him postmortem. As he took it all in, assessing my pitch, his daughter Joan and grandson Nick, seated next to Mark on the daybed, were stunned. The man who vigorously, sternly rejected this secret role for thirty years was clearly Deep Throat.

Mark still had not outright admitted his identity, and soon relapsed into coyness. However, as Joan had designed, the two watched a documentary on Watergate. Joan asked her dad, "Why do you think that Deep Throat did what he did?" Mark replied, "I wasn't out to get Nixon. I was just doing my job." That answer best defines the motive of Deep Throat, an ethical lawman.

Mark finally agreed that he would cooperate with a book or article announcing his identity, but he put on this permission one proviso: he would do so only if his friend Bob Woodward cooperated. I describe our subsequent dealings with Woodward in my book *Postgate*, so I will give here the *Reader's Digest* version of events.

I soon called Woodward to put him together with Mark. Oddly, I thought, he refused to acknowledge Mark's role and refused to cooperate in telling his story. For various reasons, as I detail in *Postgate*, I did not believe Woodward was refusing out of altruistic motives.

Woodward's refusal forced me to be Mark's megaphone. After that, I wrote an article for *Vanity Fair* magazine announcing Mark's identity. Without Woodward's cooperation, I was then forced to write the story of Deep Throat. I signed a book contract with a publisher, Public Affairs, which claimed to be independent, but which was in fact, unbeknownst to me, or evident in open sources, controlled by the *Post*, featuring *Post* editor in chief Ben Bradlee as its chairman of the board.

As I detailed in *Postgate*, the *Post*, through Public Affairs, continued to push my head into the journalistic dumpster to such an extent that I was forced to smell an unusually rancid odor, leading me to years of reexamination of the *Post*'s Watergate reporting.

As a result of my research, I determined that the Watergate "cover-up" of Richard Nixon was minor in comparison to the real Watergate cover-up by the *Washington Post*. Had Woodward cooperated with the source who launched his career, and who launched the *Post* into journalism's top tier, I never would have had the occasion to delve into this inquiry.

While *Postgate* examined the truthfulness of the reporting in lawyerlike detail, I wanted to write a more accessible, plain-spoken book that informed the broader public about what really happened in Watergate. One looking for specific factual citations to the record should look to *Postgate*'s dense notations in the compact portion of that book so devoted.

This is meant to be the book that, unlike *Postgate*, explains the narrative in an unhurried, common-sense manner, but without numerous citations. I hope that by learning what really occurred, and how it was covered up by the *Post*, we can now critically examine the modern project euphemistically termed "investigative journalism."

"Democracy Dies in Darkness," the *Washington Post* masthead daily proclaims. I agree. In accord with this aphorism, this book hopes to shed needed light on an important democratic sector, the media, or, in First Amendment language, the "press."

Enjoy.

SECTION 1
WATERGATE MYSTERIES

Image of Watergate complex in Washington, DC, public domain.

CHAPTER 1

BIG QUESTIONS FROM A SMALL BURGLARY

LET'S START AT THE BEGINNING. The most serious political scandal in United States history, arguably in the world's, is called Watergate. It began with the arrests on June 17, 1972, of five burglars (Virgilio Gonzalez, Bernard Barker, Eugenio Martinez, Frank Sturgis, and their burglary supervisor, James McCord) in the headquarters offices of the Democratic National Committee, or DNC, in Washington, DC. The scandal that unfolded over the next two years saw the only forcible removal ever of a United States president, Richard Nixon, as he faced articles of impeachment sure to cause his removal by the Senate.

Nixon had been overwhelmingly reelected, with forty-nine states in his column. Yet he was removed from office, largely through a journalistically pursued public trial. This scandal gave birth to a new era of so-called investigative journalism, which promised pursuit of governmental and business corruption without fear or favor. But it also gave the media prestige and political power it had never before enjoyed. So how did this scandal arise? And why did the media, particularly the *Washington Post*, play such a huge part?

On August 9, 1974, Nixon resigned his presidency. Eventually, forty members of his administration would be convicted of crimes, and thirty other individuals as well. Yes, Watergate may be called truly the mother of all scandals, yet the public has not yet been told, truthfully, what really happened in Watergate.

Because of the prominent role of the *Washington Post* in uncovering the scandal, especially through the stellar work of young reporters Bob Woodward and Carl Bernstein, this Pulitzer Prize-winning reporting has been universally recognized as both the birth and the crowning achievement of modern investigative journalism. This reporting advanced what had widely been understood initially to have been a "third-rate burglary," as presidential spokesman Ron Ziegler called it. The reporting, after several months of puzzlement, transmuted that third-rate burglary into a wholesale indictment of the entire presidential administration of the most powerful country on earth.

In the past, scandal reporting had been considered trashy. Watergate reporting brought aggressive investigative pieces out of these disreputable shadows, now no longer considered largely second-rate tabloid fodder. It was elevated not only into the mainstream, but also into mythological status, and it inspires all investigative journalism today.

So, if Watergate was the mother of all political scandals, then the *Post*'s Watergate reporting was the mother of all investigative journalism. Yet that journalism failed to tell us what really occurred. In effect, modern investigative journalism has been a powerful fourth branch of American government, accountable to no one. Its major figures have been recognized as powerful political players. More than one American president has eagerly read the latest offering of Bob Woodward, breathlessly anticipating how well or how poorly Woodward would paint him.

Much of American democracy today is influenced by Watergate-style journalism. It is often criticized, but nonetheless it seems to be impervious to that criticism. In any case, as meaningful as Nixon's resignation was and as impactful as the *Post* journalism was, the odd timing of the scandal's unfolding has caused little examination of the burglary itself, or its reporting. The administration's role in the burglary and the accuracy of the *Post*'s reporting of it has not been examined. How can that be, you might ask? Hundreds of thousands of news articles, three thousand in the *Post* alone, thousands of periodicals and hundreds of books have been written about Watergate. Movies have been made and television documentaries presented, continuing for almost fifty years, discussing the scandal and reporting by the *Post*. But there has been precious little analysis of the event that began Watergate: the burglary of the DNC headquarters in the Watergate Office building.

The reporting never examined in depth the details of the burglary itself, which seemed to be an open-and-shut case. After all, the burglars were caught in the act. Why should anybody go further than that? There was never a question about their participation. Rather, what excited the nation was, months later, the development of evidence that the Nixon administration's involvement was being covered up at the highest levels of the White House.

And what about Watergate journalism? Every journalism school in the country studies Watergate's reporting. High school textbooks praise it without qualification. Communications and history courses for college students not majoring in journalism treat this matter very seriously. Yet, like the burglary itself, this journalism, so universally praised, has never been scrutinized in any searching detail. How can that be?

It is counterintuitive to believe either of these proposi-
tions—that is, that neither the Watergate burglary nor the *Post's*
Watergate journalism about it has been deeply and critically
studied. Many decades after the scandal, we are going to attempt
here a deep dive into these two interrelated topics. When we
put a steady gaze to the timing of Watergate, we can begin to
understand why the key facts regarding both responsibility for
the burglary and the accuracy of the reporting about it have been
overlooked by posterity. For a number of reasons, but mainly the
initial success of the White House cover-up, followed by months
of its slow, ominous cracking, the country and the world's fascinated focus was on higher-level criminal culpability, beyond that
of the original seven defendants—that is, the five burglars caught
that morning and two nearby supervisors soon arrested. That
cracking didn't begin in earnest until around May of 1973, about
a year after the burglary of June 1972.

At this point in the scandal, April and May 1973, White House
counsel John Dean and Jeb Magruder, the deputy director of the
Committee to Reelect the President (CRP), turned prosecution
witnesses, the former against President Nixon, the latter against
recent attorney general and campaign director John Mitchell.
They successfully bargained for immunity with both regular
prosecutors and the Senate Watergate Committee. The prosecutors and the Senate Watergate Committee were now focused on
far bigger fish than the original seven burglary defendants.

Most of the attention was now placed on the possibility that
the president might be guilty, along with his close associates,
of obstructing the burglary investigation. For the next fifteen
months, the obstruction drama played out both in *Post* headlines
and in dramatic televised Senate testimony, largely following the
Post reporting. Eventually, it became a media feeding frenzy, with

outlets throughout the country forming a Greek chorus singing of Nixonian tragedy.

After the resigning Nixon departed on his helicopter from the White House lawn on August 9, 1974, media attention quickly centered around President Ford's pardon of Nixon, which roughly coincided with the trial of his inner circle, lasting several months through the fall of 1974. That inner circle included close presidential associates such as H. R. Haldeman, John Ehrlichman, and John Mitchell. Earlier in the spring of 1974, a spectacular bestselling book by Woodward and Bernstein, *All the President's Men*, featuring the mysterious supersource Deep Throat, transfixed the country. In 1976, an Oscar-winning movie of the same name, starring Robert Redford and Dustin Hoffman, followed.

Jimmy Carter's 1976 election, influenced by public revulsion at the horrors of Watergate, seemed to end the Watergate chapter of our country's history. So throughout this heady, exciting time, there had never been intense media concentration on the peculiar facts of the burglary itself, or on its specific motives.

During the first year of the scandal through May 1973, the *Post* enjoyed a virtual monopoly on the story, with no other paper or television network competing. The White House spin machine was very effective at minimizing any impact in the early months of the scandal, but it ultimately proved artless. Nixon's men were good mainly at downplaying, at distracting, but not at constructing a coherent counternarrative. So the public had never fixed in its mind what really happened in this puzzling, odd burglary. When the riveting testimony of John Dean was televised beginning in June 1973, the viewers were filling in a blank slate.

What exactly was Watergate about? The public watched and waited with bated breath for what the young White House lawyer had to say. His testimony concentrated on the president's role in the cover-up, and was largely credible and truthful regarding Nixon's actions; not surprisingly, Dean sugarcoated and muffled his own actions.

For these reasons, what otherwise were head-scratching puzzles about the burglary were put aside. The presidential scandal had become too hot to worry about seemingly small, irrelevant details. Subtle facts about the burglary and the burglars were ignored altogether.

And certainly, after the *Post* won a Pulitzer Prize, after its reporters published a bestselling book, after they were portrayed in an Oscar-winning movie, other journalists, who were now elevated vicariously in stature by the *Post*'s reporting, would not seek to criticize these canonized patron saints, Woodward, Bernstein and the *Post*. This is not to say, however, that no one brought up some obvious questions about the burglary.

Indeed, if you look at standard high school and college textbooks, they often note the lingering questions about why a president so far ahead in the polls would commission a risky program of spying and sabotage on a minor target, that is, the DNC, which had no apparent campaign information. But for years, no serious work had examined in depth the many mysteries that sprang from this initial question.

Now let us turn to the burglary and the arrests on June 17, 1972. Five men in business suits, wearing rubber gloves, were arrested at the Democratic National Committee headquarters in Washington, DC, at approximately 2:30 AM. In addition to burglary equipment, the arrested men had cameras, camera equipment such as camera clamps, and electronic devices that appeared to enable wiretapping or other electronic surveillance. They had sequentially numbered $100 bills, tear-gas guns, flashlights, and a number of other operational accoutrements.

Four of these five men were Cuban émigrés who had fled to the United States after Fidel Castro's 1959 revolution, all living in Miami. All four of the Cubans were veterans of the abortive CIA invasion of Cuba in 1961, which had attempted to wrest the island back from Castro. It was known as the Bay of Pigs, intended to overthrow the communist regime that Castro had installed.

The fifth member of the burglary team, a strange addition indeed, was James McCord, the director of security of the CRP and a recently retired CIA agent. McCord himself had been a part of the Bay of Pigs as an adviser. Think about that: all five burglars were involved in the Bay of Pigs and may have been either in the CIA or were operational assets.

Soon after these arrests, the FBI also identified and arrested E. Howard Hunt, an ostensibly retired CIA agent like McCord who, unlike McCord, apparently kept an office at the White House. The FBI also in time arrested G. Gordon Liddy, an ex-FBI agent and former White House employee. Liddy was now serving as a general counsel to the CRP.

As portrayed prominently in the book and the movie *All the President's Men*, the burglary was discovered by a building security guard, Frank Wills, who found tape on the locks of the garage-level door leading to the office building. This would allow entrance from the outside of the building. Just one and a half hours earlier, Wills had discovered and removed tape from the same door lock, leaving him to conclude that the retaping meant that there was likely a burglary in progress.

Since all five burglars on the team had entered by the time of the guard's second discovery of the tape, let's think about this plain, unblinking fact: there was no reason for that tape to have remained on the lock. The burglars could now exit at the basement level without any tape on the locks. In other words, doors without tape still allowed exit. However, they didn't allow entrance, for which tape was required to retain the locking mechanism. Since these were seemingly professional burglars, their leaving the tape on the garage door was inexplicable.

Another puzzling finding was that there was a lock still taped on the sixth floor, where the burglary was taking place. But even odder, there was tape on the lock on the eighth floor as well, where tape was seemingly never needed in the first place. The burglars, after all, had entered the building through the garage, then walked up the stairwell and arrived at the DNC offices through the sixth-floor door, which had been taped. They would exit through the same door. Why would the eighth-floor lock ever need to be taped? The burglars weren't on the eighth floor.

In the many works describing the conventional story of Watergate, no journalist or academic authority has ever adequately explained the eighth-floor tape, the sixth-floor tape, or the lack of tape removal on any of the three doors, even though these were professional operatives. But the more critical question was: why this burglary at all? And as we speak of journalists and academics, why would it be that these folks would not have screamed for answers? But they did not. The sound of silence was deafening to anyone who thought about this strange tableau.

As we noted, Nixon was far ahead in the polls and needed no campaign intelligence. Moreover, there was no campaign information to be had at the DNC headquarters well before the election season had yet been underway, usually commencing after the party conventions, getting full steam after Labor Day. Accordingly, speculation actually turned to Democratic National Committee Director Larry O'Brien. O'Brien had knowledge, it was hypothesized, of dirty Nixon secrets that may have gone far beyond the current campaign information.

One postulate about O'Brien was that he may have possessed certain dark knowledge of the funding of Nixon from his long-time supporter, reclusive billionaire Howard Hughes. Nixon's 1960 presidential campaign against John F. Kennedy had been harmed by revelation of the $205,000 loan from Hughes to Nixon's brother Donald, widely thought to be a disguised bribe of Nixon himself. We note that $205,000 in 1960 was several million dollars today. This disclosure thus had quite an effect on Nixon and that election. O'Brien had always been a suspect in the public outing of this embarrassment to Nixon. And, as we noted, Nixon thought it may have cost him the election. So, speculation about O'Brien as being the burglary's target naturally arose. But the response to this speculation would be that Larry O'Brien had not been in Washington for weeks at the time of the burglaries and would not be returning for many more. It seems, then, that there was no reasonable likelihood of gathering information possessed by Larry O'Brien since he would be speaking neither on a wiretapped phone nor in a microphoned room.

And to make this operation even more head-scratching, there had been a prior burglary of the DNC two weeks earlier, with the same burglars committing wiretapping. But the bugging monitor for these two weeks previous had not been listening to Larry O'Brien's line. If he was not listing to O'Brien's line, then to whom was he listening, and for what purpose?

Oddly, photographs developed from the prior burglary two weeks earlier, it was soon learned, showed depictions of stationery with DNC letterhead and the name of Larry O'Brien. The documents did not appear to have been photographed to read beyond the letterhead but instead seemed to be some sort of a trophy or proof of entry. The documents were spread on a carpet by two gloved hands as pictures were taken. What was the point of such "proof," which was potentially harmful evidence of a crime, with no apparent benefit to the criminal photographers? Why did the burglars feel the need to do that? One more strange fillip: the carpet on which the letters were spread was shag, and there were no shag carpets in the DNC headquarters.

Another oddity was James McCord's presence on the burglary team. McCord was readily identifiable as the director of security of the CRP, meaning that if he were arrested, the president's campaign would immediately become known as associated with the burglary. The entire team, in short, was not composed of so-called "double-blind" operatives, that is, individuals who could not be identified with their sponsors, and who hopefully themselves could not identify their sponsors. So, the stupidity of a CRP high official being placed on the team was an unforgivable sin from a covert operational perspective, since the arrest of that operative would immediately identify one sponsor as being the CRP. Yet both Hunt and McCord were trained CIA intelligence operatives with great experience and would know well not to do this unless it was necessary for some hidden purpose. As a result of this blunder, the burglary supervisor G. Gordon Liddy immediately knew upon the arrest of the burglars that, as he told his wife that night, he was sure to go to jail because James McCord was on the team. Why this occurred is one of the many mysteries of Watergate that we will try to resolve in this book.

This burglary was not rushed into operation; some form of break-ins had been under contemplation for least four months since Liddy had first proposed some sort of a burglary program. The team therefore had plenty of time to search for an operative other than McCord. With thousands of retired government security technicians living in the DC area, and with the CIA having a retired employees placement section, was there no one in the area who could have filled McCord's role and who could have been found in that four months?

Soon after the arrests, the FBI began speaking with wire-tapping monitor Alfred Baldwin III, who had readily agreed to cooperate. Baldwin told the FBI that he had been listening to what he termed "explicitly intimate" conversations between men and women. And puzzlingly, it was quickly learned by the FBI, the phone to which the monitor had been listening for the prior two weeks was the phone of a nobody, one Spencer Oliver Jr., a person not even directly working for the DNC, but instead for the Association of State Democratic Chairmen, a group with ties to the DNC but that was not part of it. So, the immediate question to the FBI, but one that was not publicly raised, was why would the Nixon administration be interested in listening to talk on the line of Spencer Oliver Jr.? In perhaps the biggest political scandal in world history, mainstream textbooks have not addressed why this obscure fellow's telephone line was targeted. Nor for the most part is the tapping of Oliver's phone even noted.

All five of the burglars played some role of the CIA's 1961 Bay of Pigs invasion, as we have discussed. And all five also trained together for our country's Second Naval Guerrilla Operation, a second planned invasion of Cuba. These well-known facts necessarily pointed to the CIA, and were highly publicized to boot.

One of the burglary supervisors was Howard Hunt, also recently retired from the CIA, hired part-time by the White House to perform "sensitive assignments." He had also been in the past a supervisor of the Cubans on both the Bay of Pigs and in the Second Naval Guerrilla Operation. At the time of the burglary, Hunt had worked contemporaneously full-time at a public relations firm located near the White House, Mullen and Company, which had offices worldwide.

The only one of the seven defendants not associated with the CIA was one G. Gordon Liddy. Liddy was general counsel of the CRP, with access to campaign funds. Liddy himself was a former agent of the FBI and most recently a White House plumber, so named because the team was charged with plugging publicity leaks emanating from the White House on national security matters. These included the Vietnam War and the smoldering India-Pakistan rivalry. There had been leaks on these confidential subjects, and the White House was very upset about them.

The five burglars made no telephone calls on the night of the arrests, yet they were represented in court by Joseph Rafferty, a criminal lawyer hired by a Mullen-associated corporate lawyer named Douglas Caddy, who was present in court at the arraignment the following morning.

Once Hunt was identified as a burglary supervisor, it became clear that Hunt, also a Mullen employee, had called Caddy, who then retained Rafferty. The question was thereby raised that if Mullen felt the need to obtain representation for the burglars, presumably out of Caddy's pocket, likely as well Mullen's, did Mullen have anything to do with the burglary? A corollary question was that, if Mullen was so deeply involved, would it be because of Hunt's connection to the CIA? Was there a connection between the two entities? Was Mullen a CIA front or cover company? In other words, was Hunt still acting as a CIA agent after retirement under cover of Mullen?

But if the burglars were acting on behalf of the CIA, we would pose the same question we put regarding the White House: what could possibly interest the CIA in calls on the line of the unprepossessing Spencer Oliver Jr?

We note one more bizarre oddity in a tableau filled with them. As the lobby of the Watergate Offices was abuzz with the arrests that morning, a man emerged from the staircase. He chatted with the guards and strolled out of the office building very calmly. By the time the guards told the police about him, the individual was nowhere in sight. He quickly became known as

Watergate's "sixth burglar," but his presence has never been adequately explored or explained. Why should this so-called sixth burglar be of such special interest to us today, as we attempt to solve the mysteries of Watergate? Has he ever been identified?

Let's ponder for a moment the likely presence of sixth man and his possible involvement in the burglary. We know that a sixth man was not in the DNC offices at the time of the arrests. And we know that none of the burglars has admitted to knowing of the sixth man in the office building that night. None of the accounts of Watergate figures, including those of the arrested individuals, acknowledges him or his presence. Woodward and Bernstein do not mention the sixth burglar in their bestselling book. Finally, the sixth burglar was not on Liddy's payroll, which did include the five arrested men. So if there was a sixth man in the Watergate Office building on the early morning of June 17, 1972, he was likely not there on a White House or CRP mission.

And even if Mullen was in some fashion a cover contractor for the CIA, the sixth burglar, unlike Hunt, was not acting under Mullen cover, nor was he ostensibly a CRP agent. And whatever his task was, it would have been of a different kind from the tasks carried out by the acknowledged five burglars. And if the sixth burglar had an agenda secret from the agenda of the five burglars, that would be highly significant, especially since the five burglars may have had an agenda secret from the White House. So, the possible sixth burglar presents one of Watergate's most intriguing and puzzling mysteries.

We leave this chapter with the overarching questions that presented themselves to the public on June 18, 1972, when the arrests were first reported. Why would Nixon forces want to break into the DNC? What were the burglars after? Was the CIA involved? If the CIA was involved, what was it after? To be sure, most of the public intuited that the burglary had to be connected to the upcoming presidential campaign but were simply puzzled as to how the burglary would advance the ball forward for the Nixon administration.

But the converse question also implicitly posed was that if the burglary was not in any way directed to the campaign, what would be its purpose? And if not directed at the campaign, wouldn't it make sense that Nixon and his inner circle likely had nothing to do with it? And if Watergate was not really an Oval Office program, did we remove a president from office for technical obstruction of an investigation into a burglary that he neither authorized nor understood the origin of?

There is no doubt, of course, that Nixon technically obstructed justice on at least two occasions. But if this is so, why didn't the Pulitzer Prize-winning newspapers tell us that his crime was technical, with no involvement in the underlying crime? In addition to this large hole in the *Post*'s reporting, the hundreds of seemingly authoritative books and articles about Watergate do not satisfactorily address these core issues. Luckily, however, there are sufficient bits and pieces of explanatory information that have been dug up by excellent researchers post-Watergate, which amount to illuminating needles in a massive haystack of otherwise intriguing but ultimately unnourishing information.

Before we get deep into the Watergate woods, let us talk about the fascinating characters involved, of most of whom you have never heard. To these intriguing personalities we will now turn.

Image of FBI Director J. Edgar Hoover, public domain.

CHAPTER 2

WHAT'S PAST IS PROLOGUE

WE DO NOT EXAGGERATE WHEN we tell you the story that will unfold on these pages will be richer than any political story in our country's history. It will detail academic but interesting historical fact going back to 1787 and the meaning of our Constitution, exploring deeply some of its key details. Some of it will concern titillating tales of men seeking paid female escort services, while some will describe out-of-control spooks listening in on these intimate calls. Some will be about the most noble, ethical, and skillful of modern law enforcement. We will present evidence of a tawdry underbelly of our country's intelligence service, an agency gone to the dark side.

These chapters will feature honest government witnesses and abject liars. The narrative will feature energetic reporting of young journalists seeking the truth without fear or favor. It will feature a presidential administration with dark secrets to hide about its churlish behavior. It will also detail the way an unattractive, awkwardly resentful politician was unfairly smeared by a partisan press emboldened by its popular success.

Some parts of the story will be uniquely personal. Others will reflect larger institutional prerogatives that transcend any individual motives. Some characters will be true patriots loyal to their country, while other characters will deviously undermine the legitimate function of the government which they swore under oath to serve. We will here profile a few of these characters and their motives.

It was July 1969 when young Maureen Kane Biner, who had just lost her husband of two years to a tragic boating accident, was pondering what to do with her life. A California girl, she decided to spend some time in South Lake Tahoe, where California meets Nevada, featuring beach and boating fun in the summer and skiing in the winter. All year long, on the Nevada side of South Lake, in the town of Stateline, there was a lively casino night life. Soon Mo befriended a glamorous German-born woman named Heidi Rikan. Heidi had lived only briefly in Tahoe and was about to return to her previous hometown, Washington, DC, to start a business. Heidi urged Mo to come with her as she drove across the country. At the time, Heidi urged, Washington, DC, was an entertaining place full of interesting people, good female government jobs, and eligible men who could make Mo forget about the tragic loss of her husband.

So after crossing the country with her friend, Mo did find a solid job in government. But more significantly, she developed a relationship with a dashing young lawyer with great ambition. His name was John Dean. Dean had been an up-and-coming government counsel and protégé of Attorney General John Mitchell. He then left the Department of Justice to take an exciting job as White House counsel to the Nixon administration.

Soon, Dean and Mo Biner began living together. When John was traveling on an extended trip, Mo would often stay with Heidi. Heidi had a wealthy boyfriend, and Mo sometimes would borrow one of Heidi's expensive furs. The two couples were friends, and the two women especially stayed in close touch.

Heidi was a guest at the small wedding of John and Maureen in October of 1972. The close friendship between Mo and Heidi would ultimately prove to be one of the strands woven into the complex fabric which we today called Watergate.

John was in a celebratory mood that October, not only because of the wedding, but also because he had just put to rest, he believed, a nagging possible embarrassment to the Nixon administration he served as White House counsel. It seems that there had been a seemingly silly, certainly odd and inexplicable, burglary of the Democratic National Committee headquarters in Washington, DC, the previous June. The original seven suspects—five burglars and two supervisors—had just been indicted. One had worked previously, perhaps not at the time of the burglary, at the White House and one at the CRP, the campaign arm of the White House.

Many had early on suspected that others in the White House or CRP would be charged beyond the original seven. But the Department of Justice announced on September 15, 1972, that no more indictments were forthcoming. As a troubleshooter for this potential scandal, Dean had deftly guided his White House clients through choppy waters. He could now relax and go on a honeymoon with Mo.

A number-two official in the FBI, one W. Mark Felt, was not pleased with this development. He was, that same September of 1972, devising a plan that he thought could possibly restart the same stalled Watergate investigation. All Felt wanted was permission for the FBI to continue to investigate and present any further findings to a grand jury. But his series of smoothly skillful bureaucratic entreaties, succinctly stating why the FBI needed to explore certain possible leads, were uniformly rebuffed by the chain of command going through the U.S. attorney in DC assigned to the prosecution, and up to the attorney general.

Felt and Dean had dueled earlier that year. A young reporter named Brit Hume had uncovered a smoking gun: a memo written by a lobbyist for the ITT Corporation, a powerful international conglomerate, dealing with what appeared to be an explicit bribe of the Nixon administration. According to the memo, written by hard-drinking lobbyist Dita Beard, ITT had agreed to pay $400,000 in cash and $400,000 in hotel rooms for the Republican National Convention in exchange for the Nixon Justice Department to drop its antitrust case objecting to ITT's purchase of the Hartford Insurance Company. Dean wanted Felt's FBI to agree with the White House that the memo was a forgery, but Felt was not buying what Dean was selling, and the FBI authenticated the memo.

When legendary FBI director J. Edgar Hoover died shortly after this, Felt, Hoover's number two and his logical successor, was passed over, likely as a result of his stubborn rectitude in refusing to politicize the Bureau in the ITT scandal. Nixon, frustrated by the obstinacy of Hoover, wanted a director he could control. Instead of Felt, Nixon named L. Patrick Gray, a malleable Republican political hack. This choice, seemingly politically safe for Nixon, ultimately became a significant causative factor in the president's eventual resignation.

Years earlier, Hoover had alerted the Kennedy brothers, President John F. and Attorney General Robert, that young, emerging civil rights leader Martin Luther King Jr. was working closely with known communists. The Kennedys feared that exposure of this link would hurt them politically as King supporters, which they were quite openly. King repeatedly denied his involvement with the two, and Robert Kennedy reluctantly ordered Hoover to wiretap King to track any communications he might have with these suspected advisers. The wiretaps, however, yielded some highly unexpected fruits, far removed from Karl Marx.

The commanding young preacher, it seemed, had a weakness for women of any color, and the matching charisma to attract them. The FBI wiretaps caught him frequently in the throes of sexual trysts, often with multiple partners, featuring loud exultations from the minister. The prudish Hoover's visceral reaction was simply shock, but his aggressive, roguish intelligence chief William Sullivan wanted to use the incriminating tapes as a weapon to bully King, perhaps shame him into resigning his civil rights leadership, which Sullivan thought was inspired by communism, or worse, to push him into suicide.

Sullivan secretly made a recorded montage of many of King's excited commentaries while in flagrante delicto and mailed a copy of the tape to King's home with an anonymous, untraceable letter, chillingly suggesting King knew what he "had to do." Hoover always suspected Sullivan of this risky and stomach-turning act, notwithstanding Sullivan's denials. Sullivan was also becoming too close for Hoover's taste to the roguish black operations of the CIA. Hoover looked down upon the Agency as a thuggish rival who might get the FBI in trouble as the Bureau helped the CIA with its domestic operations.

So, Hoover promoted above Sullivan his most capable, clever, senior agent to deal with his headstrong underling, eventually leading to Sullivan's firing. The official's name was W. Mark Felt, now after Sullivan's bitter departure in line to succeed Hoover. Felt thought that his terminated rival was a disgrace; he wanted to erase Sullivan's wrongs and clean up Felt's beloved Bureau. Indeed, Sullivan's churlish specter would later hover over the Watergate investigation led by Felt. Sullivan, at the time of the scandal out of the Bureau, would become an adviser to President Nixon on Watergate. This intriguing, bitter rivalry would profoundly affect this national debacle known as Watergate and would leave no one but the *Washington Post* unscathed.

Meanwhile, a young DC lawyer, Phillip Mackin Bailley, was making his small but lurid mark as a lawyer representing a clientele consisting largely of prostitutes, a decently lucrative client base in the swinging Washington, DC, of the early 1970s. Bailley, a stocky, boyishly handsome, blue-eyed, fun-loving Irishman with an insatiable sexual appetite, had been just a few years earlier voted by his Catholic University law school classmates, "most likely to be disbarred." He would soon prove deserving of this dubious accolade. It was not uncommon for Bailley to have close personal relationships with his prostitute clients, taking, it seemed, some fees in the form of his clients' professional services.

In the fall of 1971, one beautiful young madam named Cathy, who had dalliances with Bailley, asked Bailley if he could lure referrals from the nearby Democratic National Committee offices. Bailley dated a girl at the DNC and quickly arranged a pipeline. Her operation, Cathy assured Bailley, was protected by the CIA.

Not too long after this, Bailley was having drinks at a Georgetown bar with a large group of like-minded young men, planning their continuing deviant exploits. Bailley passed around the table a nude photo of a young college student with whom the group had had their way at a recent raucous party. One of the group, a friend of a regular attendee, was a straight arrow and became understandably shocked. His conscience told him he should report this ugly scenario to the proper authorities. Like the other events we have here described, this gathering would be one of several interconnected events that would lead to the only forcible removal of a president in United States history.

In May 1972, former Alabama governor George Wallace, a conservative Democrat, had been causing great mischief as a potential third-party presidential contender. It was unclear whether Wallace's candidacy would draw more voters away from likely Democratic nominee George McGovern or from the more conservative Republican nominee, incumbent President Richard Nixon.

On May 15, 1972, at a shopping center in the DC suburb of Laurel, Maryland, Wallace was shot and paralyzed by a would-be assassin, effectively ending Wallace's viability as a candidate. Every reporter in the country was seeking the motive of the shooter, Arthur Bremer. Was he trying to help Nixon or McGovern? Was he a Republican or Democrat? Who put him up to that? Everyone wanted to know.

Out of all the country's interested reporters, the inside story was landed by cub reporter, Bob Woodward of the *Washington Post*, whose lowly assignment was covering local crime in Montgomery County, Maryland. Scooping all others, Woodward reported convincingly that the gunman, Arthur Bremer, was a crazed loner without political motive. It seems that Woodward had developed his story through a high official he had confidentially developed within the FBI. Woodward's proven source led his editors to keep Woodward on the reporting of another local crime which also quickly became a national story: the burglary of the Democratic National Committee offices in the Watergate office building in Washington, DC, just one month after Wallace's shooting.

Months before the Watergate arrests, Washington, DC, lawyer Bernard "Bud" Fensterwald and his associate, Bob Smith, each had been hearing hilarious tales from a freewheeling friend, an alcoholic private eye long working the shadowy demimonde of Washington, DC. It seems that the investigator had been taping hookers and their johns, regularly regaling his drinking buddies with amusing recountings of the erotic proceedings.

These are just a few of the odd tableaus that would eventually unite to cause the combustion of the explosive scandal today known as Watergate.

Howard Hunt, an ostensibly "retired" CIA officer, was working in the summer of 1971 full-time for an international PR agency, Mullen and Company, when he began working part-time for the White House, hired in July 1971 by fellow Brown University alum, White House aide Charles Colson. Hunt had previously worked for the Office of Security (OS) of the CIA. He had been involved in the Bay of Pigs invasion of Cuba. Not long after his hire, the CRP hired James McCord, initially as a part-time director of security, later as a full-time employee.

McCord was recently "retired" from the CIA and also had recently worked for the OS, as had Hunt. McCord also was a Bay of Pigs veteran. Yet his hire by the CRP was not helped or facilitated by Hunt, but by White House Secret Service chief Alfred Wong. Was the simultaneous hiring of the two retired agents, both formerly with OS of the CIA, nothing more than an amazing coincidence?

McCord's job had nothing to do with the White House or with Hunt. Later, when CRP general counsel Gordon Liddy introduced the two, they acted as if they had not previously known each other. Why would they deny having known one another?

It was December 8, 1972. Dorothy Hunt, wife of Howard Hunt, was flying to Midway Airport in Chicago from Washington, DC. The approaching plane oddly lost altitude, clipped some trees as it approached Midway, causing a crash and the deaths of many on board, including Dorothy. Her body was found along with $10,000 in cash she was carrying with her. Her husband was scheduled to begin trial for the Watergate burglary just weeks later, in early January 1973. Why was she carrying cash? James McCord would later tell the Senate offhandedly that Dorothy was a "hush money" courier. But hush money to whom? Who was in Chicago that needed payment? There were no burglary or cover-up conspirators ever identified who lived in Chicago. Ever.

Those who know a bit about Watergate know that the White House was paying money to the arrested suspects mainly, it was inferred, to keep them from pointing at higher-ups in the Nixon administration, thus the term "hush money." But no one in the White House has ever written or said that Dorothy Hunt was a hush money courier, nor is there evidence she interacted with Nixon aides. In fact, her husband Howard was a hungry recipient of hush money, constantly demanding more for legal bills and financial support. Yes, perhaps he had a motive to help get the Cubans paid small amounts. But why would he, through his wife, be giving money away to someone in Chicago? None of the serial numbers on the bills matched any known White House slush fund cash and there were no burglary defendants in Chicago. To whom could she possibly be bringing money, and why? And was this hush money or something else? If McCord was giving a false explanation of Dorothy as a hush money courier, what would be his motive?

It was March 24, 1972. White House consultant Howard Hunt asked his close friend and wannabe covert operator, Liddy, to a meeting with "retired" CIA physician Dr. Edward Gunn, often called the "poisons doctor." The three discussed ways of killing or disabling by poison nettlesome columnist Jack Anderson. One of the methods they discussed was called "aspirin roulette." The CIA would put one poison pill in a victim's medicine container. After the victim takes the poison pill, the remaining tablets would all appear normal. This poisoning method, to be sure, was never employed against Anderson.

Fast-forward to a year later. In May 1973, Deep Throat met reporter Bob Woodward for one of their late-night garage meetings. Normally calm and cool, Deep Throat was greatly agitated and fearful, warning Woodward, "Everyone's life is in danger!" Did this dire warning ever materialize in a death? And if so, was aspirin roulette, a signature of the CIA poisons program, involved? Was the Gunn discussion part of a CIA operation, a White House operation, and if either one, why would Liddy be invited to the meeting? What was Hunt's purpose in inviting Liddy, at the time a campaign lawyer for a campaign committee?

Each of the vignettes we have just summarized, seemingly separate and isolated from one another, will eventually tie together as we solve the mysteries of Watergate.

Portrait of President George Washington, public domain.

CHAPTER 3

INFILTRATING THE WHITE HOUSE

WE HAVE RAISED THE STRONG possibility in Chapter 1 that the Oval Office may not have had an interest in burglarizing the DNC headquarters in June 1972, as all have historically believed, albeit while criticizing its wisdom. It certainly, we have noted, would not have had any curiosity about the calls on the phone of Spencer Oliver Jr., a minor and unimportant official, not even an employee of the DNC, who had nothing to do with the 1972 campaign. Isn't it therefore a logical conclusion this likely would not, repeat *not*, have been an authorized White House operation? We have also pointed out the strange presence of CIA connections among the burglars.

We have spoken of the employment by Mullen and Company of part-time White House consultant Howard Hunt. Mullen-associated attorney Douglas Caddy hired a lawyer for the burglars and attended the arraignment. Presumably it was Mullen paying the fee of the lawyer, Joseph Rafferty. So, was the burglary operation one sponsored by Mullen? And if so, in what capacity would Mullen be acting?

If Hunt was working for Mullen in performing this decidedly non-PR work, why would he wish to also work for the White House, as he was doing part-time? Was his work for Mullen in some form or fashion disguised work for the CIA? What good would this do for the Agency, ultimately his sponsor under this scenario? Put differently, If Mullen were tied in with the CIA in its hiring of the ostensibly retired Hunt, why would the CIA wish to be involved in the Watergate burglary, seemingly on behalf of the Nixon administration? Why would the CIA want to participate in gaining campaign strategy if that is what the burglary was after? In response, it seems reasonable to say that the CIA would have no interest at all in a domestic political campaign. So back to the original question. Why would Mullen, or for that matter, the CIA, wish to be involved in political shenanigans if the burglary fell under that umbrella?

But are we asking the wrong questions here? Maybe the question we should pose is that if the CIA had in fact infiltrated the Nixon White House through Hunt, what would the Agency stand to gain by that? And how would that purpose be furthered by breaking into the DNC?

To answer, we need an understanding of the history of our country's exercise of national security powers and the limitations on the exercise of them. These powers are seemingly in tension with the individual freedoms guaranteed by the Bill of Rights. For just one example, Fourth Amendment prohibitions disallow searches without probable cause. Yet national security often demands warrantless entries and searches of hostile foreign powers and their assets without probable cause, not seeking evidence of a crime but instead preventing foreign clandestine harm.

Basic institutional imperatives must be understood in order to understand how these two clashing principles reconciled themselves in Watergate. That is, one cherished idea is that no one should be searched, or wiretapped, a form of search, without a warrant gained under showing of probable cause that a crime had been committed and that a search would likely uncover evidence. The opposing principle is that our nation's security must be protected, and we cannot wait for an enemy's bombs to explode before taking action. It is this clash of principles that lit the spark of Watergate.

To explore these issues, we begin a brief tour through our country's political history because it will shed light on the seeds of what is viewed by history as both a cataclysmically impactful scandal and one also shrouded in mystery and intrigue. To understand Watergate, we must first learn how and when executive branch national security powers under our Constitution can be exercised when doing so would conflict with the Bill of Rights. One must understand these conflicting imperatives if one is to understand Watergate.

1787 saw the beginning of the Constitutional Convention, which ultimately resulted in our present Constitution, signed in 1789. The Bill of Rights, anticipated at the time of the ratification of the Constitution, was intended to follow shortly. It was ratified in 1791, when ten out of twelve proposed amendments were approved by a sufficient number of States. When the states agreed to the structure of the government under the Constitution, one of the large motivating factors was the glaring weakness of the executive branch's national security powers under the Articles of Confederation.

The delegates had become greatly alarmed, beginning in 1786, by what was known as Shays's Rebellion, a violent debtor protest centered in Western Massachusetts, also flaring throughout the country west of the Appalachians. In the wake of the Revolutionary War, British merchants had stopped extending credit to American merchants, insisting on payment in hard currency. So, understandably, those same merchants sought payment in hard currency from those in the interior regions.

But in the rural Western regions, there was little hard currency to be had because the farmers relied on a barter system. As debts and debtors grew from inability to pay for those items that could not be bartered, including taxes, these regions had a heavy concentration of desperate debtors. When a demanding merchant class began enforcement in rural courts, the countryside erupted. Governor John Hancock of Massachusetts, a populist, was light-handed on enforcing debt collection. But, likely sensing an uprising that even a popular man such as he could not quell, Hancock resigned in 1785 and was replaced by leading merchant James Bowdoin, who represented numerous like-minded merchants. The battle was thus joined, on one side the cash-poor farmers and tradesmen, and on the other merchants and tax collectors seeking debt repayment.

Armed rebels led by Daniel Shays prevented courts from convening, threatened tax collectors, and ultimately raised a large force of rebels. The rebellion was finally put down through the efforts of a merchant-financed private militia, but only barely. The need for a national militia was now evident to many of the influential leaders of the fledgling country.

What Shays's Rebellion dramatized was the weakness of the Articles of Confederation for national defense, where there was no provision for a national militia or commander in chief of that militia. The Federalists sought a new Constitution to remedy this weakness. Some Anti-Federalists, otherwise opposed to central concentrations of federal power, were persuaded by Shays's Rebellion to agree to a new Constitution with more robust centralized national security powers.

These considerations are spelled out in the famous *Federalist Papers*, provocative treatises written by anonymous patriots John

Jay, James Madison, and Alexander Hamilton, published in newspapers under pseudonyms. So, in 1789, following *The Federalist Papers*, the new Constitution was ratified, one that recognized the president to be the commander in chief of federal forces—an improvement, it was thought, on the prior arrangement where every state controlled its own militia.

While the Constitution required that war could be declared only with the consent of the Senate, no such consent was necessary for any national security actions of the president as commander in chief, short of a declaration of war. The lack of necessity for congressional consent for military actions approximating war, but without formal declaration of war, is certainly in a gray area of the Constitution, and subject even today to continual debate between the executive branch and the legislative branch.

But for our present purposes, it can't be doubted that there is some area of presidential national security power that needs no congressional authorization. After all, when the Constitution was ratified, it was the practice for Congress to be in session for only several months a year. It took some members of Congress weeks to travel to the Capitol, originally in Philadelphia, and it made sense that the president would not need the concurrence of Congress in the event he felt the need to take appropriate emergency national security action short of war. Shays's Rebellion was just one example of the need for such powers.

The argument has been made that the exercise of national security power should not in any way violate the Bill of Rights, a reading which would somewhat narrow the executive branch's powers. Luckily, however, for posterity, George Washington resolved that question when the ink was barely dry on the Bill of Rights.

In 1792, in Western Pennsylvania, a tax rebellion very much like Shays's Rebellion erupted, commonly call the "Whiskey

Rebellion" because the prominent source of objection was an excise tax on distilled spirits. Westerners often used whiskey as a form of currency because of the lack of circulation of sufficient hard currency, especially in outlying territories. These territories were rich in corn, rye, and other crops that could be distilled into hard liquor, which often became necessary when raw crops could not be completely sold. Because the tax, in addition, was a flat per-gallon tax to be paid in currency, it impacted more adversely the modest economies of the western states, with their low prices and part-time distillers. Distillers on the eastern seaboard, on the other hand, were usually full-time, large-volume operations with easy access to hard currency, with the ability to charge substantial prices in developed economies of the East Coast. The combination of the seemingly gross unfairness of the taxes, and the harsh hardship experienced by these pioneering farmers, caused the Whiskey Rebellion to explode, with violence widely wreaked on the hapless federal tax collectors.

When President Washington's emissaries could not subdue the rebellion, Washington himself took a force of several thousand troops and rode into western Pennsylvania. By the time he arrived, many of the rebels had melted away. But Washington did arrest and bring to Philadelphia to trial thirty rebels. What was noteworthy about his actions was that he did not resort to formal arrest or search warrants in putting down the rebellion, normally required by the Bill of Rights. Washington's actions during the Whiskey Rebellion had thus solidified the concept that the exercise of national security powers does not require adherence to the Bill of Rights. This is an important concept that we need to keep in mind in discussing Watergate. The principle has been affirmed by subsequent presidents, and as well recognized by Congress, again, with some dispute involving its gray areas.

For example, in 1863, Abraham Lincoln issued the Emancipation Proclamation, freeing the slaves in belligerent states on the basis of national security. That is, slaves were aiding the war effort, so freeing them helped national security, under Lincoln's reasoning. Several years earlier, when coming into office, Lincoln felt he had no power to free the slaves upon his own executive order because that would violate the Constitution, and more specifically the Fifth Amendment, which abjured any taking of property without just compensation. Slaves were considered property, and therefore, the reasoning went, neither the president nor Congress could free the slaves without providing just compensation for the property taken, as a government today does in eminent domain proceedings. However, once the Civil War erupted, Lincoln cleverly resorted to his national security powers to free the slaves without providing their owners any compensation.

It is notable that Lincoln did not free the slaves in the four nonbelligerent states—Delaware, Maryland, Kentucky, and Missouri—precisely because he had no national security justification. So the Emancipation Proclamation itself stands as an affirmation that the national security powers inherent in the Constitution trump the Bill of Rights.

We then fast-forward to 1942, when war with Japan had broken out after the Japanese bombed Pearl Harbor. President Roosevelt quickly, perhaps rashly, made the decision that first-generation Japanese families should be interned for the duration of the war. This decision has been criticized, and rightly so, as xenophobic, excessively reactive, and simply unnecessary, and therefore a very sad chapter in our history. But be that as it may, the Supreme Court upheld the presidential action in the *Korematsu v. United States* case, holding that the president's national security powers allowed this extraordinary deprivation of civil rights, otherwise forbidden by the Bill of Rights.

Roosevelt had in 1938 formally delegated national security intelligence powers to the FBI under J. Edgar Hoover. Hoover and Roosevelt interpreted these powers as allowing the FBI to conduct operations in the name of national security, which otherwise would not be compliant with the protections of the Bill of Rights. For example, both Roosevelt and Hoover understood and agreed that the FBI was authorized to engage in warrantless searches, sometimes called "surreptitious entries," or more colloquially, "black bag jobs." These were called "black bag jobs" because the FBI agents who conducted them often had their lock-picking tools in a little black bag of the type carried by doctors on house calls. These activities also included wiretapping in order to identify our country's enemies—at the time, Communists and Nazis. Throughout the 1940s and 1950s, the FBI regularly employed these tactics to identify Nazis and Communists. Members of Congress were regularly informed about the FBI's techniques and did not object to them.

The infamous McCarthy era[1] was in part stoked by information gained by the FBI on the continuing presence of previously identified Communists in government, most of which information was procured through surreptitious entries. While many objected to McCarthy's inflammatory public rhetoric, there was no visible opposition to the FBI's methods for surreptitiously identifying Communists.

---

1   Joseph McCarthy was a vociferously anti-Communist Republican Senator from Wisconsin in the early 1950s. The term "McCarthyism" is attributed to his practice of aggressively accusing, investigating, and smearing supposed communists and Soviet spies inside the United States government, causing them to be blacklisted and/or lose their jobs, despite little to no evidence supporting his claims. He was ultimately censured by the U.S. Senate for these tactics.

There would appear to be no doubt but that, first, the president had national security powers as described, and, secondly, that he may delegate them, and in fact *did* delegate them, to the FBI. So, World War II saw the domestic exercise of presidential national security powers both regarding the Japanese internment and their delegation to the FBI to search for Nazis and Communists without the need for warrant.

The war, of course, also required intelligence capability against foreign governments. The Office of Special Services (OSS), which worked alongside the FBI in foreign intelligence, was formed during World War II. My father himself was an FBI undercover agent in Brazil during the war. In 1947, the OSS, having been disbanded, was reformed, as it were, into a more modern bureaucratic organization called the Central Intelligence Agency (CIA).

Under its charter, the CIA was forbidden from performing domestic operations. That is, if the CIA, in its exercise of intelligence powers, sought to wiretap or surreptitiously enter the office or abode of a subject in the United States, it could not conduct that operation itself as it could in foreign countries. Rather, it would need to prevail upon the offices of the FBI, which did have those powers domestically, granted by Roosevelt to Hoover originally, and could exercise them on behalf of the CIA.

While the FBI had routinely sought to cooperate with the CIA, especially given that the two agencies needed to work together in foreign countries, the straitlaced, cautiously bureaucratic J. Edgar Hoover, director of the FBI, was mindful that any abuses of these powers, even if on behalf of the CIA, would be blamed on the FBI.

The arrangement between the FBI and CIA held steady, if not without some contretemps, through 1966. At this point, the winds of the civil rights movement were blowing fiercely. Hoover was becoming very concerned about the number of national security wiretaps that the FBI had placed. More importantly, he was skittish about what he thought were the cowboyish ventures of the CIA that the FBI was carrying out on its behalf. Those, one would suspect, dealt much with foreign governments and their representatives in the United States, such as Al Fatah (a Palestinian terrorist organization which killed members of the 1972 Israeli Olympic team), but also included spying on foreign embassies and, more sensitively, may have included sexual manipulation of blackmail targets.

At Mark Felt's trial in 1980, he was charged with violating the civil rights of the Weather Underground supporters. He noted in his testimony that Hoover had forbidden so-called "black bag jobs" or "surreptitious entries" for the entire Bureau. But Felt added that the reason for this halt was primarily the CIA's unreasonable demands on the FBI. According to Felt, Hoover determined that if he banned these capabilities across the Bureau, he could with straight face tell the CIA he was no longer going to perform them for the CIA. As you can imagine, this ban caused great upset within the CIA.

What concerned Hoover so much about the Agency's activities? We know its activities in the 1950s and 1960s were clearly egregious abuses of intelligence powers. For example, during this time, the CIA was administering psychogenic drugs to often unwitting subjects, often with disastrous results, including a suicide by the CIA's Dr. Frank Olson.

The CIA programs of which we know today were MKUltra, Operation Bluebird, and Operation Artichoke. One thing we do know is that there had been a steady intelligence operation or operations in the United States, therefore illegal, wherein the CIA surveilled prostitutes, usually cooperative, and their johns. There may well have been others, but these are bad enough. On top of the cutoff of intelligence capability, Hoover ceased formal communication with the CIA over the CIA's refusal to hand over the name of an FBI agent who had wrongly passed on information to the CIA. There were some continued informal communications between the two, and in fact Hoover's director of intelligence, William Sullivan, was likely in continuing close and supportive contact with CIA officials. In short, the CIA had lost its domestic operational capabilities traditionally exercised for it by the FBI, and it desperately wanted them back.

In May of 1969, during the height of the Vietnam War, Richard Nixon had been in office but four months when the newspapers became ablaze with headlines that the Nixon administration had begun a bombing campaign in Cambodia, designed to hit the Viet Cong supply lines. A furor erupted, causing great political damage to Nixon for ostensibly widening the war.

Henry Kissinger, Nixon's national security adviser, was livid about the leak. Furious, he called up the FBI, eventually speaking with Sullivan, who was an advocate of exercise of the FBI's robust extraconstitutional powers discussed here. Sullivan agreed, as ultimately did Hoover somewhat reluctantly, to wiretap members of Kissinger's National Security staff. Eventually, they also wiretapped prominent newsmen, two with the *New York Times* and one with CBS News's Marvin Kalb.

These taps, which were known as the "Kissinger Wiretaps," were considered extremely sensitive within the FBI. They were so explosive politically that the FBI would not even file the records in its normal register. The taps were put on in 1969 and continued through February 1971. However, the cautious Hoover let it earlier be known that this is the last time that the FBI would engage in these activities on behalf of the White House. So at least by the summer of 1970, the White House knew that it needed improved intelligence capability against the "New Left" terrorism that was now increasingly bedeviling the country. The Nixon administration also realized that the FBI would be of no direct assistance to the White House on its requests.

Sullivan also chafed under Hoover's restrictions, and was friends with many in the CIA. In consultation with the CIA, Sullivan hoped both to regain this operational capability and to use Hoover's reluctance to help the CIA as a means to overthrow Hoover and become director himself, using CIA and White House support. In short, America had a White House that had the power to order these procedures but that had no capability. It also had a CIA that had the capability but had no legal authority to order these procedures domestically, and an FBI with authority and capabilities but that was cautious in implementation of these powers for either of these two troublesome entities, the CIA and the White House.

Sullivan's first attempt to regain this capability of for the CIA was to use the White House lieutenant Tom Huston, a conservative young former Army officer. Sullivan importuned Huston to name an interagency group on intelligence to devise new capabilities for presidential approval. His purpose was to try to figure out some backdoor way for the CIA to get back these powers. The FBI, the White House, the CIA, the Defense Intelligence Agency (DIA), and the NSA were all represented on this committee. The group drew up an outline, likely authored by Sullivan, and began drafting the final so-called Huston Plan in June 1970. Its ultimate work product gave the broadest powers to these agencies, ostensibly through a committee nominally headed by Hoover, but which in reality would be headed by Sullivan. This plan, if approved by the president, would be in effect an "end around" the FBI and its limitations, and give the CIA a form of direct domestic operational capability. This would be a nifty way to overcome the limitations on the Agency's charter, which, as we discussed, forbade domestic operations.

Hoover, however, wily bureaucrat that he was, like his deputy Mark Felt, knew that once the CIA had been given an inch, it would take a mile. The FBI, which ostensibly would chair the committee overseeing all these activities, would be held responsible for any of the inevitable abuses of the powers.

In any case, on July 14, 1970, H. R. Haldeman, chief of staff to President Nixon, announced to the affected agencies that the president approved the plan. Hoover had noted on the plan his dissent and, while Sullivan acted as if he agreed with the dissent, he privately opposed it. But as Sullivan expected, the president ignored Hoover's dissent and enacted the Huston Plan. Again, this would give the CIA certain domestic operational powers, nominally under the supervision of the FBI, but without, it appeared, requiring the FBI directly to exercise the powers for the CIA.

Then Hoover, assisted by Felt, enlisted Attorney General John Mitchell to fight the now-implemented Huston Plan. Mitchell, very much respected by Nixon, pushed the president to rescind. Now that both Mitchell and Hoover opposed the Plan, Nixon withdrew authorization for it after it being in operation but for nine days.

As of late July 1970, where did this leave the White House and the CIA? The White House still needed its own intelligence resources since it could not obtain them from the FBI. The CIA needed approval for its own, perhaps questionable, domestic operations. With the FBI not cooperating, the CIA could not get that approval but through one place: the White House. And the White House, the CIA knew, was desperate to install its own operational capability.

All the forces that led the White House and the CIA not only to Watergate, but to other problematic operations including, for example, the burglary of Dr. Lewis Fielding, the psychiatrist of Daniel Ellsberg, had now been set in motion. These forces, as we will see, had the potential to bring down both the White House and the CIA, but eventually destroyed only one. With this background in mind, we can see that abuses were inevitable because the CIA was unlikely to exercise caution, and the White House was untutored in drawing the appropriate line between legal national security action and illegal political skullduggery.

In summary, the CIA's quandary forced it to seek some way to obtain presidential approval for domestic operations, now that the FBI was refusing cooperation. We have discussed that under the Constitution the president had the power to authorize national security powers domestically, that the president had the power to give the CIA authority for domestic operations, and the White House, sensing the need for more robust investigative techniques for itself, would be an easy target for CIA infiltration. This is the most lucid explanation of how Watergate began.

Image of Robert F. Bennett, public domain.

CHAPTER 4

MULLEN AND COMPANY

In Chapter 1, we elucidated the broad questions that arose from an initial view of the Watergate burglary arrests and their immediate aftermath. For example, we know that there was nothing of the DNC to be gained in campaign information, which at the time the DNC completely lacked. DNC Director Larry O'Brien may have known of much gossip, albeit not campaign gossip, but he had not been in DC for weeks and was not soon expected back.

Following the first burglary, the wiretap monitor was listening to the phone of one minor official only loosely connected to the DNC, a person known as Spencer Oliver Jr. If the burglars were not after campaign information, the question arises, why would Nixon or his Oval Office insiders care to listen to this individual? The obvious answer is that they wouldn't.

So, what was the purpose of a burglary that was the basis for perhaps world history's most impactful scandal? In the third chapter we explored the motives of both the CIA and the White House to enhance their covert domestic operational capabilities in the wake of the FBI's withdrawal from servicing both of these institutions.

We should now examine what the White House and CIA did to fill their symbiotic needs, an investigation that necessarily will delve into much that has been deeply mystifying.

What is known as Watergate began with the arrests on June 17, 1972, at 2:30 AM, of five burglars who had broken into the headquarters of the DNC located in the Watergate office building in Washington, DC. None of the five arrested men had made a telephone call from jail that night, yet when they arrived for their arraignment later that day, they had retained a private lawyer by the name of Joseph Rafferty. Woodward knew that the burglars had not made any call, which he learned from his jailhouse sources. So, he was highly curious as to how and by whom Rafferty had been retained.

Woodward alertly noticed as present at the arraignment a stylishly dressed gentleman, clearly a fish-out-of-water in the sleazy confines of the local criminal courts. He was soon identified as one Douglas Caddy, a lawyer associated with Mullen and Company. Mullen was a worldwide public relations firm with headquarters in Washington, immediately across from the White House.

The first area of mystery we encounter in connection with the Watergate arrests is the intriguing Mullen and Company. If you will recall, it was Mullen that was Howard Hunt's full-time employer, hiring him a year before he became a part-time contractor for the White House. Mullen was also the former employer of, and still closely connected with, Caddy.

One question that immediately should leap to mind is why a PR firm would hire a retired CIA operative. Hunt's job with Mullen was listed as a "copywriter," a person who pens prose for ads, brochures, and marketing materials. The job is not as absurd as it may seem for an ex-CIA man, since Hunt had some noteworthy prose writing experience, publishing approximately seventy potboiler spy novels. One, the 1949 book, *Bimini Run*, was made into a movie. Hunt, then, was an experienced writer.

In addition to being one of the chief architects of the Bay of Pigs, the attempt to overthrow Cuban dictator Fidel Castro's communist government, Hunt had also been involved in other similar capers, including a successful 1954 coup to oust Juan Jacobo Árbenz Guzmán, the president of Guatemala. Much of his experience was in high-level political manipulation and intrigue.

But while Hunt was an accomplished spy thriller novelist, the idea of a dashing undercover spy and international operator penning the praises of United Fruit bananas was a bit too much to swallow. Moreover, it would seem that there were thousands of literate English and communications majors graduating annually from college, itching for a low-paying entry job, and plenty of talented and experience freelance copywriters. So, why would Mullen wish to hire a fifty-ish ex-spy to churn out copy? The question answers itself and raises the very rational possibility that Hunt was hired for purposes other than that of a copywriter. But what would those be?

Perhaps a better question is why the CIA would want to place Hunt with Mullen. The CIA's director, Richard Helms, had personally interceded with Robert Mullen on Hunt's behalf. It is, of course, a beneficial aspect of Agency employment that the CIA would often help an ex-agent get employment postretirement. But what was so exceptional about Hunt that would cause the intercession of the director himself?

Does Helms's personal engagement tell us something about Hunt's continuing role with the Agency, that is, reporting duties to the highest levels, and its central importance? Helms's involvement certainly suggests that whatever Hunt would be doing with Mullen would yield substantial benefit to the CIA. That is only common sense.

What else do we know about Mullen? The incoming president and owner of Mullen as Hunt was about to take employment was Robert Bennett. If this name sounds familiar, we first note that Bennett's father was an influential senator from Utah, Wallace Bennett. Years later, Robert Bennett himself was elected senator from Utah.

The Bennetts were quite influential not only politically, but also within the Mormon community, in which Wallace Bennett was a prominent elder. Would these forms of influence be helpful to a PR firm? Certainly, they would help with congressional lobbying efforts and perhaps with the Mormon-assisted, reclusive billionaire Howard Hughes, a Mullen client and a businessman always desirous of help from Washington. But what skills, if any, would Hunt lend to Bennett's and Mullen's lobbying efforts? Likely none. But Mullen's relationship with Hughes, who we now know to have been a valuable CIA asset, may provide a clue.

A little bit more about Mullen. It represented United Fruit and General Foods, companies with continuing political issues in banana republics like Guatemala, and even in larger countries like Chile, where the CIA loomed large. Communist-inspired land reform constantly threatened the business interests of multinational property owners.

Another one of Mullen's clients, as we have noted, was Howard Hughes and his company, Hughes Aircraft. Recall that Hughes worked closely with the CIA on the covert raising of the *Glomar Explorer*, a sunken Soviet spy ship. So, was Mullen a CIA front or asset, like Hughes, of the CIA? Mullen's international reach, and its clients with their existential need to work with the CIA and avoid Communist land expropriation, would raise questions about whether Mullen might be some form of cover company for the CIA.

Following the burglary arrests, Caddy had fought government grand jury subpoenas, and then resisted answering questions posed by prosecutors in the grand jury on the grounds
of attorney-client privilege. He did this likely so that he would
avoid identifying CRP general counsel Gordon Liddy, one of his
clients and a burglary supervisor with Hunt. In a public court
hearing over these disputes, the government prosecutor told the
court that Caddy had revealed in his partial testimony that he
had "intimations" that Mullen was connected to the CIA. Caddy
was forced to testify in full eventually. But because grand jury
proceedings are confidential, the public never learned what
"intimations" he had about the CIA's connections to Mullen.

It is of intense interest that in the wake of these court proceedings, in order to explain this curious statement about the
CIA, the *Post* quoted Bennett as saying that Caddy "must have
been referring to the work Mullen did for Radio Free Cuba in the
1960s." Most observers knew that Radio Free Cuba was a CIA-
sponsored venture, certainly a publicly well-known program, as
opposed to a covert one. The assertion that Mullen, a public relations firm, may have worked on the Radio Free Cuba account
certainly made sense and could partially explain the company's
relationship with the Agency, perhaps or perhaps not, as understood by Caddy. But it did not answer the larger question of
whether Mullen had other deeper and continuing CIA ties. After
all, Caddy had spoken in the present tense, not past.

Was its Radio Free Cuba account the only contact with the
CIA? Did Mullen supply cover for covert CIA agents, certainly a
different job than running radio broadcasts? The public was not
told, but the *Post* reporting suggested that Mullen's role was solely
connected to the Agency as regards this limited work with Radio
Free Cuba. The *Post* never followed up again on this suggestion,
and we further note that the allusion to Radio Free Cuba was

Bennett's, not Caddy's, and not under oath. Was the *Washington Post* intentionally covering up by printing what could have been a lame flip-off? At the time, most readers would have had no facts with which to challenge the *Post*'s explanation through Bennett.

What if Mullen was in fact a CIA "front" company? That is, one which gave cover as seeming Mullen employees to CIA undercover operatives. You may recall the 2003 case of Valerie Plame, a CIA agent posted overseas under different names posing as a legitimate employee of various companies. Was Mullen one of these cover companies, shielding Hunt's role as a CIA agent? If Mullen was such a cover company, it would be logical to question whether Hunt was acting as a CIA agent when he was a part-time White House contractor on loan from Mullen, his full-time employer. If so, what inferences flow from that?

All five burglars had CIA connections of some sort, and burglar James McCord, at the time of the arrests, was director of security of the CRP. He, like Hunt, was recently retired from the Agency. The White House had claimed that it had not authorized the burglary, that is, that it was a "rogue operation" by out-of-control campaign operatives. If in fact this burglary had something to do with a covert CIA mission, then maybe the claim of a "rogue" operation, at least from the perspective of the White House, was not that far off.

Is it possible that Watergate was indeed such a rogue mission, in the sense that it should be more appropriately termed a CIA operation than it would be a White House initiative? But, we may ask, how could this have been a CIA operation if campaign cash was used? And how could it be if Gordon Liddy was involved, working for the CRP as general counsel, but never, it seems, for the CIA?

Soon after the burglary, Mark Felt (many years later to be unveiled as Bob Woodward's anonymous high-level source,

Deep Throat) was the number-two man in the FBI, in charge of the Watergate investigation. What did Mark Felt, aka Deep Throat, think about the CIA's role in this affair? When he first met with his boss, Patrick Gray, several days after the arrests, he informed Gray of his initial opinion that the burglary was, "a White House operation, a CIA operation, or both."

Was Mullen in fact a CIA contractor? We now know it was. At the request of the FBI, the CIA provided a highly confidential memo to the Bureau on June 21, 1972, just days after the arrests, admitting to having a cover arrangement with Mullen. However, throughout 1973, the Senate had been stonewalled by the CIA in the Senate requests for relevant documents. Finally, in early 1974, the Senate finally received a cache of documents from the CIA, a disclosure forced by honest CIA security agents who informed their post-Helms leadership of significant materials which had been wrongfully withheld from the Senate. They showed, among other things, this cover contract. This disclosure to the Senate, however, occurred long after the televised, widely viewed Ervin Committee Watergate hearings had concluded. The public was kept in the dark about the cover contract.

One belatedly revealed CIA document was striking. It was an internal agency report of a contact with owner Robert Mullen in February 1973, from *Time Magazine* reporter Sandy Smith, who had numerous FBI sources. He asked Mullen about whether Mullen had a cover relationship with the CIA. Clearly, the internal CIA memo of this inquiry noted, Smith had been told of Mullen's cover contract, which the Agency had revealed to the FBI following the burglary. Bennett denied all to Smith. But the internal CIA report unmistakably proved Mullen's cover status and CIA deception about it.

This arrangement means that it would not be irrational to see Watergate as having been in some manner a CIA operation, carried out undercover through Hunt and Mullen. If so, what would be the purpose of the CIA operation? Wouldn't the DNC be of only political campaign importance, however weak, to the White House, as opposed to being worthless intelligence value to the CIA? Also, since the FBI had known of the Mullen cover contract by June 21, 1972, wouldn't Mark Felt, aka Deep Throat, have also known? Of course. And if Deep Throat knew, wouldn't he have confirmed the CIA's cover relationship with Mullen to his friend, *Post* reporter Bob Woodward?

Yet we know that in more than two years after the burglary arrest, through Richard Nixon's resignation, the CIA had not been reported by the *Post* as having been involved at the time of the burglary with Hunt or Mullen. Indeed, quite to the contrary, numerous editorials and punditry in the *Post* concluded that any suggestion of CIA involvement was a ploy by the Nixon admin-istration to divert attention from its own guilt.

Let's explore for a moment the lack of reporting by the *Washington Post* of Mullen's CIA status. Did the *Post* fail to report it because it had concluded that the CIA was not involved in the burglary? Or did the *Post* have reason to so suspect, and failed to report it? If the *Post* had some basis to believe that the CIA was involved in the Watergate burglary, why wouldn't it report this stunning possibility? We will discuss this topic in later chapters.

Let us now reflect on the inferences if Mullen was a CIA cover company at the time of Watergate, having hired Hunt as an undercover CIA agent. If Mullen was a CIA cover contrac-tor, Caddy likely hired lawyers for the burglars precisely because Mullen recognized that the burglary was a CIA venture, or at least a Mullen job. But if it was a Mullen operation, wouldn't that only make sense as a CIA job?

We know now that the FBI knew about Mullen's status at least as of June 21, 1972, shortly after the burglary, and likely that someone in the FBI had eventually leaked this to Sandy Smith of *Time Magazine*, thus causing the contact by Smith with Mullen in February 1973.

June 20, 1972, or shortly before, was when Deep Throat gave Woodward the tip that Hunt was employed by the White House, which provided one of the first sensational headlines of Watergate. Wouldn't Deep Throat around the same time have told Woodward of the possibility that Hunt was also working for the CIA through Mullen? In fact, wouldn't it have been perhaps an even more sensational headline if it turned out that the head of the burglary team was also a CIA undercover operative? In that case, it would appear that, yes, he was ostensibly a White House employee, but his true employer at the time may have been the CIA. Wouldn't that revelation have put an entirely different spin on the Watergate story? Felt had suspected from the outset that the CIA may have been involved and was in continued contact with Woodward.

It's an axiom of criminal prosecutions that one who creates a false exculpatory story is likely covering up his own guilt. If the CIA was concealing Hunt's association with the Agency, was the CIA covering up its participation in the burglary? And was the *Post* covering up for the CIA?

It is therefore noteworthy that CIA records of July 10, 1972, show that Mullen's president, Bennett, had earlier made a deal with the *Post's* Bob Woodward, shortly after the burglary, that, in supposed exchange for the stories that Bennett would "feed" Woodward, a "suitably grateful" Woodward would "protect" Mullen, presumably keeping him quiet about the CIA's cover arrangement. Of course, at the time of this conversation with Woodward, which was in early summer 1972, shortly after the burglaries, Bennett had no stories to feed Woodward, who, with Deep Throat's help, hardly needed Bennett. So if Woodward kept quiet, and intentionally so, about Mullen, it was for the *Post*'s purposes, not the CIA's. With no need to help Mullen, why would the *Post* go along?

It appears that over the course of the Watergate investigation, Bennett may have been responsible in later months for at least two very lame pieces appearing in the *Post*, hardly worthy of an intentional cover-up of a major player in Washington, as well as pieces that had not been in the offing at the time of the deal.

In any case, as we end this chapter, we can conclude that at least one of the burglary team, its operational supervisor, Howard Hunt, was an undercover CIA agent at the time of the burglary. If so, was the burglary performed for CIA purposes? And if it was for the CIA, what could the target possibly have been? If Hunt was a CIA undercover operative, why would Hunt need to ply his trade under the auspices as a White House contractor? These are key questions, the answers to which lead to the ultimate unlocking of the mysteries of Watergate; we will continue to explore them in later chapters.

Image of Howard Hunt, public domain.

CHAPTER 5

HOWARD HUNT, MAN OF MYSTERY

IN PREVIOUS CHAPTERS, WE REVIEWED the very large puzzlements presented by the odd burglary of the DNC headquarters in Washington, DC. Among them, there appeared to be no campaign purpose for the White House to wiretap the DNC, even though campaign cash was used. We also talked about the enabling charter of the CIA, barring the Agency from performing domestic operations. The Agency's former collaborator who carried out those operations for the CIA inside the United States, the FBI, was now at odds with the CIA. The FBI was no longer performing those much-desired functions, which would often include break-ins and wiretaps, for the CIA.

We also noted that the White House lost the cooperation of the FBI and this same "dark ops" capability, even though the president had authority under the Constitution to order such actions noncompliant with the Fourth Amendment prohibitions against unreasonable searches and seizures, and other constitutional prohibitions such as taking property without just compensation. The FBI, which is authorized to carry such operations out, would no longer do so for White House purposes. The only way that the CIA would be able to carry out operations in the United States would be if, in some form or fashion, the CIA obtained at least a tincture of presidential approval for these operations. And while the White House lacked the capability to carry out these operations itself, it certainly had the constitutional authority to approve them or to carry them out itself.

There was every motive, as we approach 1971, following the rejection of the Huston Plan, for the CIA to seek some way to work closely with the White House. It could use that work as a basis for claiming presidential authorization to carry out its own operations. One way of doing this would be to suggest projects ostensibly for White House purposes, for an administration hungry for covert ops capability for its own ends, and carry out these missions, which were really CIA operations.

Loose talk in a White House corridor could be diarized as a request to perform what in fact was a CIA operation. The undercover agent, under this hypothesis, would be given a White House inch and proceed to take a covert CIA mile. If at some point the CIA were caught having performed such operations, they would, the CIA hoped, not be deemed illegal because the CIA would claim they were performed in good faith for the president. Severe consequences, it was hoped, could then be avoided.

We have also noted that Howard Hunt retired from the CIA in 1970 and immediately went to work for Mullen. This was right as the Huston Plan was about to be approved, or at least that is what Sullivan, Huston, and the CIA thought. If the Huston Plan was approved, the CIA would need a clever agent to carry out these operations without disturbing its ostensible supervisor, the FBI.

First, a little background about Howard Hunt. After graduating from Brown University in 1943, Hunt joined the OSS, the first solely foreign American intelligence agency, formed during

World War II. He then joined the CIA when it was founded in 1947, with a proviso in its charter that it could not perform domestic operations.

Hunt spent most of his career in undercover operations, many of them involving manipulating political influence in a government of interest—in some cases, to affect a regime change. For example, it was well known that Hunt was one of the architects and leaders of the ill-fated Bay of Pigs invasion of Cuba in 1961. As a result, much mud was slung at President Kennedy as accusations flew about whether the administration gave the invaders sufficient support, or whether the invasion was simply poorly planned by the CIA. In that invasion, Hunt worked closely with the patriotic Cuban exiles who sought to retake the island. Some of those exiles were arrested in the Watergate burglary.

After the abortive Bay of Pigs invasion, he also worked on Brigade 2506, also called—or part of—the Second Naval Guerrilla Operation, the subsequent plan to invade Cuba ultimately coming to naught, Hunt had successfully engineered the 1954 ouster of Juan Jacobo Árbenz Guzmán, the president of Guatemala, and was rumored to have worked to overthrow Salvador Allende in Chile, a task eventually effectuated after Hunt's retirement in 1973.

Hunt twice before had falsely retired from the CIA and taken undercover positions. For several years, he worked in Washington, DC, directing undercover operations based in Europe, and was also assigned to influence the American press in favor of the CIA and its initiatives, projects which he later admitted probably went beyond the elastic limits of the prohibition against domestic CIA operations.

In 1969, while Hunt was still with the Agency and OS, he importuned his fellow Brown graduate Charles Colson to hire him for White House employment. Colson was new to the job and while widely thought to be Nixon's "hatchet man." Colson was unsure of his authority and had no pressing need at the time for Hunt, in any event. But it is noteworthy that Hunt sought a job from a man known to do dirty deeds for the Oval Office. If the CIA was looking for authorization for clandestine ops, this was the man to give it, or repeat Nixonian ruminations which could be diarized as operational orders.

As Hunt later retired from regular Agency, in April of 1970, the White House interagency committee on domestic intelligence was preparing the program to become known as the Huston Plan. The plan sought to expand the capability for domestic operations by intelligence agencies other than the FBI, which was already exercising them. With a White House under Nixon now dedicated to domestic intelligence, it was unclear under the Huston Plan to what extent the White House, through Huston, or the FBI through Sullivan, would authorize the CIA to perform its own domestic operations.

Our point here is that the Huston Plan under development might make a DC-based undercover operative quite useful for the CIA. The rules were becoming gray, no longer black and white. So domestic operational possibilities were perhaps emerging for the CIA in the spring of 1970 as Hunt was supposedly retiring and the Huston Plan was readying for implementation.

In any case, it may be coincidental that around this time, on April 30, 1970, Hunt retired from the CIA and obtained a job with Mullen and Company, about which we have spoken before. Mullen could provide cover for a CIA agent, although it normally did so in foreign countries with the CIA was allowed to operate. Let us assume for a moment that Hunt was in fact selected to work with Mullen and Company to obtain domestic operations capability for the CIA, a conclusion that, as we will explore in the series, would not be irrational.

The next question would be why the Agency chose Hunt and not someone else. We know that Hunt had a vast amount of undercover operational experience, including working to influence various governments. He also had great experience stretching the elastic limits of the CIA's charter, conducting operations within the United States that Hunt later admitted might not have been permissible. But there's another qualification Hunt possessed that was unique among CIA operatives. Hunt was a graduate of Brown University. He had been active in the Brown University Club of Washington, DC. Hunt was elected to be its vice president and served for years under Charles Colson, the president of the club.

Colson was a bright, aggressive lawyer and street fighter who appealed to the more churlish instincts of President Nixon's infamous dark side. It would be rational to see that in an era when the CIA needed approval from the White House for the performance of domestic operations, and Colson was carrying out Oval Office dark ops, Hunt would be the perfect agent to get his chum's much-desired direction to be spun in the Agency's favor. All he needed, in short, to obtain some color of White House authority was a working relationship with Colson.

Under this theory, Hunt could diary a comment from Colson, "we ought to do X," or better, "the president says he want to do X," which would then be authorization to do X on behalf of the CIA, perhaps more. That would be presidential authorization through the president's agent, Colson.

Hunt had sought a White House position from Colson in 1969, while still employed with the CIA. Hunt, along with his boss, Robert Bennett, the new president of Mullen, continued to seek a part-time White House gig from Colson after Hunt joined Mullen. Interestingly, at one point in 1970, Hunt and Bennett offered Hunt's services free of charge for Colson, again to no avail. If Bennett was offering Hunt's services for free, Mullen would implicitly be subsidizing Hunt for whenever he did for the White House. We can then draw the inference that Hunt's work, ostensibly for White House benefit, would also be beneficial, perhaps *primarily* beneficial, to Mullen and Company or its client, the CIA. And of course, Hunt's proposed "free" work for the White House would likely not benefit Mullen in its public relations work since Hunt was hired for confidential and sensitive White House matters. Common sense, though, tells us that this work would benefit Mullen in its CIA relationship.

The hatchet man Colson was constantly involved in the dirty plans of the White House, much of them going nowhere beyond President Nixon's ramblings, which in turn were usually fueled by copious amounts of alcohol. It was no secret that Nixon often suggested thuggish, illegal acts, usually forgetting about the comments or later apologizing for them. These ramblings could prove very convenient for the CIA.

Later, John Ehrlichman, the counselor to the president and in Nixon's close circle, and White House aide Tom Huston would both say that they would never comply with any dark request of Nixon unless the president persisted on several occasions, on the theory that they were more ruminations than sincere commands that would not soon be regretted. Tom Huston once admitted over lunch that he made a practice of simply neglecting to carry out any questionable task that the president requested of him. Later, Nixon would invariably thank Huston for not having done so.

Huston told us he had become very concerned about newcomers to Nixon's team, who seemed all too eager to leap to carry out the president's dark suggestions without any hesitation, operating with the thought of personal advancement, not Nixon's protection. So, from the CIA's viewpoint, Hunt's attachment to

Colson, and the rich vein of presidential mutterings directed thereto, would bring the covert agent a diary full of potential White House authorizations for domestic CIA operations.

To get a bit ahead of ourselves, let's give an example of such a scheme. In late 1971, President Nixon had become upset with syndicated columnist Jack Anderson. The reporter had revealed embarrassing inside dirt on the administration's tilt toward Pakistan in the India-Pakistan silent war. According to Hunt, Colson had relayed the president's dark mutterings about Anderson in March 1972, well after the stories had impact. Hunt was years later able to seize upon slivers of anti-Anderson vitriol to claim to the Church Committee that the White House was planning to disable Jack Anderson, perhaps by poisoning or assassination. The CIA had itself been planning to disable or assassinate Anderson, the Church Committee had discovered, which would have been an illegal domestic operation. Unless, of course, the White House had approved this through Colson. Neither Nixon nor Colson had ever suggested to Hunt anything approaching poisoning, disablement, or murder. But certainly, there had been many negative thoughts spoken about Anderson. Again, White House inch, CIA mile.

But to legitimize Hunt's later discussions about disabling Anderson, Hunt claimed in testimony in 1975 that Colson had relayed such as a presidential order. This is all Hunt needed to say to support that the CIA was not acting illegally when it discussed poisoning Anderson. More on this in a later chapter, but we present this simply as an example of Hunt's seizure of loose talk to claim legality for an otherwise illegal CIA domestic operation.

The Anderson matter and the burglary of Daniel Ellsberg's psychiatrist Lewis Fielding provide two templates for Watergate. Both operations were undertaken primarily for CIA purposes, and in each case, Hunt claimed that they were undertakings the

White House had directed him to perform. The unwitting Liddy thought that Hunt was working for the White House in their poisoning-Anderson discussion with Edward Gunn, a supposedly retired CIA poisons doctor, at a lunch to which Hunt had invited the unsuspecting Liddy. They talked of poisoning Anderson, and of other ways of assassinating him, one of which was ramming Anderson's vehicle in a roundabout by hitting it with another vehicle with a certain angle proven to be deadly. At the conclusion of the meeting, Hunt asked the clueless Liddy to pay Gunn $100, winkingly telling Liddy that this was for purposes of tradecraft; Liddy complied. This payment was an act for the CIA's benefit, to show Nixon's authorization. Later, should the CIA be caught disabling or planning to disable Anderson, such as by poisoning him, Hunt and Gunn could point to this payment to show that the White House had commissioned the operation.

In June 1971, Colson contacted Hunt for his part-time hireling's first assignment with the White House. Daniel Ellsberg had just leaked the Pentagon Papers to the *New York Times*, an apparent crime, the revelation of classified national security information, certainly an act causing alarm to National Security Adviser Henry Kissinger. It was unclear to Kissinger, and eventually Nixon, if Ellsberg was in league with the Soviet Union in so doing—perhaps a farfetched conclusion from this remove—but nonetheless, the Pentagon Papers did provide some valuable information to other countries about American intelligence sources and methods. In fact, there was a strong rumor that Ellsberg had provided voluminous documents to the Soviet embassy.

Colson had told Hunt in late June 1971 that he needed his help in investigating Ellsberg, as well as for other "sensitive" projects. Hunt was hired on July 7, 1971, by the White House. We will return to that hiring session in a bit, but first note an oddity regarding the timing, which may be meaningful. Well before

Colson gave Hunt the call in June 1971, Hunt had traveled to Miami in April of 1971, where he got in touch with his old Bay of Pigs veterans. These Cuban émigrés, still ardent anti-Castro exiles, were thrilled to reunite with the legendary "Eduardo." Hunt, as Eduardo, had led them previously in the Bay of Pigs and the abandoned Second Naval Guerrilla Operation.

The feeling among the Cubans was that with Eduardo visiting, they were "back in business," as one of them had said, referring to renewed anti-Castro action. These Cubans were the operatives that eventually performed the burglary of Ellsberg's psychiatrist Dr. Lewis Fielding in Beverly Hills, California, and were later part of the two Watergate burglaries. It appears they performed other operations as well, including the wiretapping of the Chilean embassy, not an operation even remotely of interest to the White House. Why is Hunt's April contact with the Cubans so significant? Clearly, Hunt then decided to begin some sort of covert work under Mullen cover when he contacted his former operatives. But he had not yet, of course, snagged a White House job from Colson. That call came in June. Whatever he would be doing with the Cubans was not something then sought by Nixon or Colson.

Before we delve into that issue, we note that since Hunt then claimed full-time Mullen employment, this venture into Miami would have been done solely through his Mullen work. All else after his White House hire can be attributed, however implausibly, to his White House duties, such that the CIA would after this hire have either plausible deniability or plausible White House approval. But such attribution to the White House cannot be made as to his engagement with these Cuban patriots in April 1971. Our point is that Hunt could only have been reunited with the Cubans in April 1971 for CIA purposes, not those of the White House. And these were Cubans later involved in Watergate.

As Hunt was being hired by Colson in June 1971, Colson needed a formal sign-off on the hire from John Ehrlichman. At the time, Ehrlichman was extremely busy and was that day about to hop on a plane to San Clemente and the Western White House. Ehrlichman had no reason to probe what Hunt's duties would be or care about their specific features, and quickly gave Colson his perfunctory approval. Why is this important? Because in the coming year, the CIA would use virtually every department in the CIA to assist Hunt and it would claim, falsely, that Ehrlichman had asked for that widespread cooperation. Thus, the CIA would use Ehrlichman to explain what looked to be CIA operations backed by the full support of virtually every Agency department.

Hunt had used Helms's heavy-handed assistance to get his job with Mullen. Then Hunt importuned the CIA employment assistance department to seek retired CIA personnel to work on his team. He retained the CIA graphics department to prepare the GEMSTONE charts for Liddy, depicting the fatuous Hunt-inspired spy schemes he unsuccessfully presented to John Mitchell. He used other CIA sections for disguises, for weapons, for fake IDs, safe houses, surveillance equipment, for medical evaluations, each from a different department. How does the CIA explain this widespread support of a supposedly retired agent? Obviously, this support suggests that Hunt was working for the CIA undercover in his White House posting. According to the CIA, all of this came about because Ehrlichman had called General Robert Cushman of the CIA on the day of Hunt's hire, asking for "carte blanche" assistance for Hunt, in the words of Cushman. Ehrlichman strongly denied doing so, well after any criminal jeopardy would attach to him. In any case, such a request would not have been illegal. So Ehrlichman, if he made it, would not have a motive to falsify. Ehrlichman's denial, in short, is highly credible, especially in view of Ehrlichman's non-involvement with any tasks that Hunt was to perform for Colson.

In short, why would Ehrlichman ask the CIA for assistance when he had no idea what Hunt's portfolio would be? Ehrlichman later commissioned the obtaining of Ellsberg's records, but that was a month later, and it is not clear he knew Hunt was involved. The CIA's pathetic attempts to later create one-sided documents to support this "carte blanche" request are themselves evidence of guilt via fabrication of documents. If Ehrlichman is telling the truth, as he likely is, this widespread Agency assistant shows Hunt was an active agent gaining coordinated widespread CIA support, authorized from the very top of the Agency.

Later, in April of 1972, shortly before the first Watergate break-in, the alarmed CIA station chief in Miami inquired of high-level officials in Washington, DC, if they knew of Hunt's activities with various CIA Cuban assets in Miami, based on Eugenio Martinez's worried inquiries. The station chief was told very peremptorily by Langley headquarters to "cool it" and to cease further inquiry, stating that Hunt was on White House business. The response, which infuriated the station chief, was a strong indication that Hunt's activities were receiving protection from the highest levels. In any case, the best template for Hunt's undercover CIA work is not his discussion with Liddy about the disabling of columnist Jack Anderson, which we will treat more fully later. An even better example of Hunt's undercover work would be found in the burglary of Daniel Ellsberg's psychiatrist Lewis Fielding.

Please recall that if Hunt was a covert CIA infiltrator, he would want to inveigle the White House to approve an operation that Hunt would promote as good for the White House, while in fact he was doing so to gain a tincture of presidential national security authorization for an otherwise illegal CIA operation.

So, let's examine evidence of whether the Watergate burglaries were at least in part a covert CIA operation, and begin
with the Ellsberg break-in. If that burglary was in part a CIA job,
albeit one with White House approval, we can infer similarly for
the Watergate burglaries.

Image of White House, public domain.

CHAPTER 6

CIA OPERATIONS UNDER WHITE HOUSE COVER

ANY HISTORY OF THE WATERGATE scandal includes some mention of the apparent irrationality of the Nixon campaign's risky burglary of an unattractive target, the DNC, when Nixon was cruising to a lopsided win over presumed DNC nominee Senator George McGovern of South Dakota. But the same can be said of the CIA involvement in the burglaries. What of value would the CIA obtain from wiretapping the unexciting DNC? We have discussed in previous chapters the lack of motive for the White House to wiretap the DNC. But what about the CIA? Wouldn't the Agency also lack a motive?

Let us mention one longtime serious interest of the CIA: sex, a key part of its "research" into manipulation of subjects of interest. For example, in the 1950s, the CIA set up an apartment on Telegraph Hill in San Francisco, complete with a two-way mirror to watch prostitutes and drugged subjects. Sexual activity was an important avenue in the search to understand psychological control, a weapon of extortion, and a means for getting information. All of this was revealed during the Senate's Church Committee hearings in 1975, a post-Watergate investigation into intelligence agency abuses. Sexual sites operated by the CIA throughout the country, over decades, have been solidly confirmed. But more on sexual targets later.

Hunt knew he was hired by the White House in part to find ways to discredit Daniel Ellsberg. He and Mullen president Robert Bennett then helpfully suggested to the White House "Plumbers" unit that the CIA medical staff could do a psychological profile on Ellsberg, to which the Plumbers happily agreed. We would mention here that the White House Plumbers were extreme naïfs, as David Young and Egil Krogh were true Boy Scouts. A third Plumber at the time was the unguided missile, Gordon Liddy, later to go to the CRP.

The CIA produced intentionally bland and meaningless reports on Ellsberg's psychology, to the dismay of the Plumbers. Then Hunt and Bennett suggested to Krogh and Young that the CIA psychiatrists needed to have Ellsberg's psychiatric records so that its staff could do a thorough psychiatric portrait of him, presumably to be used in discrediting Ellsberg. Even if we assume a devastating future psychological profile of Ellsberg, how was that to be given wide circulation among the general public? It is not clear that any of the White House operatives were thinking along these practical, prudent lines. But the White House was not rational, given the fulminations of Kissinger and his cohort the president, such that the appetite for getting dirt on Ellsberg was insatiable. As only naïfs would do so, as Krogh and Young prepared a written memorandum to be initialed by Ehrlichman seeking approval to obtain Ellsberg's psychiatric records.

Daniel Ellsberg had been a protégé of Henry Kissinger early in the Vietnam War, and an analyst at Rand Corporation in Santa Monica. Originally, Ellsberg was a hawkish Vietnam War advocate. After some period of time, he turned ardently antiwar, and the result was his leak of the Pentagon Papers to the *New York*

Times. But his interest to the CIA may have extended beyond the Vietnam War. Ellsberg had been a very close friend of Frances FitzGerald, an outspoken antiwar advocate and author of the bestseller *Fire in the Lake,* a critical look at the Vietnam War. That the two would become friends is unremarkable, since both were strident advocates of withdrawal from the war, but what likely interested the CIA in FitzGerald was her status as the daughter of the late Desmond FitzGerald, a so-called Knight Templar of the OSS, the World War II forerunner to the modern CIA, under William Donovan.

FitzGerald became one of the leading black ops OSS operatives. His black ops work for the OSS eventually morphed into black ops work for the CIA, when it was formed in 1947. Undoubtedly, when Desmond FitzGerald died, the Agency hoped that all his dark secrets had gone with him to the grave. However, Desmond was very close with his daughter Frances, and the possibility loomed large that he had informed his daughter in his later years of his ugly activities with the Agency, while she in turn may have betrayed them to her close friend Ellsberg. It would be quite reasonable for the CIA to feel that if Ellsberg would leak the Pentagon Papers, he could also leak very significant CIA secrets learned from the FitzGeralds. What did Ellsberg know, for example, about the assassination of Ngo Dinh Deum, South Vietnam's president, and other sensitive matters? In short, the CIA may have been interested in what information had made its way to Ellsberg from FitzGerald or otherwise. It may as well have been interested in compromising sexual information that could keep Ellsberg from blowing another whistle.

Hunt wished to document White House approval for a CIA operation. Whether he suggested the written memo is unknown. But it was clearly not in the best interest of the White House, if in fact the White House thought this was an illegal operation.

At least Krogh and Young, if not Ehrlichman, knew that getting the psychiatric records would require an illegal break-in of the psychiatrist's office. Ehrlichman, somewhat plausibly, later testified that while he penned that the operation not be "traceable" to the White House, he did not think illegal means would be used. Moreover, Ehrlichman, with some justification, claimed as well that this was a national security operation. But, again, the naivete of the White House, including Ehrlichman, is shown by this amateurish documentation of its arguable crime, all national security protests notwithstanding. Another way to analyze this tableau would be to point out that if this was in fact thought by the White House to be a national security operation, there should have been prepared a national security "finding," covering all flanks. But nothing about Watergate, as we will discuss, shows any prudent legal thinking.

Ehrlichman could easily have prepared such a national security finding, signed by the president, in which it was determined that Ellsberg might be a foreign agent, therefore necessitating obtaining his psychiatric records. Such may have plausibly promised revelations by Ellsberg to the psychiatrist of matters of interest to the national security of the United States, such as admission of Russian contacts. But these eager Boy Scouts and the nonnaïve but crazed Liddy did not see the necessity of doing so, nor did Ehrlichman. Later Hunt and Liddy cased the office of Fielding and Hunt took a picture of Liddy in Fielding's parking lot, near a sign clearly denominating that it was Fielding's spot. We raise a key question here. If this in fact was a criminal action, which at least Krogh and Young thought it might be, why would this picture be taken? Isn't this evidence of a crime? But for the CIA, the picture was not evidence of a crime, but of presidential approval, since Liddy was a White House agent. The picture, in short, might prove in the future to be a CIA "get out of jail free" card, should anyone question whether the White House had authorized this mission. In fact, it later operated as a "go to jail" card for Ehrlichman. Liddy at the time of the picture was still a White House employee, working under Ehrlichman's aegis.

Likewise, you will see throughout Watergate the fine hand of the CIA in documenting White House authorization for its other domestic operations, documents that might incriminate the White House but which would save the CIA, should these operations later be discovered. It is noteworthy that the photograph of Liddy in the parking lot was taken seemingly at the behest of Hunt. If the CIA was not involved in the Ellsberg/Fielding burglary, why would the CIA receive and retain a picture of this casing operation?

More tellingly, the team who carried out the operation entered Fielding's office but claimed no success in finding Ellsberg's records. That night, however, champagne was on ice, the corks were popped, and the group appeared to celebrate. The burglary team, however, had told Hunt and Liddy that they had not been able to locate Ellsberg's psychiatric file, which would have meant that the break-in was a complete failure.

Fielding later said that Ellsberg's file had noticeably been fingered through. Also later, burglar Felipe de Diego stated that helped copy Ellsberg's file. From this, we can deduce that the CIA in fact obtained the Ellsberg psychiatric file, but that it withheld from the White House the fruits of the operation. The CIA, in short, was pursuing through Hunt its secret agenda, hidden from the White House. This is an example of the CIA's not only using White House authorization to perform domestic operations, otherwise illegal, but also of the CIA's penchant for sequestering the fruits for itself and not allowing the White House to have those same fruits.

This is a template for the Watergate burglary, in which phone calls were overheard but not recorded, so that the CIA could curate what went to the White House. Clearly, Liddy had been kept in the dark about the CIA involvement in the Fielding burglary, but all others involved on the team were CIA assets, as in Watergate. Liddy was important, not only because he provided financial support, but because he also was an unmistakable marker of White House approval. This would hold true in Watergate. Thus, the CIA would want Liddy's photo in Fielding's parking lot, just as it would want his payments for bugging devices in Watergate. Liddy's involvement, in short, was CIA's proof of White House authorization of its operations.

Before we leave this subject, let's briefly talk about two other operations in which the White House naively approved activity for its ostensible benefit, but what might have been, and seemed to have been, a CIA operation, in which the White House did not receive any expected fruits. Hunt was sent by the White House, at his suggestion, to interview one Clifton DeMott, who was said to have potential information on the Kennedy Chappaquiddick death of Mary Jo Kopechne. Hunt reported back that DeMott had no information of any value.

Hunt also interviewed Lucien Conein, a former CIA operative with suspected knowledge of the assassination of President Diem of South Vietnam, information that might help the White House to discredit the hated Kennedys. Hunt interviewed Conein in Ehrlichman's office with the intent of using a recording device hidden in the couch. According to Hunt, the recorder was not appropriately activated, so he and Conein had a long, booze-drenched conversation, which Hunt claimed not to remember. So, again, the White House received no fruits. So much for the CIA's help to the White House. Did Hunt obtain from Conein information valuable to the CIA? It was likely so. Certainly, though, as in the Fielding burglary, the White House got none.

To follow up on this theme, we can draw a reasonable inference from the evidence that the CIA had its own interest in obtaining authorization to wiretap the phone of a minor official during the Watergate break-in, while giving certain campaign operatives, at least Liddy, the false hope of obtaining information on DNC director Larry O'Brien. We do not imply by this that any particular White House personnel actually thought Larry O'Brien was to be tapped, but only that this was the justification offered to the CRP's Liddy, and would be given to anyone who learned of the wiretapping. This, in other words, was the cover story should somebody connected to the White House want to know the goal of this operation.

Now let's go to the immediate aftermath of the Watergate burglaries. Howard Hunt, after the Watergate arrests of the five burglars under his supervision, visited both the White House and Mullen offices across the street from the White House. But for whatever reason, he left his White House safe as it was, with no effort to clean it out or even to remove key materials, such as his operational diary and address book. CIA operators customarily keep diaries of their actions, including appropriate authorizations.

There were many oddities, screwups, accidents of fate, dishonesties, and much bad judgment in Watergate, all of which conspired to keep the real story of Watergate hidden. One of these was Hunt's decision to keep his distinctive clothbound Hermès notebooks in his White House safe, and not take them with him when he departed the White House on the morning of June 17, 1972. This failure was literally a history-making omission because if he had simply retrieved his notebooks and presented them in the public record, the history of this country would have taken a noticeably different turn. The public would have eventually seen that Watergate was at least in part a CIA operation, undisclosed to the White House, and Nixon would have been seen as much a victim as a victimizer. But that morning, Hunt elected, for some reason, to keep his notebooks in his White House safe, perhaps, we speculate, to lend a White House imprimatur to the notebooks.

One of the notebooks contained a list of names and addresses, which was important, but not crucial. The other notebook, however, was the diary that CIA agents are required to keep during operations. The very notion that he kept such a diary is evidence that Hunt was working as a CIA agent while performing tasks for the White House. Hunt later claimed that he had noted the authorization for the burglaries in his notebooks, and for that reason sought the return of them from the prosecutor in his pretrial discovery motion. Before we go further, let's stop right there.

What is the significance of Hunt's keeping an operational notebook? If a CIA-trained operative keeps an operational diary, the very nature of following that practice means that he is on a CIA operation. If he regularly keeps one on a posting, he is a CIA undercover agent at that posting. So, when Hunt later claimed that he kept an operational notebook for his work at the White House, this is essentially game, set, and match for the notion that Hunt was an undercover CIA operative while working at the White House beginning in July 1971.

Now let's go to Hunt's situation as it existed in the fall of 1972, several months after the burglary arrests. Indictments were issued for the Watergate burglary on September 15, 1972, naming the five burglars arrested at the site plus two supervisors—Hunt and Liddy. On October 11, 1972, following the indictment, Hunt, through his lawyers, made a discovery motion that the government prosecutors produce his clothbound Hermès notebooks and other contents of his White House safe. Why? By this time, the CIA had decided to disavow any participation in the Watergate burglary. It would naturally be in the interest of the CIA to have Hunt take one for the team and spend a couple of years in a country club prison without pointing to the CIA as being involved. But that would not be in Hunt's best interest. He previously had hopes of taking over the lucrative CIA contract of Mullen, but that contract was being terminated by the CIA because there had been too much Watergate publicity. So, that promising possibility was now gone and he no longer needed the goodwill of the CIA. He had a very warm family life with the love of his life and spouse of twenty-three years, Dorothy. She was likely a CIA agent too, terminated in the wake of the scandal from her undercover job at the Spanish embassy. She was also no longer beholden to the CIA.

Hunt knew that if he pleaded guilty, Judge John Sirica, known as "Maximum John," would figuratively hang him from the rafters. Sirica had taken on Watergate as his pet project, for which he was receiving glowing kudos from the press. Sirica was threatening stiff sentences to force identification of the sponsors of the burglaries, which he implied likely resided in the White House. Hunt had no realistic hopes of pleading guilty and achieving a lightened sentence without spilling his guts about the higher-ups ultimately responsible. But turning prosecution witness would mean that the White House would not pay his mounting legal bills. Hunt decided he would be best served by looking for an acquittal through a defense that became known as the "CIA defense"—that is, Watergate was a legitimate national security CIA mission. He wanted to retrieve his diary, which would document that White House authorization had been given for the burglaries, seemingly, we infer, by John Dean, and by hearsay through John Mitchell. Therefore, the CIA had considered this a valid national security mission, the status of which, in turn, he was reporting to the Agency as documented by his notebooks.

We note in this regard that Hunt had played regular tennis matches with Thomas Karamessines, his suspected CIA handler, the associate director of plans, a very high official in the CIA hierarchy. Did his notebook show that he had discussed these operations with Karamessines, thereby cementing the notion that this was a CIA operation? In other words, would it have shown CIA approval? Very likely it would have, and if so, Hunt at least would thereby have a good faith belief in the lawfulness of his actions, a valid defense that negates criminal intent, along with, of course, White House approval.

Moreover, Hunt's notebooks would have shown that for several other missions, such as the Fielding burglary, he had operated as a CIA agent undercover for national security purposes as authorized, he would claim, by the White House, and approved by the CIA for its own purposes. But when he reviewed the government production in response to his discovery request, the notebooks, oddly, were not included. Hunt knew that these notebooks would be central to his defense because they showed he was keeping records as required for CIA missions, and because they showed the Agency making decisions in keeping abreast of status.

John Dean had cleaned out Hunt's safe, giving most of the contents to the regularly assigned FBI agents seeking them. Some sensitive files, such as Hunt's manufactured cables about Diem's assassination, intended to falsely implicate the Kennedy administration, Dean had given to L. Patrick Gray, the interim FBI director, for his future disposal. Dean, however, kept the Hermès notebooks, and only the Hermès notebooks, for himself. Likely, we infer, the notebooks incriminated Dean. There has been no suggestion that anybody at the FBI or White House had read Hunt's Hermès notebooks other than Dean himself, after sequestering them.

When Hunt's lawyers inquired as to the whereabouts of the missing notebooks, baffled prosecutors had no answer. They then asked Dean if he had seen Hunt's notebooks. Dean told the prosecutors, disingenuously, "I don't even know what a Hermès notebook is!" He then whispered to the prosecutors about his delivery of sensitive files to Gray, which served to warn them off of any further inquiry of Dean. It is likely that Dean had frightened them into thinking Gray had kept the notebooks and was hiding them—quite sensitive information. Therefore, from Hunt's perspective, a very cogent piece of corroborate evidence for the CIA defense was now missing. His ability to make his case that this was a CIA operation was taking on water.

Even though Hunt had infiltrated the White House to document, however tendentiously, White House authorization for various CIA projects, once the highly publicized Watergate arrests occurred, the CIA wisely determined that it would be bureaucratically suicidal to emerge from the shadows to claim this burglary as its own. Therefore, the CIA would not be offering him assistance in this defense, to be sure, and indeed, quite the contrary.

Let's assume there had been no arrests, and ten years after the Watergate burglary, a congressional committee discovered the CIA had been monitoring prostitution. In that eventuality, the CIA would have been able to show White House authorization for the wiretapping, thereby rendering, at least arguably, this entire operation legal in the haze of time's passage. But in the summer of 1972, perhaps this was a not ideal timing for that claim. And it was especially inconvenient with a media—the *Washington Post*—dead set on getting Nixon.

After the burglars were arrested and Hunt was being labeled by the *Washington Post* as a White House operative, it made perfectly good sense for the CIA to deny any role in the burglary. Of course, what was good for the Agency was not good for Hunt. Luckily, Hunt had his CIA agent wife to testify for him. After all, as James McCord testified later, perhaps disingenuously, Dorothy was a courier for hush money payments. Certainly, Dorothy, an undercover agent herself, could buttress her husband's claim that this was an undercover CIA operation. Maybe McCord would testify this was a CIA operation, a somewhat more doubtful prospect, given McCord's tremendous loyalty to the Agency.

Hunt *had* Dorothy as a potential witness until December 8, 1972, just weeks before the January 1973 trial was to commence. Her United flight to Chicago crashed on that day, killing most aboard. If the CIA did not cause this crash, it was a very lucky beneficiary of it. Whether the crash was mere fortuity or was the result of CIA sabotage is not a question we can answer here. We can say, however, that within minutes of the crash, at least one CIA man and numerous FBI agents, very quickly on the scene, were sifting through the wreckage, which was somewhat unusual, almost as if the crash was anticipated. Was there some reason that the FBI had expected sabotage? Within one week of the crash, Colonel Alexander Butterfield of the White House staff, long rumored to be a defense intelligence plant, resigned to become administrator of the Federal Aviation Administration (FAA), which had responsibilities to investigate this crash.

Now Hunt had no witness on whom he could rely to corroborate his defense, and no longer had his Hermès notebooks—strong documentary corroboration. There was only one other witness who could buttress his claim that this was an undercover operation, and that was James McCord. Interestingly, if Hunt had retained his notebooks, Dorothy would not have been as important to the case as she became, and perhaps she would have lived longer.

So, the combination of no notebooks and no Dorothy was potentially deadly to his case. Hunt's only salvation would be McCord.

Three weeks later, after the crash, as the trial approached, on December 28, 1972, William Bittman, Hunt's lawyer, met with Gerald Alch, McCord's lawyer. Bittman inquired of Alch whether or not McCord would testify to the false retirement protocols of the CIA, and, ideally, testify that Watergate was an undercover CIA operation, directed by falsely retired operatives.

On December 28, after meeting with Bittman, Alch met with his client, McCord. He explored with McCord the CIA defense that Hunt had communicated to Bittman. McCord, however, was having none of it. Instead, he roundly denounced the defense as a White House effort to falsely pin this on the CIA. This reaction, ironically, was in a perverse way consistent with Hunt's defense, showing an active CIA undercover agent, McCord, defending his employer.

John Dean, thinking that a Hunt guilty plea would help him avoid his own exposure, urged Hunt to plead guilty. And Hunt, now bereft of any defense, did so. Judge Sirica made him plead guilty to all six counts. Let us stop once more to comment as we again force a Nixon team error which would have devastating consequences.

John Dean pushed hard for Hunt to cop a plea, thinking that this would be best for Dean as a potentially liable player. But by Hunt's pleading, as Dean, not a skilled lawyer, had not antici-pated, Hunt was now subject to be called to testify before the grand jury because he no longer had as a result of his plea any Fifth Amendment rights. Now, Hunt could be compelled to spill his guts to a grand jury, which would hurt, among others (we

infer), Dean. Once again, Dean's inexperience as a criminal lawyer bedeviled him, but hurt Richard Nixon far more in the end.

Hunt has written that if the notebooks had surfaced, one of
his principals would have been shown to have been John Dean.
In any case, now John Dean made an incalculable error. Hunt
had pleaded guilty, ironically per Dean's urging, and was likely
to testify soon in front of a grand jury. Dean was now vulnerable
to Hunt's future testimony, which was not likely to occur until
after his sentencing. But while Dean had blundered into exposing himself and other Nixon officials, he had also unwittingly
done much to protect the CIA, as we will see. After all, if there
was one White House official who clearly knew of the Watergate
burglary in advance, that would be John Dean. This guilty official would also be the best witness to get the president, not for
the burglary, but for the cover-up, which the unctuous Dean had
led. Dean's implication of the president would be a shiny object
drawing attention away from a rogue CIA.

In yet another irony, had the CIA's participation been made
dramatically public, as would have occurred had Hunt put on
his CIA defense at trial, Nixon perhaps could have turned the
tide and escaped his ultimate banishment by looming impeachment. Dean's client thus would have been benefited, but Dean
would not have. The notebooks presumably would have shown
Dean's direct involvement and sponsorship of the burglaries. His
conviction would have been assured no matter what happened
to Nixon. Indeed, Nixon would have had his fall guy, Dean, and
with a straight face, could have claimed profound betrayal by
both Dean (his trusted lawyer) and the CIA. But by unwittingly
protecting the CIA, Dean had made Nixon more of an unprotected target, and made his own testimony against the president
eagerly sought by both the Senate Watergate committee and the

Watergate special prosecutor. So, if Dean was a bad lawyer, he was a very skilled turncoat.

Dean would become the star witness against his former client, the president, and go on to a glamorous career as an author, speaker, and television pundit. Nixon, on the hand, would leave his theretofore successful presidency in disgrace and spend the rest of his life trying to rehabilitate his image.

We have spoken in this and the past chapters about the role of Mullen and Company as a CIA cover company and the CIA defense planned by Hunt. Finally, we have posited to you that Hunt had infiltrated the White House so that he and the Agency could claim presidential authorization for his undercover CIA actions. But for such presidential approval to legitimize his actions, they would need to be for a national security purpose. We will discuss that perceived national security purpose in future chapters.

There will be some advocates of the conventional view who will claim this rendering of a CIA defense was all nonsense, the result of a spy's fevered imagination. It would be their contention that pro-Nixon advocates have seized upon this imaginary defense, mitigating the ex-president's guilt as a last-ditch desperation pass play. It is of great interest, therefore, what Hunt had to say about this before the Senate Watergate Committee. He appeared on September 24, 1973, long after the dramatic televised hearings of May and June that had featured star witnesses Dean, Magruder, Mitchell, and Ehrlichman.

In his written opening statement, Hunt was careful to avoid saying outright that he considered himself to be working as a CIA contractor during the burglaries. At the same time, he pushed most of his CIA defense, that is, presidential authorization for a national security operation. Since no Nixon administration figure claimed a defense of national security for the burglaries, as

Ehrlichman would do for the Fielding/Ellsberg burglary, if there was such a national security purpose, it would be for that of the CIA, not of the White House or CRP.

Hunt, in his statement under oath, admitted his postretirement employment with the CIA-connected entity, which he did not name but we now know to be Mullen:

> *After retirement from the CIA, I was employed by a firm whose officials maintained a relationship with the CIA. I engaged in essentially the same kind of work I had performed for the CIA.*[2]

After claiming that the Fielding burglary was a national security operation, Hunt noted the missing notebooks that had been left in his safe, which he claimed would show his defense to the Watergate burglaries:

> *Some material was produced but significant material was withheld or destroyed. Because the government had withheld evidence, I knew there was no chance of proving my defense.*[3]

Then Hunt spoke of the effect of this destruction or withholding, which he currently blamed on the government as hurting his defense of a presidentially authorized national security operation:

> *This official misconduct deprived me of evidence which would have supported my position that my participation in the Watergate was an activity authorized within the power of the president of the*

---

2   *Select Committee on Presidential Campaign Activities, Before the United States Senate.* (1973) (testimony of Howard Hunt), 3,663.
3   Ibid.

United States. I thought it was an unwise opera-
tion, but I viewed it as lawful.[4]

To be sure, Hunt in his testimony did not admit that the true national security purpose was sexual blackmail, but, rather, instead described it in his autobiography as searching for contributions by the Fidel Castro regime to the Democrats, a sellable purpose, even though itself a cover story more favorable to the CIA than the truth. The burglars, it was speculated, were looking for "Fidelista" campaign contributions, donations either from Castro's regime or from those who were supporters of Castro, all of which would sully the Democrats. But there was never any evidence of this and at best, this has always been a cover story used to explain the presence of anti-Castro Cuban patriots on the burglary team. The Fidelista target would be a national security excuse, but it would be one to implicate the White House, not the CIA. There is not a scintilla of evidence in all the many hours of White House tapes that the White House in 1972 cared a whit about Fidelista contributions to the Democrats. Neither John Dean nor Jeb Magruder, the two young lieutenants who likely bought off on Hunt's plans to tap the DNC, with Dean likely a clear proponent, said anything about the Fidelista motive. It is a canard through which the *Post* or other anti-Nixon advocates can invent a reason, any reason, for the campaign to embark on this silly venture. Liddy, after all, was told by McCord the target was O'Brien's office—also false. But if in fact this was a national security operation, as Hunt thought it was, as did McCord in his testimony, what was its true purpose?

We know that in the Fielding burglary, the true national security purpose was obtaining the Ellsberg psychiatric records, which the CIA thought might yield confidential admissions by

---

4   Ibid., 3,664.

him, especially as would concern his Russian contacts or his knowledge of past CIA misdeeds. And we cannot discount the possibility that the Agency was looking for compromising dirt on Ellsberg. But there has been no wide public exposure of the Watergate burglar's true target. In the next chapter, we will examine the true target of the burglaries and solve yet another of the mysteries of Watergate.

Image of White House chief of staff H. R. Haldeman and
President Richard Nixon, public domain.

CHAPTER 7

THE UNDETERMINED TARGET

ONE OF THE BIGGEST MYSTERIES of the Watergate burglary has been its true purpose, about which there has been rampant and generally incredible speculation. As we noted earlier, in June 1972, it appeared that the Democrats would nominate Senator George McGovern of South Dakota as their presidential candidate. McGovern was considered a very weak opponent for Nixon, auguring an easy win for the incumbent president. Nixon's stronger opponent would have been Maine Senator Edmund Muskie. But Muskie, once favored for nomination, melted down during the primaries, most famously by crying publicly about vicious press stories revealing his wife's drinking habits. He never recovered, and McGovern soon overtook him.

As a side note, we mention that the stories about Muskie's wife may have emanated from White House sources. With this weak candidate, McGovern, on the horizon, what caused this seemingly desperate, unnecessary burglary of an unpromising source, the DNC? As of June 17, 1972, the DNC would have possession of no campaign strategies because no candidate had yet been nominated. If Nixon's campaign wanted McGovern's campaign strategies, it should logically have burgled the McGovern campaign headquarters, not the DNC.

For almost fifty years, various theories have been bruited about, none greatly convincing, suggesting an election campaign motive for the strategy. Throughout the summer of 1972 after the arrests, commentators were grappling with what seemed to be, in the words of White House press secretary Ronald Ziegler, a "third-rate burglary," seemingly bungled badly. Even FBI agents quoted by the aggressive *Washington Post* on September 9, 1972, seemed to be scratching their investigative heads: "FBI agents were not able to learn the objectives of the Watergate break-in."

The puzzlement by FBI agents likely resulted from the tap's placement on the phone of the unimportant Spencer Oliver Jr. The wiretap monitor had told the FBI he was listening to "explicitly intimate" conversations between men and women. Public attention had been focused on this question of purpose, when on September 7, 1972, the DNC held a press conference focused on revelations of a heretofore unknown witness, a "participant" not identified by name.

In that press conference of September 7, 1972, DNC Director Larry O'Brien surmised that Republicans wanted to listen to his conversations since he "had conversations with perhaps every prominent Democrat in America, including every candidate for the Democratic presidential nomination." O'Brien, the article noted, was the national campaign director for McGovern's presidential bid. We note here that such a title was largely ceremonial. O'Brien at the time would have had virtually no information about McGovern's strategies. In any case, it was suggested in the *Post* article that the Nixon White House was seeking to tap O'Brien's phone to gain access to these intimate conversations with influential Democrats. While many subscribed to O'Brien's view at that time, and others may still hold it, there are serious problems with it.

O'Brien had not been in DC for some weeks prior to the first burglary and would not return for several more following the second burglary, well after the Democratic Convention in July. We also note that the burglars were seeking a large cache of documents, as shown by the many rolls of film and camera equipment seized at the time the burglary arrests, suggesting that documents were more important than conversations. This has given rise to a number of theories, some aided by the involvement of the anti-Castro Cubans.

One theory that has taken hold over the years, to which many still subscribe, involves speculation, perhaps with a shred of evidence, that Howard Hughes had given Nixon $100,000 in cash prior to the election. Larry O'Brien, we have noted, had previously represented Hughes. Nixon always thought it was O'Brien behind the outing in 1960, during his campaign against John F. Kennedy, that Hughes had loaned $205,000 to Nixon's brother, Donald Nixon, which appeared to be disguised payment to Nixon himself.

Perhaps, it was speculated, Nixon was now looking to see what evidence O'Brien had on him in 1972. This theory would be based on speculation that Nixon was worried about the latest Hughes cash infusion, which would be supposedly leaked through O'Brien, and, again, damage Nixon's chances. But even though this speculation is still being offered fifty years later, the many hours of White House tapes released to the public contain no evidence that this was Nixon's worry, or that the worry was transmitted to John Mitchell or any of the team that entered Watergate during either the first or second burglary. If that were the purpose, Liddy would have known it and the burglars would have taken action directed at it. But they most assuredly did not.

At the time of the arrests, some camera clamps had been placed on a desktop and two drawers were open, but it was not reported where the drawers were, or on what desk the camera clamps had been placed, or what information may have been contained in that part of the office. Nor was it reported in what part of the office this activity occurred. This lack of locational clues as to the target allowed great leeway for speculation about the purpose of the burglary, virtually all of it tied to some inferred motive of Nixon. So, what light can we now shed on the purpose of the burglary? We believe that piecing together the evidence, the target can now be clearly shown, and another of the many mysteries of Watergate solved.

The wiretap monitor, Alfred Baldwin III, was an ex-FBI agent hired by James McCord to perform certain security operations. He was not hired until May 1, 1972. His first duty was chaperoning the unruly, hard-drinking Martha Mitchell, wife of Attorney General John Mitchell, on campaign trips. He was then assigned to monitor overheard conversations on the Watergate wiretaps and make notes of the conversations for transmission to McCord.

Our first clue about the wiretapping target comes from Baldwin's FBI statement, when he related his initial overhearings. When he first visited, on May 24, 1972, the monitoring station, Room 419 in the Howard Johnson hotel, no wiretaps had yet been installed. By the time they were installed, McCord had already changed rooms for a better position from which to monitor the sixth floor of the Watergate office building, across the street from the monitoring station, moving the monitoring station to Room 723. In short, no wiretaps had been in place when Baldwin stayed in Room 419. However, while Baldwin was in Room 419 on his first visit, McCord gave him a headset, on which he then listened to "a man discussing his marital problem" with a woman, seemingly a wiretapped conversation, but, again, one prior to any tap installed by the burglars.

This suggests that that there were already bugs in place at a nearby bordello, but not yet placed in the DNC, and that McCord had picked up this wiretap signal, presumably the CIA's monitoring of the escort service. The "marital problems" discussion offers a window through which to analyze the true target of the subsequent wiretaps. In his original 302 statement to the FBI,[5] Baldwin told the FBI that during the two weeks of this monitoring the first tap, he had listened to a number of "explicitly intimate" conversations.

After Baldwin gave his first press interview to the *Los Angeles Times* in late September 1972, the subsequently published story was written to emphasize Baldwin's supposed instruction from McCord to listen for "hot political gossip." The *Los Angeles Times* and the *Post* both followed up with a story of Baldwin on one occasion delivering logs to the CRP, with the suggestion that he had been delivering the logs to one of the three named Republican officials—Robert Odle or J. Glenn Sedam of the CRP or William Timmons of the White House. Of course, this report would make the wiretapping look as if it was performed for political purposes.

In their book *All the President's Men*, however, Woodward and Bernstein admit that they made a mistake in naming these officials as possible recipients. This October 6, 1972, article about these three purported log recipients helped immeasurably to cast the overhearings as targeting political gossip. We note here that the protocol in place was to transmit wiretap logs from Baldwin to McCord. McCord would then type them up and give them to Liddy, who would then refashion them again into a more profes-

---

5   FD-302 forms are used by FBI agents to "report or summarize the interviews that they conduct." They are used to record statements made by non-primary subjects.

sional looking report for subsequent delivery to CRP director Jeb Magruder. Intriguingly, McCord claimed to Liddy, falsely, that he did not have the technology to record the overheard conversations. Accordingly, it there was a desire to use these monitored conversations, the triple hearsay of this process would render them useless for evidentiary purposes. But our point here is that the content released was subject to McCord's editing. Another takeaway is that it was not McCord's job to deliver the logs other than to Liddy.

According to Liddy, he made two deliveries of wiretapped logs to Magruder, one on June 8, 1972, and one on June 15, 1972. The second delivery was right before the second burglary. According to Baldwin's testimony, he made his own separate delivery to the CRP, on instruction by McCord when McCord was out of town, which occurred June 6 through June 8. So, it would have made no sense for McCord to have logs delivered somewhere by Baldwin unless the delivery was outside the proscribed procedure. And, after all, Liddy was the person to whom to deliver the logs, and if chain of command was to be followed, McCord would have called Baldwin to deliver logs to Liddy, not to the CRP. It certainly made no sense that delivery would be made virtually at the same time Liddy was getting, at least presumably, the same logs from McCord and presenting the same materials to Magruder. Unless, of course, there was something in the materials McCord asked Baldwin to deliver that were not given to Liddy and not meant for the White House, and to a recipient not in the White House chain of command.

At some point Baldwin told investigators that the person to whom he delivered the logs may have had "two last names." We note that McCord's part-time contractor, whom we will discuss later, was named Louis "Lou" Russell, and he sometimes worked as a security guard for the CRP. Since Baldwin delivered the envelope to a security guard at the CRP, the addressee may well have been Louis Russell. But more about Russell later.

Even given the White House connections of both Liddy and Hunt, the *Post* story on Baldwin's looking for "hot political gossip," and the target of the burglary being the DNC, the natural speculation was that the Nixon administration wished to wiretap the Democrats to obtain campaign strategy. This speculation, however, today, after years after extensive study, still lacks basis in fact.

Perhaps the most important revelation about the true target comes from Anthony Lucas, a respected *New York Times* reporter who wrote the highly praised 1976 book, *Nightmare*. Collecting fragments of anecdotal evidence, Lucas suggests a possible stunning motive for the burglary:

> *Several secretaries used Oliver's phone because they thought it was the most private one in the office. They would say, "We can talk. I'm on Spencer Oliver's phone." Some of the conversations Baldwin recalls were "explicitly intimate." Ehrlichman, after debriefing Magruder in the wake of the arrests, reported, "what they were getting was mostly this fellow Oliver phoning his girlfriends all over the country. Lining up assignations." So spicy were some of the conversations on the phone that they have given rise to unconfirmed reports that the telephone was used for some sort of call girl service, catering to Congressmen and other prominent Washingtonians.*[6]

---

6   J. Anthony Lucas and Joan Hoff, *Nightmare: The Underside of the Nixon Years* (Athens, Ohio: Ohio University Press, 1999), 207.

In an impressive 1984 revisionist work, *Secret Agenda*, author Jim Hougan presents his case that the overhearings were aimed at intimate talk coming from an escort service close to the DNC headquarters on Virginia Avenue, run by whom Hougan describes as a "lush blonde" he calls by the assumed name of Tess. The targets, Hougan concludes, were this service and its conversations with DNC bigwigs, visitors from around the country who would use an empty office in the frequently absent Oliver's suite.

Now to be sure, Hougan adds a wrinkle that gives us pause. He suggests that the CIA was already electronically eavesdropping on the escort service, and only pretended to do so with the tap on the DNC line. However, contrary to Hougan, we know that Oliver's phone was tapped, but do give the impressive Hougan one of his points: that the CIA likely had independently been monitoring the bordello, as shown by Baldwin's overhearings on the headphones from Room 419, before the Oliver taps were even put in place by the burglary team.

In our view, both narratives are likely true. An already existing tap on the escort service does not preclude the subsequent tap of the DNC offices, specifically of Oliver's phone. The purpose of the DNC tap under our theory would be to legitimize the entire CIA monitoring operation since the DNC tap would have been ostensibly authorized by presidential approval, even if the others were not. In any event, we do have solid evidence, Hougan's theory notwithstanding, of a tap at the DNC because some overheard conversations did not involve women, but in fact were purely political, albeit unimportant, calls capturing Oliver speaking with the hapless Republican Harry Fleming. As a darkly humorous aside, McCord likely emphasized this political plum to Liddy to hide the true CIA purpose, after which Fleming caught severe flak from Republican higher-ups for his innocuous talk with Oliver about a bipartisan political club to which they belonged.

The great leap forward came from the 1991 bestseller *Silent Coup*, written by Len Colodny and Robert Gettlin, to whom we will refer as Colodny. Colodny named the madam of the escort service as one Cathy Dieter, which he claimed was a nom de guerre for one Heidi Rikan. A beautiful blonde of German birth, Rikan had been previously driven from DC because of heat from the vice squad, stemming from her activities at a strip club called the Blue Mirror. Colodny claimed that a lawyer for Heidi/Cathy, Phillip Mackin Bailey, had arranged for Cathy a referral system through his contact at the DNC. Colodny logically concludes that the conversations between the visiting DNC Democrats and the call girls were the target of the wiretapping, using the phone system of Spencer Oliver Jr., as overseen by his secretary, Ida "Maxie" Wells.

Oliver had empty offices and was often traveling, and Wells was in charge of entertaining visitors. Colodny summarizes the evidence of the sexual activities targeted:

> *In a recent conversation with us, Howard Hunt said that the bugging target was not Wells or Oliver, "they just happened to be on the same phone call, that's all." For corroboration that the phone was tapped in this area, and that the overheard conversations pertained to Heidi/Cathy's call girl operation, we have to leap ahead in time. The evidence establishes that in the period just after the burglars had been caught and identified and their criminal trial was imminent, the government's lead prosecutor, Assistant U.S. Atty. Earl J. Silbert, believed that the fruits of the Watergate break-in were embar-*

rassing tapes of a sexual nature. Silbert believed that Hunt had intended to use the telephone conversations that Baldwin had overheard for purposes of blackmail. The evidence includes the fact that Baldwin characterize the conversations overheard as "explicitly intimate." In addition, federal prosecutors have confirmed that the tapped conversations were "primarily sexual" and "extremely personal, intimate and potentially embarrassing."[7]

According to Colodny, at least the second burglary was ordered by Dean to find out the dirt the Democrats may have had on the Republicans, presumably of a sexual nature. Like many offended victims of unfavorable press, Dean chose to sue Colodny and his publisher over this claim. We know nothing other than that the publisher settled with Dean and his wife Maureen in some undisclosed manner. At the same time, Colodny claims to have agreed to dismissal only with the payment to *him* of an undisclosed sum from an insurer and Dean's promise not to sue Colodny in the future. So, the winner of the legal battle is unclear, and none of *Silent Coup* has been expurgated or retracted, as would be expected for a provably false allegation.

While the merits of any confidentially settled suit are difficult to judge, it appears the Dean's claim may have been motivated by what he thought an unwarranted smear of this wife Maureen, and that apart from this quibble, the essential truth of *Silent Coup* has not been discredited. But as many defamation claimants find, such litigation can often produce information far more harmful than the previously publicized work of which they

---

7   Len Colodny and Robert Gettlin, *Silent Coup: The Removal of a President* (New York: St. Martin's Press, 1991), 138–139.

are complaining. In Dean's case, prominent Democrat and DNC official Robert Strauss testified in his deposition:

> Some of the State chairmen who would come to Oliver's office and use the phone to make dates in connection with the use of the telephones. Some of the calls could have been embarrassing to some of the people who made them.[8]

Liddy, after reading *Silent Coup*, changed his tune about the purpose of the burglaries, about which he had previously been in the dark, and now claimed that the second burglary was about looking for sexual dirt that Democrats may have had on the Republicans. After this, Oliver and Wells sued Liddy, using Dean's lawyer from a previous litigation. Stalwart Fox News reporter James Rosen testified in that trial about his revealing interview with DNC Treasurer Strauss, a very highly placed Democratic official whom we quoted above. Here is what Rosen said Strauss told him:

> Democrats in from out of town for a night would want to be entertained. "It wasn't any organized thing, but I could have made the call. That lady could've made the call." The reference was to Maxie Wells. "And these people were willing to pay for sex." Those were his exact words.

Jim Hougan, who followed this litigation, later summarized Baldwin's testimony in the defamation litigation about what *he* overheard:

---

8   *Maureen and John Dean v. St. Martin's Press et al.*, 92-1807 (1996) (Robert Strauss deposition).

Baldwin was even more specific in a deposition that he later gave. According to the former FBI agent, many of the telephone conversations involved a dinner arrangement with "sex to follow." And while he never heard "prices" being discussed, Baldwin testified, he guessed that "eight out of ten" people would've thought the calls involved prostitution. But he, himself, did not. As a former FBI agent, Baldwin knew that for prostitution to occur, there has to be a promise of money, but money was never discussed, he said, or at least not in his hearing.[9]

Unfortunately for Wells and Oliver, the Baltimore jury thought the story of the prosecution referral operation was quite credible, even though the standard of proof in the civil trial such as this defamation case is usually the easier "preponderance of the evidence" test, that is, if the plaintiffs' evidence even slightly outweighs the defense, plaintiffs have proven their case. The jury still voted seven to two that Wells and Oliver had not met even this light burden. After an appeal and retrial, the second jury voted nine to zero against Wells and Oliver.

Thus, while the Dean case was settled and not tested in court, the same *Silent Coup* allegations were put to the proof in *Wells v. Liddy*, with a stinging rejection for those asserting the "political strategy" narrative of Watergate. In light of these lawsuits, how do we sum up the evidence? There are simply too many solid facts showing that the subject of the surveillance was tawdry conversation between out-of-town Democrats and the girls working for a nearby escort service. Since the only working tap was on the line of a minor Democrat, Spencer Oliver Jr., who

---

9   Jim Hougan, "On the New Inquisition," JimHougan.com, http://jimhougan.com/WatergateInquisition.html.

travelled often and had no central campaign duties, it is nearly impossible to prove the political motive speculated for decades from pro-*Post* acolytes and other anti-Nixonites.

So, we can conclude with great confidence that the motive for the wiretapping was not campaign intelligence and was likely one directed toward sexual conversations. But the questions still remain: Why would the White House care about these tawdry conversations? Why would the CIA? If Liddy was a dupe as to Watergate's real purpose, as he now claims, is there solid proof of the claimed motivation to capture such tawdry talk?

Was any Nixon official cognizant of the call girl target if Liddy was not? And to our own purposes here, why would this call girl targeting stay hidden for all these years? Wouldn't the prosecution put the call girl evidence into the public sphere? And if the CIA was involved, wouldn't the FBI and prosecutors learn that and prove it in court? And to the big question, even if all the so-called "revisionist" evidence is true, did Richard Nixon still obstruct justice? If so, why shouldn't he have deserved removal from office? Answering these questions gets us even further down the rabbit hole known as Watergate, where we hope to show you even more evidence in coming chapters solving its unsolved mysteries.

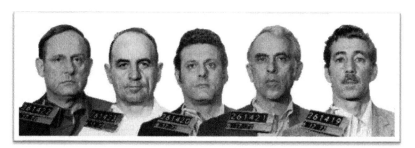

Image of arrested Watergate burglars (L-R) Bernard Barker, James McCord, Jr., Frank Sturgis, Eugenio Martinez, Virgilio Gonzalez, public domain.

CHAPTER 8

PROSECUTION AND TRIAL

ONE OF THE ENDURING MYSTERIES of Watergate is how and why the truth, if it is the truth we are describing in this book, has not yet been widely known. We have shown CIA infiltration of the White House, the targeting of sexual information, and seeming widespread deception about the burglary's true purpose. However, one of democratic society's greatest features is that of public trials, where opposing sides, using cross-examination and rules of evidence, prove their cases to a judge and jury sworn to be fair.

We have talked in past chapters about the provenance of the Watergate burglaries, especially the second burglary, where arrests were made, and evidence seized. Shouldn't the public trial of the burglary have elucidated the motives of the burglars and the principals for whom they were working? One would think so.

Felt, aka Deep Throat, was proud of the FBI's relentless investigation of these crimes. His agents had conducted, prior to the indictment of September 15, 1972, fifteen hundred interviews involving fourteen thousand work hours and three hundred thirty agents. And this was just the FBI effort prior to the indictments. Agents thereafter continued to work tirelessly supporting the prosecution up to the burglary trial conducted in January 1973. While the FBI was preparing for trial, the U.S. attorney's office assigned as its chief trial lawyer the best prosecutor it had, Earl Silbert Jr., nicknamed "Earl the Pearl," a dynamic courtroom lawyer. Silbert was joined by a tough, smart veteran prosecutor, Seymour Glanzer. The third lawyer appointed, Donald Campbell, was a wiretapping expert. These lawyers were known to be ethical, skilled, and hardworking. They put key witnesses before the grand jury to complement the FBI's preindictment investigation and were considered to have been very thorough in their trial preparation.

But those who wished to bury the truth were greatly aided by the high ethical standards of the government's trial team. This sense of prosecutorial ethics, ironically, served to keep the public in the dark about this meaningful burglary. The prosecutors planned to fully present the case to the jury as they saw it, all of which would go into the public record. But they scrupulously refrained from pretrial publicity that might be prejudicial to the defendants. So, at least prior to the trial, the public did not have an inkling about the nature of the prosecution's case, where among other evidence, it would endeavor to prove the motive and intent of the burglars, the key unknown facts about this puzzling caper.

If the burglars thought in good faith that this was a legitimate, presidentially authorized CIA operation, then each defendant so thinking would lack criminal intent. This would be called the CIA defense. What about the theory we have presented here that the burglary was in fact a CIA operation? Interestingly, the prosecutors were loath to claim CIA participation directly because they would thereby fall into the trap of authenticating a CIA defense, which would exonerate all the defendants except perhaps Liddy, who was not in any way connected to the CIA. This is so because such a defense would negate criminal intent. In any event, the prosecutors certainly anticipated that a CIA defense would likely be offered.

Although always careful to label the CIA defense as "spurious" or "phony," why did these veterans anticipate this defense? Because the evidence could fit a CIA defense. The prosecutors knew Hunt was seeking evidence appearing to support such a claim with his pretrial discovery motion to retrieve his "Hermès" notebooks. Hunt's lawyers complained to the prosecutors when no notebooks were produced in discovery. The prosecutors also knew that Hunt was working for a CIA cover company, Mullen. They saw significance in the burglars' tapping of the phone of Spencer Oliver Jr., while not listening to more significant Democrats like Larry O'Brien or Robert Strauss, the DNC's prominent treasurer. Finally, they saw strong relevance in the monitoring of the highly intimate conversations Baldwin would testify he overheard. In short, the prosecutors saw all the odd elements of Watergate that pointed to it as being anything but campaign strategy eavesdropping. This is much of the same evidence we have presented to you in earlier chapters.

Yet even today, very few in our country understand Watergate to have had these elements. Why? As we will show later, the *Washington Post*, seen as the main repository of all Watergate knowledge, has consistently slanted its reporting toward the sole and exclusive theme of Nixonian campaign evil. It has never had the motive to publish a number of very clear facts that we are here presenting in this book, even though they would not provide a defense for Nixon's commission of crimes. They would likely have, though, helped Nixon stave off impeachment and disgrace while splattering dirt on the DNC, with which the *Post* was virtually a Siamese twin.

When the *Post's* was founded in 1877, it proudly announced that it was the official organ of the Democratic Party, and it has stayed close to its political bedfellow thereafter. The *Post* and the DNC were so close in 1972 that the two institutions shared a general counsel, Joseph Califano of the prominent Democratic law firm Williams, Connolly and Califano. That firm, interestingly enough, was handling the litigation brought by the DNC against the CRP immediately after the burglary. In essence, there was at least a spiritual conflict of interest in Califano's representation of a political party against its rival party while advising a paper that claimed to be reporting fairly about both of them. In any case, simply knowing the facts, as any trial lawyer will tell you, is not the whole game, sometimes not even half of it. It is also important to put the evidence together in a coherent narrative whole so that the jury, and in this case also the jury of public opinion, can understand what really occurred.

The case the prosecutor put together, using the massive facts uncovered by the FBI's rigorous investigation and its own grand jury probe, showed a strong presence of the CIA in Watergate. At the same time, prosecutors were careful not to validate the CIA defense contemplated by Hunt and perhaps by the Cubans as well. By the time of trial, Silbert had put these facts together in a good but not perfect way. Some of his narrative fits the facts well, while other parts were less impressively inferred. It may well be, of course, that avoiding the CIA defense was part of Silbert's challenge and made him adjust the factual narrative to avoid that defense. To assert that Watergate was a legitimate CIA mission would require the element of White House approval, since the CIA could not pursue a domestic operation without special authorization from the White House. Such approval would serve to sully Silbert's chief executive, Richard Nixon, and the use of campaign funds for the burglars would also suggest a collateral

White House effort that might be for ends other than the CIA's. So, to avoid implicating his ultimate bosses at the White House, it may well be that Silbert avoided some of the inferences that we make in this book.

In any case, Silbert needed to explain both CIA involvement in the burglary, which was obvious to him, and use of campaign funds, while also fitting in the idea of the naughty talk overheard in such a way as to avoid a legitimate CIA defense, and also high White House involvement. Silbert, putting the evidence gathered in, again, a reasonable but imperfect way, intended to show that using campaign funds intended for security, Hunt went off on his own frolic and detour to get dirt on Spencer Oliver Jr.

In a truly amazing coincidence, Oliver's father, of course named Spencer Oliver Sr., was a Mullen official and a rival of Hunt's for subsequent ownership and control of the fat CIA cover contract that Mullen held. In fact, Hunt had already successfully objected to Junior's joining Mullen. Regarding this, we offer a side note. There has been speculation that Spencer Oliver Jr. was, like his father, a CIA asset and for that reason a candidate to work with Mullen. We have no opinion on that speculation but would say it is certainly consistent with the rest of the evidence.

Silbert's theory was that by getting sexual dirt on Junior, Hunt could use that information to prevent Senior from ownership of Mullen. This theory fit roughly with the evidence while exonerating the White House and avoiding a legitimate CIA defense.

So even though this overarching narrative was not a spot-on reconciliation of the facts, this presentation of the case would promise to make a very large, public splash, perhaps to be seized on by a White House seeking to explain a burglary that had it scratching its collective head, with the exception, of course, of the wily Dean. After the Hermès notebooks went missing, Hunt's wife died, and McCord refused to cooperate, Hunt, as explained, gave in to Dean's pressure to plead guilty. Therefore, Silbert would not need to combat Hunt's CIA defense with his explication of the role of the two Olivers.

Let's pause here. If there were no basis for Hunt's potential CIA defense, Silbert would not have, as he did, prepare for it. However, at this distant remove, there will still be some who claim that Hunt never seriously intended to pursue this defense. However, that the prosecutors had learned of the potential defense and were preparing for it, as Silbert and Glanzer both admitted in Silbert's later confirmation hearings, suggests that Hunt's lawyer had let it be known that such a defense was planned.

Hunt's lawyer, William Bittman, likely spoke about the defense in discussions with the prosecution over the import of the missing Hermès notebooks. After all, Bittman would have likely screamed bloody murder to the prosecutors in an effort to claim that the defense was prejudiced by the failure of the prosecution to turn over the notebooks, likely claiming possible government misconduct. As we saw in the last chapters, once Hunt had learned such evidence of misconduct by Dean in the fall of 1973, burglars Eugenio Martinez and Virgilio Gonzalez did move to withdraw their pleas on the grounds that they had always thought that the Watergate burglary was a legitimate CIA mission. They claimed the government had destroyed evidence that would have assisted their defense.

With Hunt's guilty plea, the unlucky prosecutors would lose one basis to fight for admission of key evidence to support their alternative version of CIA involvement, albeit at the time of the plea a loss that Silbert did not likely realize at the time to have been a critical one. One key component of Silbert's case was Baldwin's testimony that he monitored explicitly intimate, racy talk, which Silbert intended to hang around Oliver Jr.'s neck, and vicariously around Hunt's. Silbert intended that Baldwin only generally characterize the overhearings in his testimony, without specifying any conversation in detail. According to Silbert, this would thereby not be gratuitously embarrassing to any particular individual tied to a tawdry talk. Unfortunately for Silbert, and ultimately for the White House and the public, the Democrats were ready for Silbert, likely knowing quite well what Baldwin had overheard.

Baldwin was represented by a loyal Democrat, John Cassidento of Hartford, Connecticut, who later was awarded a judgeship with the help of the influential Joseph Califano. Through Cassidento, the Democrats knew intimately what Baldwin would say if permitted to answer and did not like what those answers would be. Indeed, Califano's firm sent a lawyer to Hartford to debrief Cassidento, with Baldwin in an adjoining room, who in turn confirmed what they likely already knew about how he would answer key questions.

In one of the many, many stupidities that led to Nixon's disgrace, immediately following the burglaries, the CRP lawyers elected not to represent Baldwin on the foolish theory that he was being paid by McCord, not the CRP through Liddy, and thus the CRP could distance itself from Baldwin. But this reflexive response was far more harmful than helpful. The Republicans thus broke the cardinal rule applicable to a party whose underling has been located by the prosecution: hire and pay for his lawyer.

Thus, if you are a drug dealer and one of your runners has been arrested, it behooves you to pay for his lawyer in the hope he will not turn against you. In addition in this strange case, by learning what Baldwin knew, the White House and CRP could have woven together a good defense. With the CRP refusing to represent Baldwin, he was eagerly represented by a loyal Democrat, Cassidento, an ally of the DNC's general counsel

(Joseph Califano). So, this was a huge mistake on the part of the Republicans, one of many that led to Richard Nixon's resignation.

The Democrats, knowing of Baldwin's expected testimony, then hired noted civil rights and ACLU lawyer Charles Morgan Jr. to prevent Baldwin's testimony about naughty DNC conversations. It was Morgan's theory that the court could block any repetition in court of an illegally overheard conversation on the grounds that it was clearly illegal to transmit any *illegally* overheard conversation. First, though, Morgan needed to smoke out Silbert to confirm that he indeed intended to introduce into evidence these meretricious conversations, so that he, Morgan, would not have the burden of unringing a bell after Silbert introduced the sensational evidence.

Morgan invited Silbert and Glanzer to lunch, where he also brought his associate, Hope Eastman, likely as a witness. As the luncheon discussion proceeded, at some point Earl Silbert dramatically pounded the table, saying, "Hunt was trying to blackmail Spencer, and I'm going to prove it!" Of course, in order to prove that Hunt was trying to blackmail Spencer Oliver Sr., the prosecution would have had to prove that Hunt was overhearing salacious conversations. Silbert's admission at the lunch of the blackmail theme in essence confirmed that the nature of the conversations was embarrassing.

The lunch tab that Morgan expended was well worth it. He now had the basis for his motion, that is, the possibility that the prosecution would present in evidence descriptions of illegally overheard conversations, conversations that suggested a bordello referral system run out of the DNC.

On the first morning of the trial when lawyers would make preliminary motions before picking the jury, Morgan appeared in court and asked permission from Judge Sirica to file a brief seeking to prohibit the prosecution from questioning Baldwin about what he had overheard. By claiming to represent both the secretary Maxie Wells and Spencer Oliver Jr., as well as the Association of State Democratic Chairmen, Morgan could point to his clients as being victims of the disclosure of such conversations in court. However, a criminal case has only two sets of parties, the government and the defense. Individuals such as Wells and Oliver were not parties to the case, and they had no standing to make a motion in court. Sirica therefore quite properly told Morgan that he could not file a brief or present argument in court, because he was not representing a party to the case.

After the midmorning recess, Sirica told Morgan he had reconsidered and would permit the filing of a brief and later argument. It is not clear whether Sirica talked to anyone at the break who persuaded him to change his mind, but change his mind he did. Morgan then postulated his theory later in open court that the prosecution was going to attempt to show blackmail as the motive for the crime.

Introduction of this evidence—or for that matter, publication of the intent to introduce such evidence—would have been sensational. For the first time, the public would have heard not about political strategies or campaign matters, but of very intimate sexual assignations between males and females. There's no doubt that the whole tenor of Watergate would have changed had the public known that these conversations were the essence of what had been overheard, and therefore the likely target of the eavesdropping.

Morgan argued that the repetition of illegally overheard conversations was illegal, and evidence of them should therefore not be introduced in court. Silbert argued to Sirica that he did not intend to offer specific details of the conversations, nor would he ask for the names of the participants on the call, and, therefore, would not actually be asking Baldwin to repeat specific conversations. It was Morgan's argument that cross-examination would allow the defense lawyers to get into the details of the conversations, which would then contravene at least his view of the law.

In our humble opinion, Morgan's argument was somewhat nonsensical because salacious matters come up at trials very frequently, and the courts have wide latitude to restrict the scope of questioning to avoid unnecessary, needlessly prejudicial testimony. In this instance, since there was nothing to be gained from getting into the details of sexual talk, the court could have easily limited the questioning to general characterization of the conversations.

More to the point, there is nothing illegal about repeating illegally overheard conversations in court. After all, that's how one proves such a crime. In other words, if a prosecutor were trying a defendant for illegally repeating an illegally overheard conversation, wouldn't he need to have a witness repeat the conversation communicated illegally? After hearing the arguments, Sirica ruled, we think properly, that the prosecution could proceed as planned and ask Baldwin to characterize the conversations.

Sirica did allow that he would give Morgan a chance for an immediate emergency appeal to the DC Court of Appeals, which Morgan promptly filed. Approximately a week later, after more briefing, once again the theme of blackmail was argued back and forth between Morgan and Silbert, this time before the court of appeals. The very liberal Democratic mainstay of the appeals court, Judge David Bazelon, wondered aloud why anyone would try to blackmail Spencer Oliver Jr., a man of modest means. This question showed that the court did not really understand the theory of the tight-lipped Silbert's case.

Eventually the court sided with Morgan and ruled that the prosecution could not ask Baldwin what was overheard. Furthermore, if at any point in the trial Silbert felt it was necessary to delve into that area, he was required to inform Judge Sirica in chambers, at which point Morgan could have an immediate right of appeal to the court of appeals. This ruling, of course, knocked the wind out of Silbert's sails. Silbert then tried a very vanilla wiretapping case, not delving into the CIA, Mullen, or naughty talk. What Morgan had astutely called his "desperation pass play" was completed for a touchdown in the closing seconds. It was helpful to this pass play that the referee was an ardent Democrat, Judge Bazelon, who, to be fair, likely thought the prosecution was simply attempting to embarrass the Democrats. It does not appear that Bazelon truly understood the theme of Silbert's case.

In another of the many quirks of the Watergate scandal, had Hunt not pled guilty and thus been allowed to pursue his CIA defense, it would have been all but impossible for the appellate court to rule as it did. But with Hunt out of the way, and no defense that necessarily required resort to the types of conversations being overheard, Silbert had nowhere to go with his theory of extortion to wrest control of Mullen and Company.

McCord and Liddy were then convicted without any sizzling testimony. Silbert did not, after Bazelon's ruling, desire to inquire into the burglars' document-copying intentions because such tends to give an alternative goal for the burglary other than wiretapping, and wiretapping was the charge that Silbert sought to prove. Accordingly, in addition to staying silent on salacious talk, the trial said nothing about the main target being document copying. The trial thus ended without the public learning one morsel about the likely purpose of this odd burglary.

Ironically, Judge Sirica made big headlines, ultimately leading to his being named *Time* Man of the Year, for raging that the prosecution had not proved the motive for the burglaries, precisely what Silbert had sought to prove! This lionizing of Sirica for presiding over what was in fact an exercise in suppression of information is an undeserved accolade in a scandal replete with undeserved plaudits and brickbats.

Meanwhile, the paper of record, the *Post*, did not print a word about the drama concerning the meretricious overhearings, that is, the central thrust of Morgan's motion and arguments about the planned blackmail theme. To be sure, the *Washington Star-News* covered the blackmail discussions that were undertaken both in Sirica's court and in Bazelon's, as did the *Baltimore Sun*. Of course, neither of these publications had wide influence, and neither paper connected blackmail with naughty talk. In short, there was never a wide public discussion of what information the blackmailers were supposedly seeking that motivated the Watergate burglary, or even an article querying about the nature of the postulated blackmail. In sum and in essence, the Watergate burglary trial was a cover-up.

But what did lie ahead could not have been comforting for the CIA. Would any of the knowledgeable witnesses crack under pressure? Would an ostensibly fearless press crack the case and tell the public that the CIA had been listening to naughty talk? What about John Dean? Would his role in the burglary be uncovered and necessarily implicate the CIA, since both were interested in lurid assignations? Putting aside the CIA, would the Nixon administration learn who within it was behind the burglary? Would the public learn about the DNC's bordello referral program, greatly embarrassing the Democrats, who had been on offense since the burglary arrests?

The failure of the prosecution to put on evidence of the blackmail theme, prevented by the court of appeals, kept the still-clueless White House from looking anew at this burglary, that is, to ascertain who, if anyone, in the administration would care about listening to sex talk and why. This revelation would certainly have buttressed the straitlaced Mitchell's claim that he did not authorize the burglary. It would have supported Nixon's claim that he did not believe that the White House had been involved in the burglary, and therefore was not covering up for his administration. It would as well tend to absolve the still-suspected Colson, who may have been a "hatchet man" but not a petty dirt gatherer. Nixon's Teutonic, bare-knuckle Oval Office, cynical though it may have been, would have better fish to fillet than the sex life of a Montana State chairman, not the least pertinent to a presidential campaign.

But what was significant about the trial was that it kept both the CIA and the DNC from being exposed for their sexual projects and also for the moment prevented the Nixon administration from focusing on its cover-up counsel, John Dean. At the end of the burglary trial, the White House had no idea that its chief in-house defense lawyer, Dean, was withholding from his clients his own involvement in the scandal. As well, the White House and the public had heard little about the central role of the CIA. In the two years following the burglary trial, having successfully kept from public view their participation in Watergate, the CIA, the DNC, and Dean would now all strive to keep these cats in the bag. How they did that successfully will lead us to exploring several more of the mysteries of Watergate.

Image of White House counsel John Dean, public domain.

CHAPTER 9

JOHN DEAN, CLEVER COUNSEL OR CONFLICTED QUISLING?

IN PAST CHAPTERS, WE HAVE explored the question of the motives behind the odd Watergate burglary. We have talked of CIA infiltration of the White House and its interest in sex for manipulation of subjects. Unfortunately, Hunt's guilty plea and the limiting of evidence by the appellate court kept the public from learning much of this at trial.

While we have focused on the CIA's potential involvement in the burglary, the fact remains that Liddy's presence and use of campaign cash meant that this operation had been approved *somewhere* in the Nixon administration, even if not in the Oval Office. But where and why? Let us now turn to the extremely interesting Watergate actor John Dean.

Preceding the Nazi invasion of Norway during World War II, Germany was aided by a Norwegian military officer who was covertly collaborating with it, Vidkun Quisling. His treachery was so dramatic that the name Quisling is generically used to designate any covertly traitorous member of a governing group. John Dean may well be seen, politically speaking, as the Quisling of Watergate, if our view of the scandal is correct.

John Dean is clearly the most intriguing of Watergate characters. To some, Dean has been viewed as a Boy Scout caught in bad company. To others, he was simply a classic squealer, saving his own skin by turning on his superiors. Presently, of course, he is the sainted voice of the anticonservative rhetoricians one hears on CNN and MSNBC. To yet others, however, he is the very embodiment of treachery—a White House counsel who turned on his client after leading the client astray with bad advice.

First, he sponsored, it would appear from our vantage point, the burglary, although he would deny it. Then he sucked an unwitting Richard Nixon into its cover-up, destroying what had been a successful presidency. And, finally, he sold out his own client to avoid jail time, at least according to those who think that John Dean was the ultimate Quisling. The last of these descriptions in our view is closest to accurate. But why does it make a difference? Because understanding Dean is a necessary tool of comprehension of that still ongoing mystery known as Watergate.

Understanding Dean's intellectual and legal capability is important. First, he has always been shrewd, albeit on the shady side. He was fired from his first job as a lawyer after just four months for ethical lapses, secretly pursuing a television license in competition with a client. He was then able to obtain a series of jobs through political connections, having married the daughter of a senator. He had a reputation among his coworkers as an idea thief, to such an extent that some of his colleagues locked their papers in a drawer before leaving for the night, for fear Dean would co-opt their valuable insights. But in a career marked by cleverness and shrewd calculation, there is little in his background to show his ability to think out a troublesome dispute as would a skillful lawyer. Yet in Watergate, he became the chief legal adviser for the entire White House, CRP, and Nixon administration team, without the group relying in any substantial way on outside legal advice.

Few, if any, observers have done an analysis of what would have happened in Watergate had Dean possessed the experience, training, and skill of a good lawyer. We will return to this subject as various events unfold, and in some cases, comment on forms of alternative history that may have transpired had prudent legal thinking been employed. But for now, let us focus on Dean's place in the Nixon White House hierarchy.

John Ehrlichman was a Seattle lawyer who worked for Nixon in the 1968 election, whom Nixon brought with him to the White House. One of Ehrlichman's titles was counselor to the president. In essence, Ehrlichman handled duties normally performed by White House counsel, even though his job was somewhat more elevated than that. Ehrlichman was not, in any case, particularly well suited for a job as a political lawyer. He was by all accounts an intelligent man, but he had practiced law in the real estate field in Seattle, meaning he was not a troubleshooter for corporate shenanigans as some lawyers are. Nor was he a litigator who understood lawyerlike strategies in dealing with his client's troubles and conflicts. That said, his loyalty, cunning, and sharp intelligence were valued by Nixon, and soon Ehrlichman was given the added portfolio of heading Nixon's Domestic Affairs Council.

The White House therefore searched for someone to take over the seemingly menial legal duties that had been performed under Ehrlichman's umbrella, but which he now had to give over to a lower staff lawyer. John Dean at the time was a young attorney on his way up in the Justice Department bureaucracy, garnering essentially political positions, eventually occupying a senior niche in the Department. Political appointees in the Department of Justice, as the term implies, do not rise in the organization by litigation skills and experience as do "line" DOJ lawyers.

In the political environs of the DOJ, Dean's cleverness made him into something of a political star, and he was a natural target for recruitment by the White House for a job which, interestingly, Attorney General John Mitchell advised him to reject.

Dean, however, like a moth to a flame, could not resist a job that could be made into a very prestigious position. His appointment carried with it the name of White House counsel, an overblown title. Unlike White House counsel in other administrations, Dean had no contact with the president for well over two years on the job. He was essentially a glorified legal flunky, performing menial tasks. But he was shrewd enough to use the title of the position to enhance his power and profile.

Dean soon saw that his rise to prominence would greatly depend on developing some political opposition intelligence capability. So as Dean brought in lawyers to serve under him for what he called his "law firm," to enhance his profile he sought intelligence responsibilities, a euphemism for harvesting compromising information on opponents. He first caught Nixon's eye as the coordinator of the White House response team to the massive May Day, 1971, protest against the Vietnam War, where thousands of demonstrators attempted to close down the city.

Dean was an integral part of the jailing of ten thousand protesters in the practice field of RFK Stadium. This, of course, was an egregious affront to civil liberties since the vast majority of those arrested were peaceful protesters. The appalling lack of sanitary facilities and attention to civilized constitutional standards turned these arrests into a politically divisive issue. But what was important was that in the eyes of the churlish Nixon and his Oval Office team, Dean had shown his stuff.

Dean candidly recounts in his first book, *Blind Ambition*, his autobiography, that he sought a role in campaign-related intelligence before the 1972 campaign, hoping, it appears, to be the beginnings of the more permanent intelligence portfolio. His challenge was that the president's chief of staff, H. R. Haldeman, was the undoubted czar of opposition intelligence within the White House. Thus, part of understanding Watergate is understanding Dean's drive to achieve tangible intelligence results during the short time that the campaign would be ongoing and flush with campaign cash, while working for an organization, the CRP, which Haldeman intentionally ignored as the White House intelligence czar.

In Haldeman's eyes, the campaign was an unattractive, thankless outpost to which he banished rival John Mitchell and had rid himself of his inept aide, Jeb Magruder. So, Dean had something of an open field with the CRP, the malleable Magruder, and campaign cash, even though he was still a White House official with no official CRP duties.

As we discussed in Chapter Two, the FBI had indicated its unwillingness to perform intelligence operations for the White House after placing the controversial Kissinger wiretaps in 1969 and 1970. After the Huston Plan bit the dust in July 1970, there was ever more need for an in-house intelligence gathering capability that went beyond Haldeman's bandwidth as chief of staff. Recognizing this gap, the Oval Office hired a former New York police detective, Jack Caulfield, to perform investigations for the White House.

Caulfield kept under wraps his Runyonesque gumshoe, Tony Ulasewicz, a former NYPD police detective with wide connections in the gray, seamy areas of dirt gathering. Nixon, Haldeman, and Ehrlichman were already on their way to building an in-house intelligence and investigative team, using Caulfield and Ulasewicz, which would substitute for what they thought to be a recalcitrant FBI.

The ambitious Dean had used Caulfield and Ulasewicz on a number of occasions, as he sought to build up his own intelligence portfolio with this available resource. But the most noteworthy use of this investigative team, as we near Watergate, occurred in the fall of 1971. In 1971, a prominent call girl ring had been prosecuted in New York City, gaining notoriety not only because of its rich and famous, albeit confidential, clientele, but also because it was run by a glamorous, self-promoting madam named Xaviera Hollander, known in the press as "the Happy Hooker." After being busted, she authored a popular bestselling book.

Around October 1971, Dean sent Ulasewicz, via Caulfield, to New York City to attempt to get the names of Hollander's clientele, hopefully snaring many prominent Democrats. Presumably, Dean would try to use this information to discredit Nixon's enemies. And at the least, he could win points by boasting to the Oval Office that he had this sleaze in his portfolio. Unfortunately for Dean, Ulasewicz did in fact find prominent Democrats on the Happy Hooker client rolls, but also snared many Republicans, rendering the detective's dossier unusable.

So, we know the theme of Democrats and hookers was intelligence dirt that interested Dean. It would not be unreasonable to see Watergate as simply a continuation of Dean's same hunger for advancement, by grabbing such meretricious dirt where he could find it. In that regard, we will now turn to a highly illuminating venture by the shady triumvirate of Dean, Caulfield, and Ulasewicz.

After the Happy Hooker venture, perhaps a month later, in or around November of 1971, Dean sent Ulasewicz on what the detective thought was an odd casing mission. Ulasewicz was instructed by Dean to case the offices of the DNC headquarters in the Watergate office building. Ulasewicz was puzzled by the request, later reporting back to Dean, describing the DNC offices, which he managed to walk through, as being much like any other offices, with filing cabinets, desks, phones, and the like. It was also, he reported, unprotected, with little security in place.

So, we ask, what was it that so interested Dean in the fall of 1971 in the Democratic National Committee headquarters? And what was the significance of the timing of Ulasewicz's mission occurring in late fall 1971?

We have spoken about the naughty boy and girl talk overheard on the DNC phones and also about Dean's interest in hooker dirt on Democrats. Was the DNC casing mission of Ulasewicz similar to his Happy Hooker assignment? We also ask whether and when Dean knew about the referrals from the DNC headquarters. If he did know about them in the fall of 1971, such knowledge would cast an entirely new light on the central question of the Watergate burglary goal. If in fact, months later in May and June of 1972, Watergate break-ins were directed toward these referrals, such tends to support the testimony of John Mitchell that he did not authorize the Watergate break-ins, since there was no indication Mitchell would be interested in scandalous information. Put differently, history's tumbling easily to believe Magruder's later testimony that Mitchell authorized the burglaries would seem reasonable as long as the break-ins were for campaign dirt. But not if they were, in fact, for sexual dirt.

Ulasewicz's two missions also support the corollary idea that the Watergate break-ins were not campaign-related events. If not campaign missions, Richard Nixon may have been lured into his clear but insubstantial obstruction of justice liability under false pretenses, thinking that he was protecting unknown persons in his administration who had performed silly, useless, campaign spying. Put differently, if Richard Nixon had known that the Watergate burglaries were not campaign related, he would not have suspected, as he did, that someone in his inner circle was involved, and therefore would not have been as motivated to engage in a cover-up. Rather, he would have investigated the identity of the bungling junior aide who foolishly sponsored this fiasco and shown him the plank to walk.

Indeed, Mark Felt, in his first meeting after the arrests with his superior Patrick Gray, importuned Gray, on June 21, 1972, to urge the president to do just that, to wit, to help the FBI find the foolish junior aides who sponsored this amateurish venture.

Dean's Ulasewicz casing mission of the DNC also shed some light on his recruitment of G. Gordon Liddy to join the CRP around that very same time. In November and December 1971, the CRP, per Mitchell, was looking for a general counsel, mainly to handle fundraising issues as a new campaign contribution disclosure law was to begin effective April 7, 1972. Dean's very capable associate and right-hand man, Fred Fielding, was being interviewed about his interest in the job. Dean discouraged Fielding's hire and instead pushed Liddy toward the job.

Liddy was known as a smart, knowledgeable former FBI agent, but also as an unguided missile, with the mindset that he would do anything to help country and cause, regardless of its legality. He was very close in his Plumber's Unit work with Howard Hunt, whose stories of undercover intrigue greatly influenced him. So, Dean, in essence, hoped to get a twofer— the eager Liddy, as well as his influential buddy, Hunt, using the budget of the soon-to-be cash-rich CRP to help with daring investigative assignments to fill Dean's newly created intelligence portfolio.

Although the CRP general counsel, one would think, should care mainly about fundraising, Dean talked Liddy into accepting the position by emphasizing the sensitive, covert intelligence gathering aspects of the job, promising him "half a million for openers" for a well-funded intelligence program. Liddy eagerly accepted after Dean made this promise. Because Dean could credibly be seen as both a Mitchell man, since Dean came from Mitchell's DOJ, and a Haldeman man (Dean was very close to Gordon Strachan, the chief aide to Haldeman), this promise of a generous budget was credible to Liddy. Liddy, in turn, was eager for the cloak-and-dagger work his new White House "Plumber's Unit" buddy Hunt had romantically described from his CIA days. Moreover, as we will treat later, Hunt had whetted Liddy's appetite for adventure by casing, then burglarizing, the office of Dr. Lewis Fielding, the psychiatrist for Pentagon Papers leaker Daniel Ellsberg.

Watergate began, by all conventional accounts, with Liddy's presentations of his "security" plan to Mitchell, while Mitchell was still attorney general, the first such presentation occurring on January 27, 1972. Mitchell had planned on soon leaving to head the CRP, temporarily being managed by Jeb Magruder, a former Haldeman aide. But in substance and effect, in late January and early February, Mitchell was not only attorney general, but he was also acting de facto as head of the president's reelection campaign.

This first January 27 presentation of Liddy to Mitchell contained a vast and bewildering array of proposed illegal acts, from wiretapping to kidnapping, even involving a "chase plane" to electronically monitor another opponent's plane. All of this was stitched together as part of Liddy's so-called "GEMSTONE" proposal, professionally presented on impressive CIA-prepared charts. After the acerbic Mitchell quickly turned down the plan, Liddy, encouraged by Dean to believe the main issue was cost, quickly followed with a second plan on February 4, scaled down to $500,000 from the original $1,000,000 presentation.

The second plan was not accepted by Mitchell, and although the attorney general was known to be an impenetrable stoneface, anyone with an ounce of intuition would have known that he was horrified by the presentation. His displeasure at once again being presented with fatuous, harebrained schemes was so obvious that Dean interrupted Liddy, solemnly to intone that this sort of thing should not be discussed in the attorney general's office. We do note that for years, commentators have assumed that these wild schemes were hatched solely in Liddy's imagination. In fact, they reveal the thinking of one conversant with the latest CIA techniques, and may well have been the brainchild of Howard Hunt, looking for White House approval of a whole variety of imaginative CIA operations and techniques.

To be sure, Dean later claimed to have been so offended by Liddy's February 4 presentation that he immediately went to Haldeman's office to tell him that he was disavowing anything Liddy was doing. This later claim of sanctimony does not pass the laugh test, however. It was Dean who encouraged the first plan of January 27, far more outrageous than the February 4 scheme. And Liddy's book, which was not published until 1980, does not reveal Dean as being horrified at the plans so much as chastened by Mitchell's obvious displeasure. In any case, Haldeman disputes being told any such thing by Dean, and given his highly meticulous notetaking, Haldeman has the better side of the dispute. In summary, it does not appear that Dean was disavowing Liddy or his fevered schemes but was simply acknowledging that Mitchell was obviously not buying what Liddy, with Dean's encouragement, was selling.

Liddy's book supports Haldeman, since Liddy claims Dean simply encouraged a cheaper plan at the conclusion of the second meeting, where, once again, the attorney general's substantive disapproval was manifest to everyone but perhaps the clueless Liddy. At the very least, Dean's participation in Liddy's absurdly illegal proposals made it clear that Dean had approved the schemes, and, if Liddy is to be believed, that Dean remained the driving force behind what became known as the Watergate burglaries.

For the moment, we will skip the immediate events preceding each burglary and concentrate on Dean's role in the cover-up. Let's assume for the moment, and we will delve into more evidence later, that Dean was a sponsor of the burglary. Howard Hunt testified before Congress in early 1974 that one of his principals was Dean. This testimony garnered no headlines and there was no analysis by Congress or the president as to the implications of his testimony, which should have been shocking, considering Dean's dramatic protestations of innocence in his televised 1973 Senate testimony. By the time Hunt so testified, to no headlines, Nixon was on his way out of office, while the rest of his aides were about to be tried for cover-up.

If in fact Dean was a sponsor, this tends not only to exculpate Mitchell, and vicariously Nixon, on the burglary scheme, but also points to a noncampaign-related dirt-gathering project. So let us slow down a bit and reflect on the possibility that Dean may have been the main political sponsor of these burglaries, even though his superiors may not have known his role.

We know that President Nixon committed two clear acts of obstruction. On June 23, 1972, he directed the CIA to call the FBI off its Mexican Money Trail investigation, and on March 21, 1973, Nixon at least arguably agreed to Dean's plan to raise $1,000,000 in hush money for Hunt. Both of these two acts were carried out on the advice of Dean. But Dean was likely protecting himself more than the president in each case.

At the same time, Dean had concealed from all in the Oval Office his apparent role in the sponsorship of the burglary, which if known would have caused him to proceed to the firing squad. Such a role, of course, exculpates John Mitchell and Charles Colson, both continually suspect in Nixon's eyes, in spite of their fervent denials. Now, we say Dean's "apparent role" because Dean today denies directing or sponsoring the burglaries. We do not take on the burden of here marshalling all the evidence against Dean. But it suffices to say that there is a live issue on this score, given Dean's continuing denial, but that strong evidence, in our view, points to his active sponsorship. We will not here attempt to do more to resolve this issue, which will be treated further when we discuss Liddy's later book.

But if Dean was so involved, then, contrary to everything Dean had told Nixon, and upon which Nixon had relied, there was White House culpability in the burglary, even if only through this junior aide Dean, to go along with what Nixon suspected of the CRP. If Dean was involved, in other words, he concealed that important fact from his client. If the burglary was directed at sexual talk, and Dean knew it, he hid that evidence as well, highly exculpatory evidence for his client the president. Finally, this seeming involvement of Dean, which he still denies, would have severely handicapped his credibility and reliability as a witness against Nixon and Nixon's top aides.

We said earlier that we would talk from time to time about the blunders of the Nixon administration in defeating Watergate charges. Dean's early legal advice, or better put, his failure to give good advice, ultimately resulted in the only removal of a president in United States history. As we noted earlier, Dean was not only potentially personally involved in the burglary, and thus legally conflicted, but also had little skill or experience as either a litigator or a corporate troubleshooter.

But Liddy presented any skilled litigator with an easy way to mitigate both White House and CRP guilt in the burglary. Liddy had informed the young lawyer that he would do anything Dean wanted, to the point of volunteering to stand on a street corner and be shot. If Liddy merely had his lawyer admit to the public that Liddy had gone rogue, because he was convinced the DNC had import national security information related to Fidel Castro, or some similar justification, this would be consistent with the use of campaign cash by Liddy while serving to exculpate all others.

But Dean was not experienced in either criminal or civil defense and ignored the fall guy of all fall guys in Liddy. In this treatment we will point out other major blunders by Nixon's counsel, albeit resulting in all his clients suffering far more than he.

In this chapter, we have discussed Dean's blind ambition to feather his intelligence nest with scandalous intelligence about Democrats. But how does this desire explain the inexplicable second break-in? Wasn't he already hearing such naughty talk as was available? And why, again, would either Dean or the CIA have the burglars break in the second time? The answer to this question holds a key to our nation's most impactful scandal.

With this brief explication of Dean's place in the scheme of Watergate, we can begin to understand Watergate's mysteries.

Image of CIA seal, public domain.

CHAPTER 10

THE CIA AND SEX

THE CONVENTIONAL EXPLANATION FOR THE Watergate burglary has always been that of a silly bungled campaign-spying operation in which the Nixon campaign was seeking Democratic strategic information in the DNC headquarters. We have spoken in earlier chapters about Baldwin's overhearing conversations of apparent prostitutes and their johns. We have also covered the prosecutors' plan to show the burglars' interest in these tawdry assignations, based upon the purported motive that Hunt was looking to extort Spencer Oliver Sr., an executive with Hunt's full-time employer Mullen and Company. Supposedly, Hunt wished to push Oliver to step aside, or at least sought to convince higher-ups to favor Hunt over Oliver, as the two vied for control of the fat Mullen CIA cover contract.

But if the prosecution was correct, Watergate would not have been an authorized covert CIA operation, but a frolic and detour by Hunt for his own personal business purposes. Hunt was unable to present at trial his supposed explanation of why the CIA wished this to be seen as a presidentially approved Agency operation, which he would do in pursuing his CIA defense. The public was thereby deprived of viewing the highly sensitive inner workings of the CIA and of an intriguing aspect of Watergate, one that would render Nixon a victim of intelligence agency abuse, with both prosecution and defense arguing for CIA involvement, albeit of two different kinds.

Any student of Watergate should explore the CIA's interest in sexually explicit talk, that is to say, its institutional motive. The CIA has always had an interest in sex as a means of manipulating or gaining information from a subject of interest. One such CIA initiative that was publicly revealed only because of the Senate's Church Committee hearings in 1975 was the operation of Colonel George H. White in the 1950s in San Francisco. White recruited prostitutes, then set up what he thought to be an alluring sex pad, complete with red velvet-flocked wallpaper, on San Francisco's fashionably hip Telegraph Hill.

Through a two-way mirror, White watched the proceedings, often fueled by a dose of some experimental drug supplied by the CIA and served up by the cooperating prostitutes to their johns. The idea was to determine the best time and method for gaining information. One answer on timing: immediately following sex.

But White's operation may have been among the more innocent of CIA research projects, similar to other "business as usual" CIA sex pads around the country. Jack Anderson revealed in 1976, in the wake of the Church Committee hearings, that the CIA had for years maintained widespread, untraceable sexual safe houses. Likely in cooperation with local vice squads, foreign officials, defectors, and traveling agents would be entertained. Influence, more accurately extortion, was also a likely use. After the Watergate arrests, McCord's assistant Robert Houston cleared his office of tapes and documents. When Richard Helms was relieved as CIA director in early 1973, he destroyed a massive cache of tapes, certainly audio and perhaps video, explaining suavely later that they were not related to Watergate.

More darkly, the CIA had pursued a stomach-turning set of illegal domestic programs called MKUltra, Project Bluebird, and Project Artichoke. In these experiments on unwitting humans, a subject would be given a dose of some psychogenic drug to assess his reactions. The administration of a large dose of LSD led the CIA's Dr. Frank Olson to leap out of a building to his death in the early 1950s.

I personally was assigned a matter as an assistant U.S. attorney in which an unwitting New York tennis pro checked into a local VA hospital for depression and anxiety issues. He was given massive doses of LSD without his knowledge, far beyond that which today a recreational user would need to get to Strawberry Fields. Over the following days, the nursing staff carefully noted the excruciating pain and extreme distress of the overwhelmed patient until he finally passed to his eternal reward. I know this because I read those records. The hospital, the state, and the federal officials lied to the widow, after which they sent each other congratulatory letters for keeping the matter concealed.

Correspondence included the state attorney general for New York, later a U.S. senator, Jacob Javits, Eisenhower administration Attorney General Herbert Brownell, and others. To this day I shudder at the casual cruelty displayed by these records and the congratulatory notes that followed. My point here is that nothing was and is beyond the pale for the CIA.

In the late 1960s and early 1970s, as brilliantly unearthed by author Jim Hougan, the CIA took great interest in the research of Duke University psychology and neuroscience departments into building what they termed "psychological machines," replicating subjects of interest. With enough information about a person, it was hypothesized, one could in essence build a psychological avatar that the CIA could then learn to manipulate. Of course, sexual information, including odd proclivities of the subject, was considered highly useful in such endeavors. Any such research within the CIA would have been conducted within the OS.

Within the OS was an even more secretive office called the Security Research Staff (SRS). James McCord, whom we know to later be the security director for the CRP, had been assigned to the OS and reportedly was active in the even more secretive and clandestine SRS. Howard Hunt had been assigned to the OS, and possibly the SRS, prior to his retirement as well.

In the wake of the Watergate burglaries, and with a suspicion that the CIA was somehow involved, President Nixon had removed Richard Helms from his CIA post as director, effective January 1973. At this point, Helms destroyed massive files, including considerable hours of taped materials. In addition to taped conversations from bugging foreign embassies and entities, there may have been a substantial library of taped sexual encounters. Whatever secrets those files held are of course lost to posterity, deepening much of the mystery surrounding Watergate.

The secrets in these non-Watergate files, which may have been subpoenaed if the burglary trial or the Ervin Committee hearings revealed the CIA's involvement in Watergate, were so sensitive that lives were threatened, and perhaps taken. But we can derive some hint from our limited knowledge of the CIA's history that one of its covert activities was an operation we call Watergate. But what clues do we have that the CIA, and Hunt, were interested in sexual information, and therefore were interested in using Watergate, and any claimed approval by the White House of it, as a way of immunizing the prostitute taping operation?

One set of hints comes from a statement of CIA employee Rob Roy Ratliff, dated January 17, 1974, uncovered late in the day as a result of two honest CIA security officers. Much of it is redacted for public consumption, but what is revealed is helpful. Ratliff had been assigned to the White House as a CIA liaison, primarily facilitating transfers of secure pouches between the White House and the CIA, usually from the White House NSC staff. Ratliff had been told by his predecessor that Hunt routinely put documents in these pouches, again suggesting an ongoing CIA relationship with Hunt. Ratliff's predecessor had told him that he had read some of Hunt's transmissions, and that Hunt routinely documented gossip, primarily of a sexual nature, about White House habitats. Ratliff himself had happened to see one transmission of the same ilk. Certainly, part of Hunt's duties involved spying on and reporting to his Agency about insider sexual gossip for which his undercover employer had a demonstrated appetite.

Perhaps a stronger piece of evidence emerged in the FBI's very thorough investigation of the burglary, and all leads coming and going. The FBI interviewed one Miriam Furbershaw, a former CIA analyst who had rented her Rockville, Maryland, in-law apartment to James McCord. McCord had led her to believe that his actual residence was far away, whereas in fact it was nearby. That McCord rented from Furbershaw likely stemmed from his belief that an ex-CIA employee would not give up an Agency agent, and is therefore itself some circumstantial suggestion that McCord was acting undercover for the CIA.

Unluckily for McCord, Furbershaw ran a tight ship, and she had a strict "no women" rule for her renters. After he received several visits from distraught, highly emotional young women, Furbershaw evicted McCord. Given the recognized rectitude of the hardline Baptist McCord, it is highly improbable that these young women were for McCord's pleasure. The implication is therefore presented that McCord had been importuning the young ladies into doing more than providing sexual favors, and what other distressing tasks they were asked to perform would be left to our spy thriller imaginations. Covert drugging of their customers, of course, would be a logical explanation for the emotionality shown by McCord's female visitors. But we are speculating here to a degree as to the motives for this widespread distress.

Another important curiosity which arose from the Furbershaw interview was the discovery by a telephone company technician that McCord's apartment had stored a considerable amount of bugging material, about which he duly informed Furbershaw. From Furbershaw's and Ratliff's statements, along with the CIA's history of skullduggery in human research, we can infer a motive for the CIA to gain presidential approval to legalize the instant program as well as its other illegal domestic programs.

There is one more key piece of evidence corroborated by three credible witnesses concerning Lou Russell. Russell was a veteran DC investigator who, as discussed, worked for McCord and Associates, McCord's private security firm that he formed after retirement. More about Russell in coming chapters. For our present purposes, the three witnesses each told of Russell's hilarious recounting of his electronically overhearing prostitutes and their johns. And this was *before* Watergate. The witnesses, Treasury agent Kennard Smith, investigator Bob Smith, and Russell's friend and well-known lawyer Bud Fensterwald, were all reliable, and each told from his own vantage point stories consistent with those of the others. In short, Russell had been taping prostitutes plying their trade, and had been listening to the proceedings to his great amusement, presumably on behalf of the CIA as McCord's contractor.

What conclusions can we draw from all of this, and what questions are thereby raised? First, it seems the CIA would have a motive to tape prostitutes with influential johns, and likely had been doing so. If so, we conclude that such a domestic program, unless approved by the president in some form or fashion, was illegal. Those involved, if caught, could go to jail and lose pensions. If a wide swath of CIA employees were involved, especially if considerable documentation had been amassed, it would not be beneath the CIA to threaten to kill anyone who threatened to expose the program. And to expose the program in relation to Watergate would have also been to expose the flimsy tissue of presidential approval for that operation, procured ostensibly by deceit, thus arguably invalid in any case, and worse, criminal. More frighteningly, such exposure would likely reveal other actions that lacked even the patina of presidential approval, and thus were clearly criminal. So, yes, murder would not have been beyond the contemplation of an Agency that assassinates officials in other countries.

How would the CIA obtain such approval for its covert prostitute taping operation? It would need, one would infer, approval by person with legal authorization from the president, sufficient under the Constitution to validate a national security operation. Wouldn't the best way to obtain such approval be to entice one of Nixon's all too eager lieutenants to authorize an operation for the seemingly political benefit of the lieutenant?

In *Blind Ambition*, Dean makes no secret of the careerist value of developing one's own opposition intelligence portfolio. We, of course, will never have on-camera confessions by those with clear motive to continue the concealment of their crimes. But in coming chapters, we should examine the circumstantial evidence for corroboration that the Watergate burglaries were meant to sanitize an otherwise illegal prostitute taping operation of the CIA, while providing opposition intelligence for an ambitious young White House lieutenant.

Let us add a couple of smaller notes to this discussion. The week before the second break-in, James McCord gave an odd assignment to his underling Alfred Baldwin III. The order dictated to Liddy by Magruder on Monday, June 12, to go into the DNC a second time, was vehemently opposed by Howard Hunt, presumably representing the Agency's view. If our analysis of the matter is close to correct, the CIA would neither need nor want a second break-in. Why? Because, at least under our theory, no more benefit and only risk was involved from the CIA's perspective. The CIA had already established presidential authorization for a program of wiretapping escorts and their johns. What were the risks it foresaw, and what did it need to do in that regard?

That week, McCord gave Baldwin a seemingly bizarre assignment, one at which he had never previously hinted and certainly one Liddy never heard of or authorized. Baldwin, McCord said, was to have some "fun" that week of June 12. McCord would provide some expense money for Baldwin to frequent DC's most notorious hooker haven—and that is saying something—the cocktail lounge in the Watergate Hotel next to the Watergate office building. He was supposed to watch for "big shots" hooking up. What has never been explained is how, among the many besuited apparent big leaguers in the lounge, Baldwin was supposed to know who was important or for that matter what their names were or, finally, what actions would be taken even if identified.

But Baldwin did frequent the lounge that week and got inebriated on several nights. He indeed witnessed much activity which, without a camera, would be meaningless to posterity. How do we analyze this strange tableau? We suspect that McCord was confident that as an OS agent, and more importantly, as an SRS officer, he could later justify all of this on national security grounds, and Baldwin's mission would fortify his justification.

This was all part of the mission, McCord would explain, to see who was subject to blackmail and thus a national security risk. This, we presume, would be part and parcel of any CIA defense for the Watergate eavesdropping, if caught. SRS had a mission of ferreting out security risks, sex always having been a main factor in blackmail or foreign recruitment. This was, as shown by Baldwin's mission that week, to look for these security risks. For various reasons that will become more apparent later, McCord was worried that the burglars' mission, if his young Nixon lieutenant sponsors found the documents they were seeking, would expose the CIA's role in the prostitute operation.

There is still to this day a case to be made that under certain circumstances, McCord might need to intentionally "blow" the operation, presumably if it got too close to an Agency nerve. Jim Hougan is one highly astute observer who believes that to have been a distinct possibility. That said, the operation was blown unintentionally before it was necessary to blow it intentionally. The evidence in support is solid, and we will give you only a few tantalizing tidbits.

Before McCord left the CRP office that Friday, according to CRP Deputy Security Officer Penny Gleason, McCord gave a goodbye talk, as if that day would be his last at work, telling all how much he had appreciated working with them. Also, local Metropolitan Police Department (MPD) Lieutenant Carl Shoffler decided that night to pull overtime, and to do so in an unmarked car as a plainclothes officer. But because of an injury, Shoffler had been working at a desk assignment for months. And more curiously, June 17 was Shoffler's birthday, for celebration of which his family had already decamped to relatives in Pennsylvania. Shoffler, common sense would say, would be pulling a late-night shift only if something big had been expected while he was waiting, parked a block from the DNC.

Some suggestion has been made that Baldwin had been in touch with Shoffler before that night. A former coworker of Shoffler's, John Chung, has claimed that Shoffler later confessed to him his foreknowledge of the burglary, adamantly denied later by Shoffler. We risk this possible digression simply to note that there were a number of secret agenda in place that night, including clear deception of Liddy as to both burglaries. Before we leave this intriguing subject, we note that at the time of the burglary, Shoffler was certain to be the first police responder should there be a radio call that night.

Let us talk more about the CIA's sexual information mission. Within the CIA's secretive OS, as we have noted, there was an even more secretive department, the SRS, headed by General Paul Gaynor. Its role was to sniff out disloyal or risky national security threats. Gaynor personally was obsessed that there might be a so called "Manchurian candidate," named after a hit movie in which a harmless, all-American-looking Soviet mole had penetrated the U.S. political system to chart the doom of America.

Gaynor was obsessed with sex as a compromising tool against foreign governments, or as a way of extracting information. But it was also a tool used by foreign governments against American agents and officials. So attentive to sexual blackmail was Gaynor that he compiled a massive three-hundred-thousand-person file on every convicted, suspected, rumored, arrested, or perhaps different-seeming person with actual, alleged, or suspected homosexual leanings. It was known in that part of the CIA as Gaynor's "fag file," a name that tells you all you need to know about the state of enlightenment of Gaynor's group. To be fair, in the late 1960s and early 1970s, homosexuality had not yet been widely accepted and was therefore, in absurd but nonetheless widely accepted circular reasoning, a source of blackmail and national security risk.

One reasonably infers as well that Gaynor was also interested in heterosexual sex, especially if in some way verboten, as in prostitution. To use an example from current times, recall the somewhat odd excuse of the otherwise intelligent Sally Yates, then acting attorney general, an Obama holdover at the beginning of the Trump administration who justified on the basis of potential blackmail targeting her attention to the "peeing prostitute" rumor regarding President-Elect Trump. So, sex as a basis for an investigation of national security risk has not been eradicated, even today.

But what, one may ask, did Gaynor's obsession with sex have to do with Watergate? For one thing, both James McCord and Howard Hunt had worked for Gaynor in the SRS. It is therefore relevant if they were falsely retired as of the time of Watergate, or, put differently, currently working for Gaynor. Gaynor's SRS staff often received information on sexual deviation from the DC chief of police, Captain Roy E. Blick. One of the Blick's intelligence officers was Garey Bittenbender, who had a recent but close liaison with the CRP through James McCord. The names of Gaynor, Blick, and Bittenbender will come up in future chapters. Another tie-in in a tableau filled with apparent coincidences that may not be coincidental at all, Shoffler was so interested in Blick's veritable museum of sexual information and deviant devices that he was known around MPD as "Little Blick."

Let us leave this subject with one thought: if sexual talk was a target in Watergate, it is a logical inference that the CIA was involved, especially if on the burglary team there were two supposedly retired SRS operatives, James McCord and Howard Hunt.

Image of Cathy Dieter/Heidi Rikan on sailboat, © Kathy Dickerson.

CHAPTER 11

WHITE HOUSE CALL GIRL

As WE HAVE EXPLAINED IN previous chapters, the conventional view of Watergate has little place for the facts we have shown, and there has been no attempt to explain any of them by mainstream historians as part of a consistent narrative whole. This is the narrative, in short, that was put forth by the *Washington Post*.

We have thus far put together pieces of evidence that, when assembled, make for a satisfying, fact-based story. But the evidence we have put forth still admittedly requires some inference from circumstantial evidence, as in most disputes.

To explain, circumstantial evidence is considered just as valid as direct evidence under the law, to be weighed under all the facts and circumstances present. A criminal defendant, for example, may testify that he did not shoot the victim, which is classic direct evidence. In that situation, circumstantial evidence—his fingerprints on the weapon, purchase of the weapon by him, his threats to the victim, and witness testimony that the victim and the defendant were seen together arguing shortly before the shooting—would appear far stronger than the direct evidence of his denial. So, circumstantial evidence is often much stronger than direct evidence and must be judged with reference to the particular situation.

The circumstantial evidence we have shown in the first ten chapters is a sufficient basis for a jury of public opinion to find in favor of our interpretation, specifically that Watergate was, at its core, a covert operation surveilling sexual activity for intelligence, not campaign, purposes. But, of course, the more we can fill in the gaps with evidence closer to the fact to be inferred, the more credible would be our solution to the mysteries under our microscope. For our counternarrative to be strongly proven, someone in the White House would need to have been interested in listening to Oliver's line, such that Hunt could draw out approval of the project. We could imagine that a White House/ CRP aide was fooled, as was Liddy, into thinking that the proposed burglary was to be for campaign purposes. But such would mean that Hunt's team had taken upon itself quite a heavy burden of convincing the aide to burglarize a worthless campaign target.

Significantly, we have shown an attraction by Dean to prostitution dirt on Democrats. Finally, we put forth Tony Ulasewicz's casing of the DNC offices in the late fall of 1971, on command by Dean, just as Dean was recruiting Liddy to go to the CRP with promises of funding and an intelligence operation. From all of this, we may infer Dean's interest in the knowledge of a hooker referral pipeline into the DNC.

If that matter were left here without such proof, we would still have a solid case, but one subject to principled argument and opposition. Fortunately, we have the benefit of brilliant pieces of research aiding us, valuably dug up by authors Len Colodny and Phil Stanford, who have been, to no one's surprise, excoriated by those invested in the *Post*'s conventional reporting of conservative Nixonian venality.

Let's start with the unidentified lush blonde, called "Tess" by Jim Hougan, who describes her as running a call girl operation out of the Columbia Plaza apartments on Virginia Avenue, just blocks from the Watergate office building. The madam ran her operation under the name Cathy Dieter, we learn from Len Colodny, and was a beautiful blonde of German birth. Cathy Dieter was one and the same as Heidi Rikan, a girlfriend of DC underworld gambling boss Joe Nesline, according to Colodny. Rikan had been a stripper at the Blue Mirror lounge in DC, leaving the District under heat from the vice squad. After spending some time in South Lake Tahoe, which has four major casinos and plenty of high-priced prostitutes, Heidi returned by automobile to DC, where she began her call girl business at the Columbia Plaza.

For reasons we will explain, the identity of Rikan with Dieter will be important in stitching together our evidence. And for that reason, her identity has been ignored by those wishing to ignore solid proof of any revisionist narrative. Author Phil Stanford located Rikan's sister and Rikan's former maid, who in turn related Rikan's admission during her old age: "I was a White House call girl." This statement, somewhat inflating Heidi's status, is important because it corroborates a statement by lawyer Phillip Mackin Bailley to Len Colodny, identifying Rikan as the same person as the Cathy Dieter who ran the Columbia Plaza service.

Stanford documents, via her lawyer Bailley, that the ring had been taping prostitutes and their johns under the protection of the CIA. The operation's bouncer, according to Bailley's interview with Stanford, was a burly man called Russ, a former minor league ball player. It is in this escort service that the needs of the CIA, Hunt, Dean and the DNC all appear to merge.

Appropriately, Bailley's fledgling law practice numbered among its clients a fair number of prostitutes. Bailley had a wide circle of acquaintances and often boasted about his numerous Democratic party contacts. One of his clients, whom he considered a girlfriend, perhaps without reciprocation, was the aforementioned lush blonde of whom Jim Hougan speaks.

The Watergate area was a hooker-rich environment because of the many high rollers living in, working in, and/or visiting the area. Cathy let Bailley know she was looking for a good referral source, and at one point asked him if he had any contacts at the DNC offices down the street, known to have a constant stream of well-heeled visitors. Perhaps, she offered, Bailley could set up a referral program with the DNC. Bailley, who prided himself in his connections with both Democrats and women, allowed as how he might enlist a girlfriend at the DNC to assist.

Let us pause right here. There is no doubt that Cathy's request made business sense. Every professional needs referral sources, after all. But we should here add another detail that Bailley soon learned. Cathy was being protected by the CIA, a very good way to avoid arrest and harassment by law enforcement officials. Cathy's request of Bailley was seemingly motivated, as Adam Smith would approve of, by profit. But from our remove, as we study the odd details of Watergate, there would have also been a strong motive for her benefactor, the CIA, to push her to develop such a referral program with the DNC. So, in short, we do not know if the CIA was behind her request or not, though it certainly would have been consistent with the Agency's motives. After all, if there were such a referral program involving Democrats, this just might interest an ambitious young White House aide, who in turn would authorize a break-in under White House imprimatur.

In fact, Bailley did have a girlfriend of the DNC, whom he called Champagne, the predecessor to Maxie Wells. Per Bailley, as an employee of the DNC, Champagne set up Cathy's referral program. According to Bailley's later interviews with Colodny, an out-of-town visitor to the DNC would be asked if he was looking for female companionship, and if he was, he would be directed to the usually empty office in Spencer Oliver's suite. Oliver was out of town often, so his office was often unoccupied, but he also kept an empty office for visitors and had the only private phone system in the DNC office.

His group, the Association of State Democratic Chairmen, was not formally part of the DNC, and thus owned its own phone system. So, its calls did not go through the DNC switchboard, and visitors to his office who used his phone would have privacy. No one could listen, at least not through the switchboard, nor would there be a record of who called. The visitor was instructed to call a particular number and let it ring twice, whereupon he would wait for call back. When he received the call back, a young woman would be on the line and he would be supplied by Champagne, or perhaps later Maxie, with her picture, whereupon he could then begin a discussion of plans for the evening. So, this arrangement would explain the target of the eavesdropping, which the burglary team had been carrying out for two weeks after the first burglary, as monitored by Baldwin prior to the arrests.

Now let us tie this arrangement to our narrative with some further details. Bailley had occasion to visit the apartment where Cathy's operation was, where, as we related, he met a burly man by the name of Russ, seemingly the muscle or security for the operation. Bailley was given a drink, and in the absence of Cathy, wandered about the apartment looking for a bathroom. He opened a door only to find a man in a closet-like space with recording equipment and headphones monitoring something, presumably activities in the adjoining bedroom. The startled monitor did not take kindly to Bailley's intervention and sternly told him to return whence he came, and quite ominously, to forget what he observed. A chastened Bailley readily agreed and retreated.

Obviously, the observations of Bailley, chronicled by both Colodny and Stanford, in fact constitute direct evidence of our narrative. Before we leave Bailley, let us foreshadow subsequent events. Bailley was later arrested on a morals charge not directly related to either Watergate or Cathy, but his knowledge of the arrangements we have described was threatening to someone.

Somewhat out of the blue, the court hearing his morals case—a crony, it seems, of the corrupt Maryland political system that yielded Nixon's vice president, Spiro Agnew—quickly shuttled Bailley off to a mental hospital rather than publicizing anything Bailley knew, an assignment which occurred shortly after the Watergate arrests. Prosecutors had not asked for that assignment and certainly Bailley's lawyers did not. Obviously, someone wanted Bailley to remain quiet and to stay out of the picture.

Later in John Dean's litigation against Colodny, and in Maxie Wells's case against Liddy, Bailley was often dismissed as insane. We take serious issue with this claim and from this remove, the assertion, as Bailley would agree, was preposterous. But in defending their position on Watergate, Dean, Oliver, Wells, and the *Post* have all retreated to Bailley's alleged insanity, in our view a fig leaf. The insanity trope has been convenient to overcome his clear observations of the call girl business run by Cathy and protected by Russ, where taping of the prostitution was ongoing. This evidence now explains why Dean in October/November 1971, had Ulasewicz case the DNC. Bailley's later arrest and indictment, as we have noted, stemming from his priapistic tendencies, would ultimately cause Dean to order a second break-in of the DNC and literally change world history. We will talk more about this later.

We have noted the interest of arresting officer Lieutenant Shoffler in the sexual files of MPD Captain Roy Blick. What is the significance of Blick and his files? Blick, in short, was obsessed, much like the CIA's General Gaynor, with the intelligence aspects of illicit sex. The assumption to be inferred is that sex is a common tool of leverage, blackmail, and in our nation's capital, compromise of national security. Blick was so obsessed with sex that he maintained in his office what he called his "sex museum," of which he was quite proud, containing the accoutrements of wildly varied sexual perversion, whips and chains being the most conventional. Blick was especially proud of his "fucking machine," which he proudly showed to office visitors. We assure you we are not making this up.

In light of the foregoing, we must ask whether "Little Blick" Shoffler, who was rumored also to have been friendly with Alfred Baldwin, the wiretap monitor, was aware of the wiretapping in advance. To be sure, there have been years of speculation connecting Shoffler to advance knowledge of the break-in, on the conspiracy theory that the operation was intentionally blown. There is some inference and opinion leading to that conclusion, and I would, for the sake of interest, love to confirm such a mysterious conspiracy. But, alas, I cannot. It is of far more concrete evidentiary interest that in making the arrests Shoffler noticed one burglar reaching into a suit pocket to grab something, at which point he and Shoffler had a fierce wrestling match.

We note here, parenthetically, that Shoffler or his partner had observed a Raleigh's tag on the lining of the burglar's suit, which the *Post* reported. But the *Post* did not report the wrestling match, or the items sought in that breast pocket. Why wasn't at least the wrestling match reported? The item in the burglar's pocket we will discuss in a future chapter.

Is there any other connection of Shoffler and Blick to Watergate? For one thing, one of the intelligence officers in DC with whom Blick and Shoffler worked was one Garey Bittenbender. One of Bittenbender's jobs was to act as a liaison not only with the CIA, but also the CRP. Bittenbender at the time of the Watergate arrests was only twenty-three years old, and had known McCord only since March of 1972, when Bittenbender shared intelligence from MPD about a demonstration to occur in front of the CRP headquarters. That they had known each other for only a short time, and only in McCord's capacity as a CRP security director, not as a CIA agent, will have huge significance as we move forward.

Let us here throw in another curiosity. From 1969 through 1971, the entire military establishment had been desperately seeking secondhand intelligence or were directly spying on the White House, hoping especially to learn of foreign policy gambits of President Nixon and his national security adviser, Henry Kissinger. The military suspected these two of being way too friendly with Communist regimes. Nixon, it will surprise many, had very strong critics on the Right. One spy ring run by Navy big shots was exposed in late 1971, after documents had been pilfered from Henry Kissinger and sent to the Navy.

President Nixon decided to keep the scandal quiet. It was known as the "Moorer/Radford Affair" (named after an Admiral William Moorer and Yeoman Theodore Radford, who regularly stole the documents from Kissinger's "burn bag"). The spy affair is brilliantly covered by Len Colodny in *Silent Coup*, in which Colodny seeks to hook up to Bob Woodward and Watergate, along with General Alexander Haig. For a more detailed discussion of that tableau, I would recommend reference to *Silent*

Coup. While fascinating, we do not connect this spy ring, or its uncovering, directly to Watergate. Rather, it demonstrates generally the hunger of the DC intelligence community for information about the White House.

Let us now delve into another curiosity. The White House taping system was publicly announced in Watergate Committee testimony in June 1973 by a White House aide, Colonel Alexander Butterfield. Butterfield, in our view, was likely one more intelligence agency plant within the White House. To be sure, none of our narrative depends on Butterfield's status, but there are interesting observations to make from it.

It is unclear whether the Senate Watergate Committee was tipped off about Butterfield's knowledge of the taping system. It has always seemed odd to us that this obscure White House aide would be called to testify so early in the Ervin Hearings at a time when Butterfield should not have been seen as a major witness, but it was when the CIA was desperate to pin the whole affair on the White House and avoid any exposure of its own role. Put differently, many far more central characters had still not yet appeared when the committee decided to call Colonel Butterfield, an obscure and seemingly uninvolved administrator. It is even money as to whether the Agency pushed the committee, or had Butterfield push the committee, to have Butterfield testify early in the proceedings, ahead of far more prominent potential witnesses.

Butterfield, movie-star handsome, was on his way to general's stars within a short time frame when he joined the White House after writing his college friend, H. R. Haldeman, asking for a job. His job was obscure and backroom, yet to take it he was required to resign his commission by the military. Yet the White House did not require such resignation. In contrast, General Alexander Haig not only served in the White House in uniform, but received promotions while serving. Resigning of this commission suggested interagency protocol, wherein spying for one agency such as the CIA would forbid working for rival, to wit, Air Force intelligence. The point here is that placing himself in a position to listen to all Oval Office conversations would be of incalculable value to anyone wishing to spy on Nixon's inner circle. In any case, within one week after Dorothy Hunt's plane crashed near Midway Airport in Chicago, Butterfield resigned his White House post to head the FAA, which was investigating that plane crash.

While we are discussing the taping system revealed to the Senate by Butterfield, perhaps here it is the place in which we might clear one minor mystery of Watergate, about which you will read only in my book, *Postgate*. I have interviewed two very solid sources to explain why Richard Nixon did not burn the Oval Office tapes earlier and avoid presenting proof of his criminal liability. In essence, Richard Nixon preserved the tapes because he was hopeful of never again paying a cent in income tax for the rest of his life.

Let us explain. We all know that charitable contributions constitute a deduction from one's taxes. If you make $50,000 and give a $1,000 contribution to charity, you pay taxes only on income of $49,000. We all know that. But let's say Picasso had contributed a painting worth $5,000,000,000 to charity. He could have deducted only the cost of the paint brushes, canvas, and the like, not the painting's market value since he did not pay to acquire the painting. The Constitution, however, gives the president ownership of his "presidential papers." Tape is considered a presidential record and thus part of presidential papers. I do not pretend to follow the tax logic, but apparently this constitutional provision would allow a president to deduct the full market value of the papers, so Richard Nixon could donate his tapes, a portion each year, have them appraised, and deduct the value of these tapes. With enough tapes, he could wipe out income for the rest of his life after leaving office. So clearly Nixon did not want to burn his tapes early on, even though he knew that they might contain compromising White House conversations. By the time he was forced to produce the tapes, however, any lawyer who wished to keep his bar card would not advise the president to destroy them. Indeed, at a certain point, burning the tapes might be an impeachable act, that is, obstruction of justice. Had Nixon been advised to burn the tapes prior to their being subpoenaed, or at least before a court ruled on Nixon's claim of executive privilege, destruction of the tapes could have been justified and thus not worthy of impeachment. In any case, many have questioned Nixon's steadfast refusal early on to burn the tapes, and this is the best explanation.

We have discussed before the Agency's adamant opposition to the second burglary as expressed by Howard Hunt. We do know from a public statement from legendary Nixon advance man Ron "Roadrunner" Walker that many young Nixon administration aides frequented the same Columbia Plaza operation run by Cathy/Heidi. With all the documents that the burglars were assigned to copy in that second burglary, was the Agency afraid that such documents would reveal information showing that the Agency was in fact also spying on White House aides through its monitoring of the bordello? Perhaps the most obvious concern of the CIA was to protect the Columbia Plaza operation from any detection of its role at all, whether or not any Nixonite would be outed in the materials. At the very least, the CIA would wish the White House not to learn that this call girl operation was protected by the CIA, and, in general, the CIA wished to keep all the fruits of its operations, including any listing of johns, tapes, or transcripts, sequestered from the White House.

We will leave for another chapter how the CIA took steps to curate and sequester any sensitive fruits of the second burglary. For now, it suffices to say that the CIA had a longstanding institutional interest in the use of sex for intelligence purposes.

Image of journalist Jack Anderson, public domain.

CHAPTER 12

THE DOG WHO DIDN'T BARK: JACK ANDERSON

IN A SHERLOCK HOLMES SHORT story by Arthur Conan Doyle, "The Adventure of Silver Blaze," the perpetrator's identity is proven not by something that happened, but by something that did not: the dog that didn't bark. In the highly intriguing swirl of events surrounding Watergate, none is more engaging than the participation, or rather lack of same, of world-renowned muck-raking columnist Jack Anderson: the dog that didn't bark.

To those of you that do not recognize the name, Jack Anderson was for a number of years the king of the muckrakers, the old-fashioned, turn-of-the-century name for scandal-seeking investigative reporters, a moniker that reveals the low esteem in which investigators had been held pre-Watergate. Anderson, the syndicated columnist and successor to longtime scandal-seeker, syndicated columnist Drew Pearson, was at the height of his powers in late 1971 and early 1972, at least briefly emerging from the lower echelons of respectability. He had just won a Pulitzer Prize for his 1971 reporting on the Nixon administration's tilt toward Pakistan in the India-Pakistan war, reporting based on leaked confidential national security documents.

The reporting was controversial because the Nixon administration had maintained a pose of neutrality. An unfortunate but unintended byproduct of America's silent support of Pakistan was the Pakistani crushing of the minority Bengalis in East Pakistan, ultimately giving rise to an independent Bangladesh. It suffices for present purposes to confirm that Anderson was a man of great investigative resources, from whom nothing in Washington of a scandalous political note could escape, unlike today, when numerous media outlets fancy themselves investigative reporters but few if any fulfill their claims to competence.

Anderson was the only nationally known media outlet for sensational exposés, and because of that fact alone, received numerous tips. In early 1972, Anderson, whose sources were legendary and his sleuthing indefatigable, exploded another bombshell when his associate Brit Hume broke a scandal eclipsed only by the Watergate burglary arrests soon to follow. Hume had been provided a memo, seemingly authored by hard-drinking ITT lobbyist Dita Beard, boasting of a corrupt deal in which the Nixon administration would drop its objections, expressed through an antitrust lawsuit, to stop ITT's purchase of the Hartford Insurance Company, in exchange for $400,000 in cash, a considerable sum in 1972, and a $400,000 block of rooms for the planned San Diego Republican Convention. In short, Anderson's team was formidable, energetic, and fearless. It is with this legendary muckraking in mind that we note an incident that Watergate researchers rarely scrutinize, an incident which we believe has much to do with a successful cover-up of many of the facts we are disclosing here.

In late 1971 and early 1972, word was making its way around the New York intelligence street that the Nixon administration was planning a break-in of the DNC headquarters in Washington, DC. Let's reflect on that date. Why is this timing significant?

Liddy, while preparing, with the encouragement of Dean, his infamous GEMSTONE plan in January 1972, probably starting in midmonth, had never considered the DNC to be anything other than a remote option, and at that only one exercisable during the heat of the campaign, when the headquarters might actually have meaningful information. As of December 1971 and January 1972, he had no plans formulated to break into the DNC headquarters, and as of December, it seems, had formulated no burglary plans at all. The highly disputable May 1973 testimony of Jeb Magruder, John Mitchell's CRP deputy director, stated that Mitchell had suggested the Watergate target on March 30, 1972, the first time Magruder allegedly heard about that target, and the day Mitchell, according to Magruder, first approved any break-in program.

For various reasons not pertinent here, Magruder's testimony was in all likelihood false. But the point we make here is that among all White House aides, Watergate's DNC offices had not received mention before March 30, 1972, even if one believes Magruder. These earlier rumors making their way around the New York intelligence milieu were soon received by one A. J. Woolston-Smith, a former British spy with connections to American intelligence. Oddly, "Woolly," as he was known, was on the scent as early of a possible DNC Watergate break-in as early as December 1971, before Liddy even began formulating the elements of his fatuous GEMSTONE scheme.

In early 1972, the rumors were so strong that Woolly passed them on to William Haddad, a small-time New York City muckraker and publisher of the small, now defunct *Manhattan Tribune*. Soon, not knowing what to do with this information, Haddad passed on to Jack Anderson what he said was a detailed dossier for the world's most prestigious and resourceful muckraker to investigate.

The timing and source of the rumors provide two meaning-ful inferences. First, it was the intelligence community (read, CIA) that was likely behind the rumors and therefore likely a sponsor or cosponsor of the planned break-in. And second, per-haps someone in the administration, unbeknownst to others, was planning on signing off on this break-in once a budget was approved. But that someone was clearly not Gordon Liddy, who had no plans to go into Watergate and was not even formulat-ing GEMSTONE in December of 1971. But during December, Dean was pushing Liddy to take the CRP General Counsel position with promises of a healthy intelligence budget. And in November, please recall, Dean had a puzzled Ulasewicz case the DNC headquarters.

The rumors asserted that the reason for the break-in would be to look for evidence of Fidelista contributions, that is, money from the Castro regime donated to the Democratic party. Since this justification for either Watergate burglary was never in the minds of any White House official, and because it was a later justification for the burglaries put forth by Howard Hunt and also by the Cuban members of the team, at least as they under-stood the purpose, we can only conclude that this rumor about the DNC break-in came ultimately from the CIA, likely through Hunt, McCord, or the Cubans. Remember, the Fidelista motive was a way that the CIA could claim that this was a national security operation, and at the same time claim it was not a CIA national security operation, but one for the White House's pur-poses. And, of course, the White House had no such motive, and had never discussed a Fidelista type of investigation.

What came next is even more intriguing. This hot, delicious scoop was thrown in Jack Anderson's lap by Haddad, accord-ing to him part of a very lengthy and detailed submissions, and then was followed by second long and detailed summation after

Anderson did not respond to the first. Anderson later claimed that he did not respond until he got what he termed was a "sloppy, one-page letter" from Haddad in early April 1972, after Haddad had claimed to have long before sent the two detailed dossiers. At that point, according to Anderson, he did brief checking and found nothing to corroborate the tip, promptly dropping it. He later claimed, absurdly so, that he must have misplaced the first two detailed dossiers that Haddad had sent him.

One curiosity about this tale is that Anderson's supposed belated assessment of the tip did not occur until, conveniently, two weeks *after* Mitchell's alleged March 30, 1972, approval of the program. This was convenient timing because the previous referrals, after all, were inculpatory of the CIA, having occurred before Watergate was an alleged gleam in Mitchell's eye—even a fabricated gleam, as put forth by Magruder in his tale. In other words, Magruder claimed that he had no thoughts of a Watergate break-in until Mitchell supposedly ordered it on March 30, 1972.

Liddy had vaguely contemplated, albeit not in a written plan, a Watergate DNC break-in by March, but it was far down his list, likely never to occur, and he was upset when he was first told in April to go into the Watergate, which he considered of no intelligence value at the time. It was not Liddy, then, who had come up with the Watergate scheme in early 1972.

If Anderson had admitted to having notice of the DNC break before March 30, 1972, he would be pointing the finger at the true instigator, the CIA, and, as we will describe, he did not want to do that for reasons we will discuss. But whether or not Anderson is deemed to be credible about losing these potentially career-enhancing files from Haddad, and, even more incredibly, never finding them, that there were those earlier rumors completely destroys Magruder's suspect testimony about Mitchell being the March 30, 1972, father of the ill-advised caper, always vehemently denied by the former Attorney General.

But Haddad's tip places at least some of the planning for the break-in, as Mark Felt wisely hypothesized, in the lap of the CIA, planning begun at least by late 1971. Of course, the most solid inference from Anderson's receipt early on of the Haddad files is that the columnist was the dog that didn't bark. In the Holmes novel, the detective infers that the dog knew the intruder who killed a horse, so failed to bark and alarm others. In the case of Jack Anderson, he may have failed to bark, but not just because he knew of the CIA's involvement, but because he also believed his life was threatened if he revealed what the CIA was about to do and ruined their program.

In fact, around the time Haddad sent the first dossier, in January 1972, the CIA began a blatant intimidation operation aimed at frightening Anderson. Are the two connected, to wit, the intimidation program and the receipt by Anderson of the planned break-in of Watergate? It certainly makes sense.

That there was obviously and ominously threatening behavior by the CIA directed toward Anderson showed that the CIA's actions were meant to blatantly intimidate, rather than to secretly plan an assassination of the columnist. Clearly visible cars were stationed near the Anderson residence beginning in February, after surveillance of him in January, with the stalking agents openly displaying cameras. They were so obvious with their stalking that Anderson's children began laughingly taunting the agents. This intimidation project was known in CIA files as Operation Mudhen. There is no evidence that the White House knew of or authorized this operation.

As we discussed earlier, any domestic CIA operation is illegal without presidential approval. Howard Hunt, consistent with our analysis, in order to absolve the CIA of criminal culpability for Operation Mudhen, claimed years later that Charles Colson had authorized an assassination or disabling by poisoning of the columnist, supposedly because of his painfully embarrassing exposé of the Nixon administration regarding India and Pakistan. According to Hunt's testimony in 1975, Colson ordered him to explore these thuggish techniques in mid-March 1972, exploring ways to assassinate or disable Anderson. Colson had heatedly denied any such order, but, like all other White House officials of the time, did not have nice things to say about Anderson. Perhaps more to the point, most were not inclined to believe anything Colson said, given the general attitude toward Nixon, and Colson's role as Nixon's "hatchet man."

Consistent with our theorizing elsewhere, Hunt could easily have conjured up, falsely, presidential approval for disabling Anderson, as was much of his purpose all along—to legalize the CIA's assassination planning. In later years, Colson and Anderson became quite friendly. So, Anderson took advantage of this friendship and asked Colson, now free from any criminal jeopardy, to confirm his assassination order as claimed by Hunt. Colson angrily denounced the notion, highly credibly. Moreover, there is not a peep on the many hours of White House tapes and thousands of White House documents suggesting any such order or plans, even though there was plenty of grousing about Anderson in 1971. If there were a plot against Anderson, common sense suggests, there would have been, per normal Oval Office ways, substantial discussion of how to disable or kill him. Perhaps, more significantly, if the White House had really authorized an operation against Jack Anderson to be implemented by Hunt and the CIA, there would have been reports to the White House about the operation, but there is no such evidence.

Moreover, Operation Mudhen started in January 1972, and was clearly carried out by CIA agents before Liddy or Hunt even discussed Anderson. It is CIA documents, not White House records, that call this Operation Mudhen. The CIA, in short, does not deny the stalking and intimidation, but simply claims it was concerned with Anderson's possible publishing of Russian intelligence. We are to believe, per the CIA, that the Agency was stalking and intimidating Anderson, but it was the White House that was considering his assassination. Many readers were born at night, but not last night. The CIA claim does not pass the straight face test.

At a key juncture of Operation Mudhen, Anderson and CIA Chief Richard Helms had lunch on March 17, 1972, at the Montpelier Room restaurant in the Madison Hotel. The discussion was per an invitation to the columnist from the director himself, and perhaps some preliminary understanding may have been reached at the lunch.

Helms later claimed that the lunch was designed to obtain Anderson's promise not to unearth CIA documents about Russia. For several reasons, the supposed discussion of Russian documents made no sense because Anderson's source for the Russian documents, Yeoman Radford, had been taken out of play several months earlier. While there was no threat from Radford, there was a threat that Anderson would blow the cover off a Watergate operation that the CIA hoped would legalize many other illegal domestic operations. In short, none of the CIA's story, that the White House ordered an assassination plot against Anderson, makes sense. But clearly there was in fact a three-month CIA Operation Mudhen designed to intimidate Anderson from reporting something the CIA did not want reported. The Russian documents were simply a ruse to justify stalking and threatening the reporter.

We can also infer, very importantly for our discussion, that the timing of Operation Mudhen, from January until mid-April

1972, is consistent with the DNC break-in tips that Anderson was receiving from William Haddad. It is therefore a rational hypothesis that the Mudhen operation was to intimidate Anderson from blowing the lid off the CIA's plans to bug the DNC's Watergate offices, the plans that had been relayed by Woolston-Smith to Haddad, and on to Anderson.

While Anderson and Helms may have made progress toward some tentative understanding during their Montpelier Room lunch on March 17, we infer that the dispute was not concluded with finality until early to mid-April, when the ostentatious home surveillance of Anderson stopped. This timing suggests that Anderson then agreed to put down his pen on some unknown subject with timing nicely fitting with Liddy's having been recently pointed toward Watergate. In other words, Liddy was not given the go-ahead on Watergate until it was clear that Anderson would not be exposing the operation. This connection of Anderson with Watergate is nothing, of course, about which Liddy knew anything. All that Magruder had earlier reported from his meeting with Mitchell was than the "program" was approved. Liddy was not told about the Watergate target until weeks later even though, according to Magruder's later story, Mitchell targeted Watergate on March 30. None of this makes sense per the conventional narrative.

Many observers have wondered why there was such a long delay after Mitchell's supposed March 30, 1972, order to conduct the break-in. Liddy was not informed of the order until the end of April, not long after Anderson agreed to see no evil sometime in mid-April. To be sure, on March 24, 1972, one week after Helms and Anderson lunched, Hunt invited Liddy to meet with Dr. Edward Gunn, a supposedly retired CIA poisons doctor, to discuss ways of killing or disabling Anderson. At the conclusion of the meeting, Hunt suggested Liddy pay Gunn $100, which

Liddy assumed was part of tradecraft, and which he did with a crisp $100 bill.

From our view of the evidence, that $100 bill is equivalent to the casing photo of Lewis Fielding, that is to say, proof of White House approval, should the CIA ever need to prove White House authorization of whatever it intended to do to Jack Anderson. That Hunt had Liddy pay Gunn $100 was clearly designed to put a Nixon stamp on any killing or disabling that may have later occurred. The bets here are that the $100 bill was preserved in CIA evidence lockers, fingerprints intact. Clearly this meeting was part of Operation Mudhen, designed to protect the CIA should it be caught poisoning, killing, or disabling Anderson.

Therefore, a logical inference is that the intimidation of Operation Mudhen, which was admitted by the CIA, caused Anderson to be a dog that did not bark about the Watergate plans. Had the muckraker revealed a potential break-in, all that would have transpired was the scuttling of plans, to no great acclaim for Anderson. On the other hand, to the CIA, ruining its DNC scheme would have prevented it from receiving what it likely saw as a pension-saving get-out-of-jail-free card, giving White House sanction to what normally would be seen as widespread Agency illegality in its prostitute taping program.

Why is Operation Mudhen, we may ask, pertinent to our exploration of the Watergate mysteries? First, as we suggested earlier, it as a template for the Watergate burglaries, that is, a CIA operation that could be blamed, at least partially, on the White House. As Hunt sucked Liddy into the Gunn meeting, we suggest that Hunt likely lured Dean into the enticing fruits of the DNC prostitution calls. And, of course, this is consistent with the CIA, through Hunt and Bennett, luring the White House into the Fielding burglary with visions of discrediting Daniel Ellsberg, certain to please the chief executive.

If Operation Mudhen was about hushing the Haddad dossier, it is circumstantial proof that the CIA was behind Watergate. In later days, the CIA would show its willingness, as in Mudhen, to protect its illegal operations with threatened murder.

It is impossible to believe that the dogged, highly engaged Anderson received two explosive dossiers from Haddad, lost them, and remembered nothing about them. To conclude this discussion, we note that the world's fiercest, loudest Pulitzer Prize-winning dog, Jack Anderson, did not bark after months of CIA intimidation convinced him to stay silent. Anderson's silence is strong proof that the CIA was involved in Watergate, through the dog that didn't bark.

Image of John and Maureen Dean on their wedding day, with
Cathy Dieter as the bridesmaid, public domain.

CHAPTER 13

JOHN DEAN'S HISTORICAL BLUNDER

AT THIS FAR REMOVE, THERE can be little doubt but that the CIA had achieved its main goal, at least as we have here hypothesized, in the first burglary of late May 1972. The Agency had made a clear record that the White House, certainly through White House counsel Dean, less certainly through Attorney General Mitchell, approved its program of taping prostitutes. It could now point to the payment of the burglars from CRP funds controlled also by the White House, which Hunt would say was authorized by Dean and Mitchell, both lawyers acting on behalf of the president. Any bugs purchased for the first burglary were paid for by the White House and could therefore be used with impunity in subsequent missions. This claimed approval could be stretched a long way to include ratification of the entire prostitute taping program of past and future years.

But when Hunt learned to his surprise on June 12 of the plans to break into the DNC a second time, he voiced adamant opposition to Liddy, ultimately to no avail. Hunt understood that the CIA had achieved its goal with the White House approval of wiretapping prostitutes. A second entry would be all risk and no reward for the Agency. Liddy also disapproved, mainly because of the strain on his budget for a seemingly barren target, which had produced little so far. But his dislike for Magruder kept him from appearing too fearful, a big bugaboo for the macho man Liddy, who despised the putatively spineless Magruder.

In the first burglary, the CIA-controlled Cubans photographed only a few documents, to Liddy's chagrin. Indeed, the only photographs later produced were seemingly of trophy papers spread on a carpet by gloved hands, complete with identifying DNC letterhead. Because of these photos, there would be no doubt in any future inquiry that the team, financed by White House money, broke into the DNC. But these pictures had no intelligence or informational value. The photographs also had the purpose of corroborating that the break-in was aimed at Larry O'Brien, whose letterhead was photographed. Proof of the targeting of O'Brien was also an important justification for those in the White House and CRP who might learn of the operation, not knowing of the true secret agenda of the break-in.

So, if there was now to be a second break-in seeking massive document copying, how do we now explain this mission if only a few documents were copied on the first burglary? With Hunt's opposition and a clear lack of necessity under our presidential approval hypothesis, the impetus for this second break-in appears to come from non-CIA personnel, in other words, from the White House or the CRP, and certainly someone other than the hotly opposed Liddy. Who would that be, and why? One candidate for giving this order, Magruder, was a notorious weakling and a nonstarter, who we can infer received his oppo document copying orders from above him. The only logical candidate for the order is Dean who, we must add, still denies all.

Magruder first gave Liddy a heads-up about the possible second burglary on the afternoon of June 9, 1972, and issued the order the following Monday, June 12. Did something happen that day, June 9, 1972, which caused what appears to have been this sudden desire, not evidenced before, to copy copious documents? In response, let us return to talk a bit about the adventures of our engaging bad boy, prostitution lawyer Phillip Mackin Bailley.

On one festive but reckless occasion, Bailley met with his like-minded buddies and passed around nude pictures of a woman, a University of Maryland student, with whom many of them on one wild night had had their way, termed colloquially, "pulling a train." Unfortunately for the mad barrister, one sybarite brought with him a straight government lawyer who, shocked, blew the whistle on the whole affair. It turns out that one of the several train engineers had given the girl twenty dollars on that steamy night. The sex now became technically prostitution because of the money having been transferred, and Bailley had brought the girl across state lines for immoral purposes, a Mann Act violation, which is a federal crime.

His office was raided, with address books and other documents seized in April 1972. The indictment came back June 8, 1972. On June 9, 1972, the following day, the *Washington Star-News* wrote about the indictment, which was limited to several similarly victimized young ladies, the first being the University of Maryland coed we've spoken about, with no claim of a call girl "ring." But the article about the indictment went far beyond these few individual cases and spoke far more broadly of a call girl "ring" run by Bailley, which involved executive office employees, including "one lawyer at the White House."

On June 9, after reading the article, an alarmed John Dean telephoned Bailley's federal prosecutor, John Rudy, summoning him to the White House to bring with him all the evidence he had uncovered. The ostensible purpose of the meeting was for

Dean to investigate the involvement of the executive office building personnel, and indeed, he thereafter terminated one involved young lady. Dean examined the address books of Bailley, in which there were five references, unbeknownst to Rudy, to Dean's then girlfriend, Maureen Biner, aka "M.B.," "Clout," or "M.Biner." The reference to "Clout" was to her White House counsel boyfriend, a man of presumed influence.

Dean reportedly mumbled to Rudy that the article likely had been leaked by Democrats. While Dean denies ordering the second break-in, others have in later years affirmed his role, most significantly Hunt and Magruder. Certainly, the *Star-News* article gave him a possible motive to seek the large cache of documents the burglars planned on copying. Magruder told Liddy in essence that the target was the dirt the Democrats had on the Republicans, emphatically slamming his hand on his left lower desk drawer, where Republicans normally kept their oppo dirt, telling Liddy, "We want what they have in here!" Magruder did not specify the location of the targeted desk, which Liddy assumed was O'Brien's. But we know that the *Star-News* article referred to "one lawyer at the White House" and it is also undeniable that Maureen Biner, later Maureen Dean, had known the madam, Cathy Dieter, through her real name Heidi Rikan, remaining very close with her. All of this is simply part of the circumstantial evidence suggesting that Dean might have felt vulnerable to the reference in the June 9 *Star-News* article about "one lawyer from the White House" having been involved in a "call girl ring."

How does Dean's involvement in either or both of these burglaries, more importantly the second, affect our analysis of Nixon's guilt and the shaping of the cover-up? It is hard to discern where in the cover-up Dean's raging conflict of interest ended and his legal ineptitude began.

When Dean first spoke with Gordon Liddy after the burglary arrests, the crazed but martially disciplined Liddy offered, if deemed necessary, to be shot. But he certainly offered to keep his mouth shut. An experienced litigation lawyer would know that Liddy had been a central figure who could have provided everyone a defense, in short, a fall guy. And, to boot, he would not need to perjure himself to do so. All that was required was a public pronouncement from Liddy's lawyer that Liddy was off on his own rogue operation in the burglary. Such an approach would have given all the defendants some leeway to fashion a defense, with Magruder claiming that his disbursement of CRP funds to Liddy was intended for more traditional security measures.

Secondly, it is widely recognized that even for employees charged with a crime, the employer can and should indemnify these employees and agents for legal expenses unless and until the court determines that the employee acted in bad faith and not in the interest of the employer. The CRP could thus have provided a sound basis for openly providing indemnity payment for the defendants' legal fees, and even continued salaries while on administrative leave for employees such as Liddy. But it is clear that the calm but desperate Dean never considered any sophisticated legal strategies. Ultimately, the White House relied upon as White House counsel, a lawyer with four months of private legal experience, none in litigation, whose limited private practice work was marred by charges of unethical conduct.

Let's discuss now what Dean did do. For the next nine months postarrest, he professed to his superiors that he knew of no White House involvement in the burglary, which became Nixon's lifeline, but one Dean knew was false. Of course, because Dean was both conflicted and inexperienced, he did not advise his clients early on about avoiding obstruction of justice or cover-up criminal liability. So, Dean's advice at the outset, with no disclosure to his colleagues of his exposure, was abominable.

Citing John Mitchell, in our view likely falsely, Dean advised the president's inner circle to tell the CIA to call off the FBI's Mexican Money Trail investigation on the grounds of potential interference with a CIA operation. This was untrue, at least, as far as the inner circle knew, even though, coincidentally, Watergate was in fact a CIA operation. How do we know that Dean did not get this advice from Mitchell? Colodny proves quite strongly that Dean had no opportunity to confer with Mitchell before offering this extremely silly advice.

But halting this innocuous Mexican part of the investigation was all risk and no reward. Any good lawyer would know that the investigators would eventually prove CRP funding of the burglary, so why bother to stop the Mexican investigation, which was essentially meaningless money trolling?

It has been suggested that Nixon did not wish exposure of a major anonymous donor, Dwayne Andreas, an explanation that makes sense. But, that said, Andreas's contribution would ultimately have been discovered by the FBI and, in any case, likely would have remained confidential with the FBI. So, this act of obstruction concocted by Dean was both silly and harmful because eventually it became the basis on which Nixon's advisers told him he must resign from office. This act of obstruction was clearly shown on the White House tapes produced in July 1974, after which Nixon resigned within a month.

The other somewhat less clear act of presidential obstruction occurred, again on the advice of Dean, in his March 21, 1973, Oval Office meeting with Nixon, where he lured Nixon into arguably committing to raise $1,000,000 for Howard Hunt. Trying to prevent his own exposure, Dean was pushing Nixon to assert executive or attorney-client privilege to prevent Dean from testifying. Dean tried to force this protection for him by revealing for the first time to Nixon the potential culpability of Haldeman aide Gordon Strachan, thus implicating Haldeman, and Dwight Chapin, Nixon's aide, uncomfortably close to the president himself. Dean was hoping that these revelations to Nixon would cause him to assert executive privilege over any of the inner circle testifying, which, of course, would include Dean. Dean, it is obvious today, was still concealing his own substantive criminal liability for the burglary.

Dean, after sucking Nixon into seemingly agreeing to raise money for Hunt, but not convincing him to assert privilege, immediately went to his own counsel for advice. Dean then began cutting deals with the prosecutors, using his knowledge of Nixon's Dean-inspired cover-up as bait. Dean, as we all know, became the first and most powerful witness against Nixon.

While testifying like he was a Boy Scout caught in bad company, Dean professed no prior knowledge or preapproval of the burglaries. With no one else to contradict him, Dean easily escaped exposure for the burglaries, while admitting, as he must, to the cover-up. Thereafter, Nixon's criminal guilt was based upon his obstruction of justice, counseled by this conflicted and unethical lawyer. With the other burglary defendants silent, except for the dishonest Magruder, who implicated Mitchell falsely, there was no opportunity for the public to comprehend the significant but hidden unanswered questions of Watergate.

Was the burglary an event having nothing to do with the campaign other than the campaign contributions paying for it? Another question: was it an operation geared to listening to prostitutes? Another question: was it in an initiative pushed by the CIA? One more: were the Democrats running a prostitute referral operation? Was Nixon lured into obstruction by fraudulent, conflicted counsel? If any of the above questions are answered in the affirmative, an entirely new front would have been opened in the impeachment inquiry, and many honest legislators and sympathetic citizens would have been drawn to Nixon's defense.

Unfortunately, each of the major testifying witnesses had strong motives to lie: McCord, Magruder, Dean, and, after pleading guilty, Hunt. The public was fooled, and our history written deceptively. Could journalists, though, have found and printed the truth? Could the country have been enlightened by a media more concerned with the facts than by partisan effect?

Let's consider the effect that partisan reporting can have on our nation's history. Had the *Post* reporters published what they knew about the tawdry nature of the sexual assignations being overheard, more investigation would have been required. Eventually it would identify a call girl operation. Fine, one may respond, but how would that help us get to the bottom of this? First, we would learn that the madam was one Cathy Dieter, then eventually she would be revealed to be Heidi Rikan, the "lush blonde" to whom we have been referrin

So, what, you may ask, if we can identify Heidi Rikan as Cathy Dieter's true identity? Well, Heidi Rikan was Maureen Biner Dean's best friend, as Maureen wrote later in her own book, meeting Rikan in South Lake Tahoe before driving with her to live in DC. Our point is that if the *Post* had revealed the truth about the sexual target, and if the public had known of the true missions of the two burglaries, it would have later looked askance upon the testimony of burglar James McCord to the effect that the CIA was not involved. And Jeb Magruder's testimony that the straitlaced John Mitchell suggested the Watergate break-in for intelligence purposes would have been out-loud laughable. But the public never learned of this important set of facts.

Image of CIA agent and Watergate burglar James McCord, public domain.

CHAPTER 14

JAMES MCCORD, CIPHER

WE TURN NOW TO JAMES McCord, cipher. Prior to this chapter, we presented what we believe is at least a plausible case explaining the otherwise inexplicable mysteries of Watergate. We have shown you the complete lack of campaign information available at the DNC headquarters in June 1972, not worth the expense and risk of one burglary, much less two. We have also presented the legal and constitutional framework which prevented the CIA from pursuing domestic operations, even though it had both the capability and desire to do so. We have reviewed the president's national security powers, which would allow him to authorize an operation otherwise illegal, or at least not compliant with the Bill of Rights.

We have presented evidence that Hunt's employer, Mullen and Company, was authorized to provide "cover" for CIA agents, and that Hunt was contemplating a CIA defense to the Watergate burglary charges. We have shown also that a substantial part of the monitored conversations in Watergate were of a salacious nature, and that the Agency had for years performed sexually related "research," as it were. It may have been doing just that at a particular Columbia Plaza bordello.

We have shown you two instances in which the CIA engaged in domestic operations: the Fielding burglary and the plot against Jack Anderson, to both of which it could later claim White House authorization. And we have demonstrated that the phone lines being monitored in Watergate were those of the unimportant Spencer Oliver Jr., who had a private phone system, an empty office within his suite, and was often out of town. All of this, we would submit, goes a long way to explaining many of Watergate's lingering mysteries. But it does not explain them all, and perhaps to some jurors in the court of public opinion, it does not show proof beyond a reasonable doubt of primary CIA responsibility for Watergate. We believe that the evidence regarding Watergate burglar James McCord solves many of these perceived shortcomings.

On March 23, 1973, convicted Watergate burglary defendants G. Gordon Liddy and James McCord were to be sentenced by Judge "Maximum John" Sirica. Sirica had been loudly and consistently demanding that the prosecutors, and for that matter the defendants, explain what motivated the seven members of the team to commit the burglary. The appellate court ruling obtained by Morgan had prevented the prosecution from doing just that, as least as the prosecution viewed the evidence.

Prior to trial, Howard Hunt had also taken his own steps in that direction, contemplating a CIA defense, which would have explained much but was stymied both by his wife's death and Dean's withholding, then destroying, Hunt's operational notebooks. The evidence thus blocked would have shown facts consistent with those we are here advocating. But what glimpses and glimmers of evidence the public had thus far seen pointed toward a burglary directed out of the highest levels of the White House for campaign purposes. It is our belief, expressed here, that this was a substantially false view of the evidence. Fragmentary evidence, though, had by fall of 1972 brought the scandal to a sim-mering state from what had been a moribund curiosity.

Dramatically, on March 23, 1973, McCord opaquely alluded in his letter to Judge Sirica of something he had written to White House detective Jack Caulfield in December 1972. In that December letter to Caulfield, McCord warned that if CIA Director Richard Helms was fired from his CIA post, "every tree in the forest will fall." In fact, Nixon did remove Director Helms from his post in January 1973, sending him to Iran to be the American ambassador. On March 23, 1973, someone should have yelled, "Timber!"

In open court, Judge Sirica read aloud a March 19 letter sent by Agency die-hard McCord. There had been perjury com-mitted in the trial, McCord wrote. The White House had both threatened him and offered him clemency, he told the court. The White House had tried falsely to blame the burglary on the CIA, and Nixon higher-ups were involved.

Although all of McCord's knowledge of high officials' involvement was hearsay, the letter was a bombshell, creating sensational stories throughout the media. By the time McCord was questioned in public about his allegations, John Dean had turned prosecution witnesses against Richard Nixon on the cov-er-up, and CRP Deputy Director Jeb Magruder had pointed at his boss, John Mitchell, in our view falsely, for authorizing the burglary. These two guilty administration lieutenants, in other words, played their get out of jail free cards by implicating their bosses. While Dean's testimony was truthful as it implicated Nixon, he omitted his own false and conflicted advice that drew the president into a cover-up of a burglary he never understood.

There was no reason now for the heavily partisan Watergate Senate Committee, or the press, to drill down on questions about the odd, inexplicable burglary. Or, for that matter, to question the idiosyncratic James McCord about any holes in his story. For those interested in the possibility that the CIA was looking for presidential authorization for its otherwise illegal intelligence operations, McCord provided a big clue which no legislator or journalist seemed to notice at the time.

Hawaiian Senator Daniel Inouye had asked McCord the obvious question: how could a person like you, Mr. McCord, law-abiding his entire life and a loyal, patriotic government agent, have so willingly broken the law? It was a good question. McCord answered, as he previously told the *Post*, that he thought the burglary was legal because it was authorized by the attorney general as a national security operation. No media outlet pounced on this important testimony, which is absolutely in line with this book.

This answer confirmed that theory we put forth in Chapter Two and following chapters of the motive of the CIA to infiltrate the White House and the CRP. It shows that McCord had in mind the authorization by the attorney general as rendering a national security operation legal for acts that would otherwise have been illegal. This was the Agency's cover story. McCord simply refrained from admitting that the "national security" purpose was one determined by the CIA. After all, no one in the White House or the CRP had claimed Watergate to have been a national security operation. The only person so claiming, at least with Hunt now having abandoned his CIA defense, was a recently retired CIA agent, one we submit here was continuing undercover in that role. Hunt later claimed that this was a national security operation, although an unwise one, but therefore legal. Very cutely, he did not in later statements name the CIA, from which his pension came, but was clear that these were the types of operations he had performed for the CIA.

What was it, McCord should have been asked, that made a DNC break-in an arguable national security matter? As a national security veteran, Mr. McCord, why would you think that breaking into the DNC had anything to do with national security? How would tapping Larry O'Brien's phone protect our country? Unfortunately, these questions were not asked, and it is not clear that there would have been a credible answer, at least not one that McCord would have wished to volunteer.

As the scandal unfolded, it was revealed that Eugenio Martinez and Virgilio Gonzalez both had thought Watergate to have been a legitimate national security operation, indeed, a CIA operation. But their belief was widely chalked up to the "duped Cuban" theme, that is, that Hunt fooled them, and the *Post* did much to support this angle. But no one could claim that the veteran McCord was a dupe.

McCord made another odd statement that was not pursued. He testified that during the first break-in, he was to wiretap the phone of Larry O'Brien and, curiously, one other Democrat official at the team's discretion. The latter direction, clearly falsely concocted by McCord, justified what should have been seen as an inexplicable tap of the peripheral figure Oliver. But, again, what he said about the method of placing the O'Brien tap should have been seized upon immediately. The veteran agent claimed he had tapped O'Brien by clipping, in an office near Oliver's, a "call director" line going to O'Brien's phone. This would have been a line routed to the subject phone from the switchboard, then routed again from that place to O'Brien's office. O'Brien might have, say, twenty different lines coming into his office, fifteen of them, for example, routed from various parts throughout the office. When analyzed, this claim proves to be nonsensical.

Even if the call director were effective when listening to O'Brien through that one line, it would not capture O'Brien on any of the other lines, which would have been achieved if O'Brien's phone itself would have been tapped. The calls through this call director may have been highly unfruitful and involving pedestrian matters, that is, whatever occupied the person from whose phone the call director ran, and McCord expressed no knowledge of whose phone that was. Indeed, the calls routed to O'Brien from that line could have been possibly involved matters meant for O'Brien's secretary. In any case, this seems, if true, a highly ineffective way to tap the alleged main target, O'Brien, while the direct tap on Oliver's private line would have been quite effective in capturing all calls on Oliver's phone system. So even if one was to believe the patently absurd "call director" testimony, doesn't it mean that the true targeted phone was that of Oliver, not of O'Brien? Indeed, if, as the *Post* has suggested for years, the aim of the first burglary was to tap O'Brien, wouldn't the burglars go to his office? By McCord's own admission they did not get near O'Brien's office during the first burglary, even though at the time, as we later learned, McCord told Liddy otherwise, claiming he had planted a super-sophisticated room bug in a piece of O'Brien furniture.

Of course, while this "second tap" theory, as we will call it, was at least marginally credible so long as Liddy remained silent, we now know that this was not what Liddy had actually authorized: a phone and a room bug directly on O'Brien, with no mention of a second or discretionary tap. McCord never explained, nor was he asked, why his team did not simply enter O'Brien's office to put a tap on his phone.

Since the burglars made no phone calls from the jail on the morning of the arrest, it is our deduction that McCord likely thought the CIA would admit its participation and then claim that this was a presidentially sanctioned CIA operation, and therefore legal, consistent with McCord's Senate testimony.

Indeed, at his arraignment, McCord had softly whispered, "CIA" to the judge when asked from which Agency he had retired, consistent with his thinking that the Agency would tell the court privately to hush the whole affair, which Hunt described in his autobiography as a standard CIA practice.

McCord's whisper, then, may have been a tip-off that McCord believed the CIA would claim the operation was a legal national security operation and quietly extract the defendants from the charges, as was the defendants' expectation, per later complaints of Martinez and Gonzalez.

Another important event had occurred prior to the arraignment, as the defendants had been waiting to be led to court. DC intelligence officer Garey Bittenbender, who worked with McCord while McCord was with the CRP, saw McCord under arrest and asked him what had happened. McCord, according to Bittenbender's statement to the MPD, as referenced by the FBI, replied that he had been on a CIA operation. If Bittenbender was telling the truth, that would support a unanimous verdict in favor of the CIA infiltration theory we here offer. When questioned before the Senate, however, McCord blithely testified that he never said that, and that Bittenbender must have mistakenly assumed he was still working for the CIA, since McCord had known the detective through the liaison between the CIA and the DC intelligence. The senators, eager to dismiss any notion of CIA involvement, offered no cross-examination on this highly vulnerable point.

But we note, first, that Bittenbender gave this statement to the FBI shortly after the arrest, but, even more importantly, had interviewed McCord at length later in his jail cell. How likely is it, we ask, that a trained intelligence officer would misunderstand McCord's statement dealing directly with Bittenbender's area of expertise, intelligence operations? We put a Bittenbender mistake in the "highly unlikely" category and conclude that McCord was at the time anticipating his own CIA defense before the Agency decided otherwise. But the death blow to McCord's testimony should have been that Bittenbender, only twenty-three at the time, first met McCord when he was with the CRP, advising him of a possible demonstration. There is no evidence that the two knew each other when McCord was with the CIA, and in any case, McCord's CIA duties had nothing to do with political demonstrations or local policing work. He was interested in potentially disloyal Americans.

But for those who might still credit McCord on this testimony, there is another large nail to shut his perjurer's coffin. Penny Gleason, McCord's deputy security officer at CRP, was questioned by the FBI on July 1, two weeks after McCord's arrest. She related that Bittenbender had visited her at the CRP offices the afternoon of the arrests, highly concerned about his friend McCord. What was so important about Gleason's statement was her notation that Bittenbender had visited McCord on multiple occasions while McCord was with the CRP, after McCord had ostensibly retired from the CIA. So Bittenbender could not have been confused about McCord's ostensible present employment for the CRP at the time of the arrest, as McCord tried to convince the Senate was the case. Moreover, Bittenbender told the FBI that he first had met McCord while liaising with him in McCord's role as a CRP director of security, not as a CIA man. Bittenbender, then, was not confused.

Bittenbender's statement thus rings true, and McCord's false. Bittenbender, in short, would be attuned to the distinction between a CRP operation and a CIA mission. More importantly, he was a current friend of McCord's who had stayed in touch with him, whereas McCord's testimony suggested that he and Bittenbender had only a now-distant past relationship.

There is another bit of information quite intriguingly offered by Gleason to the FBI. McCord had in his office a photograph of Richard Helms, then the CIA director, signed by Helms with a note to McCord reading, "with deep appreciation, Dick." The word "deep" was underlined twice—hardly, one might say, the best deep cover practice! This picture was removed by McCord's loyal assistant Robert Huston soon after the arrests, along with a large cache of materials, including tapes, in McCord's cabinet. But simply this picture, suggesting that McCord was operating under deep cover, is itself decent evidence of McCord's continuing role as a CIA agent.

In another anomaly, McCord, the last burglar in the Watergate building the night of the burglary, did not remove the tape from the locks, even though he told his worried fellow burglars he had done so. This was necessary reassurance for the burglars since the presence of tape on the locks might lead to their arrests. They knew that previously that night tapes had been discovered on the locks and removed, seemingly by security personnel. We will analyze later the likely cause of this apparent recklessness and why McCord would have lied to his fellow burglars.

We will deal as well with other evidence implicating McCord in subsequent chapters. But we will leave you with where perhaps we should have begun. How was McCord able to place himself in the CRP? John Mitchell wanted as the head of his security in the CRP an individual with *personal* security experience. He had commissioned White House detective Jack Caulfield to find him such a person. Caulfield, however, had no federal experience and was not familiar with accessing retired government personnel. Nor was he a personal security expert himself. He turned, understandably, to the head of the White House Secret Service detail, Alfred Wong. With hundreds of retired Secret Service agents living in and around the DC area, all of whom presumably would have personal security experience, one would think that Wong could with no difficulty find such a retiree for the job. Wong, however, could not, to Caulfield's chagrin, find anyone better than McCord, who was a former CIA security agent, but with not a shred of personal security experience.

Wong had for years been friendly with McCord, who had lent Wong numerous CIA technicians for use in the White House. It has been speculated that these technicians may have planted undetectable bugs throughout the White House for monitoring by the CIA. But for our present purposes, it is enough to say that McCord and his likely sponsor, the CIA, used a favor from Wong to place McCord in an apparent undercover post.

McCord began part-time employment with the CRP in September 1971, soon after Hunt was hired by the White House. He went full-time in January 1972, just as Gordon Liddy was transferring to the CRP, with his big Dean-encouraged plans for an expensive intelligence operation. It is likely McCord sought an undercover role with the CRP so that Hunt could enlist him as an operative in future CIA work, performed under the cover of a CRP operation. McCord committed to the CRP full-time only after he was assured that the undercover operations led by Liddy would be run through the CRP.

It was January 1972 when Liddy knew he would need to hire a reliable wireman to implement the GEMSTONE plans he was about to propose to Mitchell. As we discussed earlier, any such wireman, that is, someone who knows how to wiretap, should be double-blind, or at least single-blind, that is, not readily recognizable as an agent of the CRP. A double-blind retiree, of course, would not know for whom he was working, and anyone who arrested him would not have any clue that he was working for the CRP. But in the next five months, to Liddy's frustration, Hunt could not find one such wireman. Liddy then was stuck with McCord as the only available person capable of filling the slot. If there was in fact a secret CIA agenda at play, a wily and loyal wireman like McCord was necessary. After all, a wireman would need to tap Oliver's phone while pretending he was in fact placing a room bug in O'Brien's office. Hunt and the CIA both needed, someone to direct the operation toward the CIA's true objective while fooling Liddy into thinking that the operation as Liddy had understood it went as planned.

Was McCord's employment, then, an infiltration by the CIA, where campaign money, an attorney general who ostensibly directed the campaign, a White House counsel Dean, interested as he was in building his own intelligence portfolio, a DNC referral system to a CIA-protected bordello, and a daring but easily duped Liddy made an enticing mix for an Agency that sought to legitimize an otherwise illegal CIA program of surveilling prostitution?

As we continue to explore other veins of evidence, let us see if we can offer additional proof that the Watergate burglaries, even though approved by the White House and CRP lieutenants, likely Dean and Magruder, were at their cores CIA operations into which the CIA had inveigled these unwitting junior lieutenants.

As we move through other areas of evidence, let us keep in mind several questions we have raised about McCord. Why didn't McCord remove the tape after he entered the Watergate that night? Was it mere negligence? Were the burglars really trying to wiretap or record Larry O'Brien? Was there evidence that McCord lied to Liddy about his activities, which would suggest a secret CIA agenda? And who was the man named Pennington who picked up McCord at the jail, as police personnel informed the FBI? Did he have any connection to the CIA? What evidence, if any, is there that the burglars were looking for information other than political strategies?

In December 1972 and January 1973, as the burglary case was hurtling toward trial, McCord wrote five worried notes about the status of the case. Please recall that this was the period in which Hunt was preparing his CIA defense and prosecutors Earl Silbert and Seymour Glanzer were preparing to oppose it as "phony" and "spurious." Meanwhile, these prosecutors were preparing a case whose outlines were centered on Mullen's CIA cover contract and Hunt's seeming search for sexual dirt in his electronic surveillance of Spencer Oliver Jr., son of Hunt rival and Mullen executive Spencer Oliver Sr. So, this was a crucial time in pretrial preparation, and it should not be surprising that McCord would wish to advise his employer as to the rapidly evolving status of the case. But McCord did not send these concerned notes to the CRP, his ostensible full-time employer; instead, he forwarded them to the CIA, which we contend her was his true employer. What means did he employ to send these letters?

He sent them to the Agency through a man named Pennington. Let us examine some of these communications of McCord to his former, perhaps current, boss at the SRS, Paul Gaynor. In two prominent letters sent while Hunt and his lawyer, William Bittman, were pressing McCord and his lawyer, Gerald Alch, to support the CIA defense, McCord expressed the danger to the CIA of the expected testimony of Bittenbender. Let us examine this worried correspondence. On December 22, 1972, right after Hunt and Hunt's lawyers' first initiative to McCord and Alch, on December 21, McCord wrote Gaynor as follows:

> *Dear Paul, there is tremendous pressure to put the operation off on the company. Don't worry about me, no matter what you hear, the way to head this*

off is to flood the newspapers with leaks or anon-
ymous letters that the plan is to place the blame
on the company for the operation. This is of imme-
diate importance because the plans are in the for-
mative stage now and can be preempted now if the
story is leaked so as the press is alert. It may not be
headed off later when it is too late. The fix is on.
One of the police officers in the MPD intelligence
department to testify that one of the defendants
told him that the defendants were company people,
and it was a company operation. He has probably
been promised a promotion for changing his story
to this effect. Be careful in your dealing with him.
I will do all I can to keep you informed. Keep the
faith. [emphasis in original]

This note was obviously referring to Bittenbender. A week
later, after Gerald Alch, McCord's lawyer, met with William
Bittman, Hunt's lawyer, and then met with McCord to explore
the CIA defense, McCord wrote Gaynor on December 29. Here
is a portion of the letter:

...The fixed police officer's report, that of Garey
Bittenbender...The impact of his statement is one
which can be read two ways, giving them a fall-
back position. 1) That I claimed to him at the time
of arraignment that this was a CIA operation, and
2) that this was an operation that we (the Cubans
and I) cooked up on our own. No such statements
were made. They are absolutely false. Bittenbender
incidentally has a twin brother, as I recall. I have
never met him, to my knowledge. I assume he also
works in the intelligence division.

Elsewhere in the letter, McCord told Gaynor that he needed "evidence of perjury" by Bittenbender before the trial: "I know he is lying." When McCord references the "fixed police officer's report," note that this is not a reference to an FBI report prepared by an FBI agent, but Bittenbender's full MPD statement of his own, referenced in an FBI report, but fully contained in the MPD files.

In the summer of 1973, at the Ervin Committee hearings, McCord again admitted that Bittenbender had given a statement detailing McCord's admission that this was a CIA operation, claiming only that Bittenbender must have been confused. But McCord and the Democratic questioners all agreed that Bittenbender had in fact made that statement about McCord's admission.

Why bother with this clear issue? Because some, stupidly in our view, perhaps dishonestly, try to defeat the CIA involvement by asserting that Bittenbender never made such a statement, ignoring his full interview of McCord after initially running into him, in a later meeting in McCord's jail cell, memorialized in the MPD files and admitted by all concerned.

What about the allegations that a fix was in? Nixon's men did not know about Bittenbender and Silbert wished to stay miles away from such an admission because it spelled an acquittal if in fact this was a CIA mission. Only Hunt wished to use this statement, and he eventually pleaded guilty.

Before the burglaries, McCord had prepared that spring a research paper on columnist Jack Anderson. You will recall that the CIA had been for some months in 1972, ending in April, openly stalking Anderson, part of an acknowledged CIA venture, which Helms later said was meant to assure Anderson would not release information about Russia. This story did not ring true, and in any case, was itself an admission to a seemingly illegal, perhaps ambiguously so, domestic CIA operation. Again, as in the case of the five status reports, McCord did not give this paper to the CRP, but to the CIA, and more precisely, to the SRS, his former and/or present employer. Again, he did so through a man named Pennington.

If McCord's research paper was a CIA mission, it was also an arguably illegal domestic operation, an investigation of a U.S. citizen living in the United States. McCord denied that he had done the research for the CIA, but once he had finished it, volunteered it to his former employer on the off chance the Agency would find it useful. Since McCord was not doing this for the CRP, and he claimed it was not meant for the CIA, who exactly commissioned it? That was never explained. Was it an amazing coincidence that McCord decided to spend time researching Anderson while, by gosh, the CIA was ominously stalking Anderson to prevent him from spilling the beans about the planned DNC mission?

In any case, we will delve deeper into McCord through the intriguing Pennington in future chapters as we explore the mysteries of Watergate.

Image of Watergate bugging device, public domain.

CHAPTER 15

MICHAEL STEVENS, BUG FABRICATOR

WE HAVE TALKED ABOUT RETIRED CIA agent James McCord, around whom, we suggest, strong swirls of suspicion should have arisen. But when questioned by credulous senators enjoying their fifteen minutes of televised heroism, McCord couldn't have been more emphatic in his story, without any pushback from these senators. No, he adamantly testified, the CIA had nothing to do with the burglaries. That, he noted, was a story concocted by the White House. He angrily rejected, he said, the completely unsupported suggestions of Hunt and Hunt's lawyers that the case be defended as a lawful CIA operation. And, no, he had never told DC intelligence officer Garey Bittenbender that the burglary had been a CIA operation. Bittenbender must have been confused, because of McCord's DC liaison work while with the CIA. Yes, O'Brien was tapped on a "call director" from another telephone in another office, via a line directed toward O'Brien's phone from elsewhere on the floor. This testimony is exactly what we would expect an undercover CIA agent to give when his operation was blown. Agents are *supposed to lie*, especially about a blown operation.

Certainly, the senators had no taste for challenging someone whose testimony was roasting Nixon, and it was unclear that they were skilled enough to cross-examine him even had they so wished. In the senators' defense, they did not have the extremely thorough FBI Watergate file, nor had the CIA yet produced to the Senate the full scope of documents the Senate had requested. There was only limited ammunition for cross-examination in any case. Moreover, there was zero effort by the Senate to perform even minimal investigation, such as, for example, determining that Bittenbender was twenty-three years old, and unlikely knew McCord from the spook's CIA days as asserted so vehemently. To slice and dice Nixon did not require such effort.

We mentioned earlier the odd testimony of McCord to the effect that he thought the burglaries were to be a national security operation. Yet no one had asked McCord exactly what an experienced national security agent like McCord thought was the national security purpose for listening to what McCord had supposedly told Baldwin to seek, "hot political gossip." These two cover stories in effect collided, both of course false to a degree. So, as McCord was being interviewed, first in closed Senate session beginning in May 1973, and publicly shortly thereafter, there was no reason for the wider public to sense the deep CIA penetration into the Watergate operation.

If McCord was not admitting having been undercover, the FBI records were not yet available showing the Mullen contract, and if Hunt's CIA trial defense was abandoned, was there any other basis upon which the public could have sensed a suspicion of Agency involvement?

Those of you who have read the book or seen the movie *All the President's Men* should recall probably the most frightening episode in the story. It was mid-May 1973 when Deep Throat burst into the garage where Woodward was waiting, quivering and visibly shaking. "Everyone's life is in danger!" he urged. Also, he told Woodward, beware of wiretapping. The CIA was desperate. According to Deep Throat, as relayed by Woodward, the CIA was worried less about Watergate itself than about what evidence would then be discovered about other CIA activities, presumably as a result of CIA involvement in Watergate. This, of course, is squarely consistent with the inferences we raise in this work.

Woodward furtively hand-signaled "CIA" to Bernstein after meeting in his apartment. Then the two hustled to the home of editor in chief Ben Bradlee in the middle of the night, where they fearfully huddled in Bradlee's back yard. They were terrified. While the audience gains no resolution of this fearsome threat in the movie, the book assures us that nothing came of this frightening incident, and that after days of caution, the group had resumed normal activities. All of this may have made sense when most observers thought Deep Throat to be a principled White House insider without professional knowledge of the CIA, and therefore the recipient of a false rumor.

But once we learned that Deep Throat was in fact the head of the FBI's Watergate investigation, then we should have questioned whether Deep Throat really had bad information and irrationally relied upon it. Was this preternaturally savvy and cool Mark Felt being needlessly hysterical? Unlikely. Deep Throat's now-revealed identity should give us pause and make us rethink that there was in fact nothing to justify Deep Throat's frightened warning. Of course, if the CIA was so concerned institutionally, such that it was contemplating murder to keep certain secrets, then two conclusions may be warranted. First, that the CIA was involved in Watergate. Second, Watergate, as we hypothesize here, was just the tip of the iceberg of illicit CIA domestic activities, and indeed the whole purpose of Watergate was to legitimize those activities.

If Watergate was so important to the Agency that it risked the illegal Operation Mudhen, inferentially to intimidate tattletale Jack Anderson from outing the operation in advance, even to the point of the Agency's mulling his murder, certainly the CIA would consider murder to squelch exposure after the operation had been carried out and blown, as it was here.

Thus, not irrationally, McCord thought as he was proceeding to arraignment that the CIA would claim the presidential authorization so easily proven in Watergate. But the Agency now calculated that with a bright spotlight on Watergate, questions would be asked about prior similar CIA operations, which would then be the Agency's death knell. In other words, such would be quite consistent with the rationale that Deep Throat gave to Woodward that May night for the CIA's threatening behavior. Put differently, if the CIA connection were to be discovered in, say, 1990, the haze of memory, summoned after several succeeding administrations, could allow the Agency to claim with a straight face a broader presidential legitimation of prostitute monitoring. In short, all would have gone well in that hypothetical 1990 discussion, perhaps in an oversight hearing by a congressional committee.

But in May 1973, questioning would be too searching, and events and documents would be too fresh in memory and availability to make a larger claim of broad authorization beyond Watergate. In short, the danger of discovery of long-standing illegal operations loomed. Does our theory make sense?

If we look at the book *All the President's Men*, it seems that our organizing hypothesis is right on the money because there, regarding his garage meeting with Deep Throat of May 16–17, 1973, Woodward states that the CIA was not so much afraid of what might be uncovered in Watergate, but where such inquiry would lead as to other CIA operations:

Deep Throat had told him they could meet earlier, say about 11:00 P.M.

Cabs were easier to find at that hour, and the trip did not take as long as usual, but Deep Throat was in the garage when Woodward arrived. He was pacing about nervously. His lower jaw seemed to quiver. Deep Throat began talking, almost in a monologue. He had only a few minutes; he raced through a series of statements. Woodward listened obediently. It was clear that a transformation had come over his friend. Woodward had dozens of questions, but Deep Throat held up his hand.

"That's the situation," he said when he had finished. "I must go this second. You can understand. Be—well, I'll say it.—be cautious."

He stepped away and hurried from the garage.[10]

That night, Woodward asked Bernstein to come over to his apartment after Woodward had met with Deep Throat. When Bernstein got there, Woodward acted very secretively, closed the drapes, put on a piano concerto on his phonograph, and the reporters wrote, "Woodward put his finger over his lips to indicate silence." At the dining room table, Woodward typed out a note and passed it to Bernstein: *Everyone's life is in danger.* So obviously that had come from Deep Throat.

Another phrase that Woodward typed out for Bernstein that night: *Deep Throat says that electronic surveillance is going on and we had better watch it.* Then Bernstein signaled that he wanted

---

10   Carl Bernstein and Bob Woodward, *All the President's Men* (New York: Simon & Schuster, 1974), 317.

something to write with. Woodward gave him a pen. *Who is doing it?* Bernstein wrote. C-I-A, Woodward mouthed silently.

> *Bernstein was disbelieving. While the Rachmaninoff piano concerto played on, Woodward began typing as Bernstein read over his shoulder:*

> *...The covert activities involve the whole U.S. Intelligence community and are incredible. Deep Throat refused to give specifics because it is against the law.*

> *The cover-up had little to do with Watergate, but was mainly to protect covert operations...*[11]

These passages say, in essence, what we have been postulating. If outed now, the CIA could claim presidential authorization for Watergate, but not for the long parade of prior horrors. The passage is quite consistent with our organizing framework, and is in fact strongly probative.

But what particular event spurred the gut-wrenching garage warnings? Since Mark Felt was head of the FBI investigation, we would expect to find the answer in FBI 302 files.

In the 302 reports dated May 12 and May 14, 1973, the FBI detailed the statements of the fabricator of bugs purchased by McCord, some still on order. The fabricator had come out of the cold to seek FBI protection. He related to the FBI that he believed his life was being threatened in the ominous calls he was receiving. The bug fabricator, consistent with Deep Throat's exclamation, thought his life was in danger.

A federal investigator, who we sense was likely Mark Felt, assessed that the best way to protect this bug fabricator was

---

11   Ibid., 318.

to reveal his story in print. On March 14 and March 16, 1973, each article occurring two days after one of the two FBI reports, *Chicago Today* printed two chillingly sensational stories about the knowledge of the bug fabricator, quoting an "investigator" as the source of the story.

These two stories should have been, but were not, nationally explosive. But that failure of resonance was because they never made it into the *Post* headlines or even in its buried inside news. In short, even though the *Post* through Woodward had the chilling story direct from Deep Throat, it never made print. Woodward's terrifying meeting with Deep Throat was the night of May 16–17, certainly as a result to the bug fabricator's statements to the FBI. What was this story and why should it have upended the conventional view of the Watergate scandal?

The *Chicago Today* stories revealed that the bug fabricator, a government-approved contractor, could legally deliver devices only if ordered by a government intelligence agency. To this bug fabricator, McCord claimed to be acting as a CIA agent. The mere fact that the bugs were ordered from this fabricator strongly suggests CIA involvement, since he could deal only with an approved intelligence agency.

We could speculate that the bug contractor could have assumed, without proof, McCord's Agency bona fides, given his knowledge of McCord's previous experience with the CIA. But according to the *Chicago Today* story, the contractor (using the assumed name Michael Stevens) asked and received from McCord a letter on CIA stationery attesting that the order was for a CIA operation. How would we know that this letter from the CIA attesting to McCord's bona fides wasn't a phony letter? Because the bug fabricator had followed up on McCord's letter by calling the Agency, where he spoke to one of his close contacts. The Agency contact verified that McCord, using his operational alias, could order the bugs as a CIA agent and that the bugs were for a CIA project. This is extremely strong proof that the bugs were for a CIA project and that McCord was a CIA contractor.

But there was even more. McCord still had on order with Stevens at the time of the Watergate arrests six bugs costing $18,000, which were set to uplink to a CIA satellite used to monitor Vietnam double agents. For younger readers, satellites were extremely rare in 1972, and neither the White House nor the Republicans had any satellite capability. Indeed, it was rare for anyone other than sophisticated intelligence agencies to have satellite capability in that era. There is no other way to explain the ordering of these satellite-linking bugs other than as part of a CIA operation. The revelation should have been a sensational story in the *Washington Post*, clearly available through Mark Felt and through *Chicago Today*. But nothing whatsoever about Stevens or his story was printed in the *Post*.

The *Post* had at least firsthand knowledge of dire garage warnings from the head of the investigation, Deep Throat. The credibility given to these threats by Deep Throat/Felt assures us, and should have assured the *Post*, that Stevens's fear was rational. Even more disturbingly, Stevens had related both to the FBI and *Chicago Today* that in December 1972, Dorothy Hunt, wife of Howard Hunt, was traveling to Chicago to pay Stevens $10,000. That Dorothy Hunt was a "hush money courier" appears to be verified by no less an authority than James McCord himself in his Senate testimony. It may well have been, however, that the $10,000 was not true *hush money* at all, but rather money designed to persuade Stevens to testify to support Hunt's planned CIA defense. But in any case, the money was intended for Stevens, he told the FBI.

Other evidence added to that offered by Stevens is even more ominous. Not only was Dorothy Hunt's body found with $10,000 when her United flight crashed, but also on board was a young DC television reporter, Michelle Clark, who may have been, we infer, traveling to Chicago for this very story, one to be written in cooperation with Dorothy Hunt. Witnesses had seen the two talking together before boarding the flight.

Please recall that in early December 1972, Howard Hunt was still planning an energetic CIA defense. Whatever inference we draw here about the purpose of the payment of the $10,000, it is unmistakable that Dorothy Hunt's cash was for the purpose of paying Stevens. But why would Stevens and other witnesses need to be paid off by the White House? After all, no one at the White House had known of Stevens, and federal investigators were not questioning Stevens in December 1972.

To the White House as of December, it was already beyond dispute that CRP money had paid for the bugs. So why would the White House care about silencing Stevens in May 1973? It wouldn't; that's the simple answer. But the CIA certainly would. And that was the source of Stevens's fear. We note also that the serial numbers of the cash found with Dorothy's body after the plane crash did not match any known White House slush fund monies. If Dorothy Hunt was carrying money intended for Stevens as he so understood, it was not to hush up a witness against the White House, we may reasonably infer.

Let us note again that Dorothy Hunt was at the time preparing with her husband Howard his CIA defense, mainly so that he could continue his life with Dorothy. So, we can infer he was likely at odds with the Agency in December 1972 regarding this contemplated defense, a plan which would not have escaped the Agency's notice.

Dorothy had just been fired from her job at the Spanish embassy, presumably as an undercover CIA agent. Were Hunt and his wife working hard to shut up a CIA contractor to protect the Agency? In response, it only makes sense that Dorothy Hunt was travelling to Chicago to enlist Stevens in her husband's defense, a story perhaps to be transcribed and authenticated by the reporter, Michelle Clark, whose published stories would act as an insurance policy guaranteeing Stevens would stay alive. To be sure, we note that the presence of the reporter may be a red herring because her parents' home was in Chicago and perhaps her presence on the flight was coincidental.

The only retort offered to the blockbuster *Chicago Today* allegations was thin. McCord's new CIA-connected lawyer, Bud Fensterwald, told the paper regarding Stevens that his client simply "picked his name out of a phone book" as a bug supplier. Of course, we can see today that the statement makes no sense. An experienced CIA agent does not pick a bug fabricator out of a phone book, for these highly sensitive and sophisticated bugs, especially ones that link to a CIA satellite. How many CIA-approved bug suppliers were listed in the yellow pages in 1972?

The $10,000 cash, said Fensterwald, was in part to pay Stevens for money still owing for the bugs and part for Hunt's use to buy a motel. It seems unlikely that one would buy a motel with cash and without a written contract. Any portion of the $10,000 does not seem like a sufficient sum with which to buy a motel, or make a down payment, even taking in to account 1972 prices. So, not very convincing as to the motel and also not convincing that Dorothy and Howard Hunt would care if the contractor had been stiffed when they faced a life without income and legal bills. Were they really using cash to pay off a CRP debt to a bug fabricator? Highly unlikely.

By May 1973, Dorothy Hunt was long dead. Hunt was keeping his mouth shut as a defendant who had pleaded guilty in January 1973 and now wished to stay in good Agency graces. What was it that the CIA would fear in May 1973, that might cause lives to be threatened as Deep Throat so ominously warned?

What would be clearly proven in May 1973 by Stevens was that James McCord was working under an operational name for the CIA and ordered not only the bugs planted in Watergate but had on order additional satellite-linking bugs. We also know that McCord had never told Liddy about ordering these bugs. Please recall that Liddy had been told by McCord that he ordered one $30,000 room bug, to be implanted in the first burglary. McCord's dealings with Michael Stevens prove, beyond reasonable doubt, CIA complicity in Watergate, and as well a secret CIA agenda hidden from Liddy and other Nixonites. The fears expressed both by Stevens and Mark Felt also serve to buttress our view of Operation Mudhen as an intimidation of a possible whistleblower.

This frightening episode also corroborates one other aspect of Watergate. It is beyond a doubt that Watergate's paper of record, which won a Pulitzer Prize for its investigative journalism, failed to tell the public at the time anything about this horrendous tableau. It did not report, for example, that lives were being threatened by the CIA, that it appeared that the CIA was covering up its involvement in Watergate, or that the Agency was worried about other skeletons in its closet.

Before we leave this chapter, let us keep in mind the question of whether the CIA had credibly been threatening lives. If so, our theories of both CIA involvement in Watergate and a wider, multiyear illegal domestic prostitution-monitoring program would appear to some degree corroborated. Moreover, Stevens is a strong marker of McCord's activity outside of Nixon channels. There are more such markers to be discovered in coming chapters.

Image of Lou Russell, public domain.

CHAPTER 16

LOU RUSSELL, SIXTH BURGLAR

MANY STRANDS OF THE HIDDEN story we have thus far uncovered meet in the person of Lou Russell, an important character in the Watergate saga, but one whose name very few people have ever heard.

As we noted in *Postgate*, any sketch of this shadowy figure should emphasize his central part in the drama which we call Watergate—one, however, little understood by posterity. As we will show, Russell was in all probability the man who emerged into the Watergate office building lobby shortly after the arrest of the five burglars, soon to disappear before the police could question him. Russell, in other words, was seemingly the legendary "sixth burglar." He was at the time an independent contractor performing services for James McCord's private security company.

As we discussed in prior chapters, the involvement in the burglary of other key actors—McCord, Hunt, Magruder, Dean, Baldwin—is clear and, but for Dean, admitted. Their motives, identity of their true principals, and nature of their actions can all be subject to good faith debate, since all have testified in material particulars inconsistently with the evidence we have shown here. But Russell stands apart.

Any involvement whatsoever of Russell in the burglary has earth-shaking import. If he was involved, it would be only in his role as McCord's own independent contractor, on McCord's tab, unreimbursed by the CRP. It would be one thing if McCord had made a buck from Russell's labor for services provided to other McCord clients, if there were any prior to June of 1972. But it would be quite another if the payments made to Russell by the allegedly financially strapped McCord were for Russell's services on Watergate. Any such services would strongly implicate a hidden agenda, likely one of the CIA.

If Russell's work was needed for Liddy's operation, as Liddy understood it, Liddy would have known and would have paid him, as he did to the five arrested burglars. Surely Russell's only possible role in Watergate, assuming he had one, would be as an off-the-books CIA contractor, hidden from Liddy. Simply put, if Russell was involved in Watergate, so was the CIA secretly.

Who was Lou Russell? He had a long history in the shadowy venues of DC detective work, starting out as an investigator in the early 1950s for the infamous House Un-American Activities Committee, or HUAC, which sought to root out Communists in government. A beefy former minor league baseball player, Russell was a heavy drinker as well as a frequent consort of prostitutes. Since at least February 1972, he was part-time contractor for McCord and Associates, ostensibly to provide security for CRP headquarters.

Russell did not have his own bank account and cashed his checks through intelligence community friends, one of whom, Bud Fensterwald, eventually became McCord's criminal lawyer in March 1973, to implement McCord's posttrial strategy of lashing out at the Nixon administration. Significantly, prior to the Watergate burglary, Russell had told several acquaintances including Fensterwald, Fensterwald associate Bob Smith, and former treasury agent Kennard Smith, that he had been taping prostitutes and their johns with the cooperation of the prostitutes.

In *White House Call Girl*, Phil Stanford describes the observation of a lawyer for the Columbia Plaza call girl ring, our favorite debauchee Phillip Mackin Bailley, as having observed in the madam's apartment a burly man going by the name of Russ, seemingly acting as bordello security, who had been a former professional baseball player. But in perhaps the oddest and most telling note of all, Russell had worked for General Security Services (GSS) for less than a year, ending in April 1972. His resignation occurred shortly before the first Watergate burglary and soon after Jeb Magruder claimed he had the go-ahead to authorize the break-in, later to direct Liddy to the DNC headquarters.

As this was occurring, McCord hired Russell to work for the CRP in security after he worked for GSS at the Watergate Office Building. This GSS job is likely more than a stunning coincidence. As a security guard, he would have had the key to the DNC offices and the opportunity to get an impression or copy of any desk key he so wished.

In wiretap monitor Alfred Baldwin's statement, published on October 5, 1972, in the *Los Angeles Times*, he mentioned seeing from his Howard Johnson hotel room McCord in the DNC office suite on May 26, 1972. Baldwin claimed to have been occupying Room 419 at the time, which on May 26 was well before the break-in on May 30.

By May 30, Baldwin had been moved to Room 723 for improved monitoring of the now inserted bugs. If he is correct about seeing McCord, McCord likely, through Russell's security keys, already had access to the DNC office suite. Moreover, on May 26, before the first break-in, McCord had Baldwin listen to tawdry eavesdropped conversations, handing Baldwin his earphones. This would imply, as suggested by Hougan, that the CIA was already electronically eavesdropping on the bordello, having no connection to the first burglary to be carried out several days later.

In any case, in the hubbub of the June 17 arrests, a man entered the Watergate lobby from the stairwell, chatted up the guards, and departed before the guards thought to tell the police. If Russell was involved that night as this "sixth burglar" who quickly exited the lobby after the arrests, that meant the CIA was clandestinely part of the operation and that the eavesdropping likely was targeting prostitution calls.

Unlike in the Stevens scenario, no analyst can claim that the CIA was merely aiding a solely White House operation as a favor to a former agent, as the CIA asserted it had done for Hunt. If Russell was involved, then McCord was an active undercover agent at the time, acting for the CIA. Merely raising the issue of Russell's participation in the burglary operation, hidden from the other burglars, would suggest a plausible revisionist narrative of the Watergate burglary, directly at odds with the conventional version published by the Watergate paper of record, the *Washington Post.*

Early on in its reporting, on June 20, 1972, before the *Post* had become palpably dishonest, it published a note that the police were investigating a sixth participant: "Police sources say they were still looking for a sixth person believed to have been involved in this incident."

Strangely, after this intriguing note the *Post* thereafter went radio silent on the question of the sixth burglar. Had Woodstein learned about the sixth burglar from the police or the FBI? Likely from both.

If Russell was involved with the burglary operation that night, he most likely was the sixth burglar of Watergate lore, unknown to his fellow burglars other than McCord. His participation would explain the tape that McCord allowed to remain on the basement door lock as well as on the sixth floor and eight floor locks. It would also clarify not only why McCord lied to others about having removed the tape (which would allow Russell's subsequent entrance), but also would explain his false statement to Liddy that a DNC employee continued to occupy the office from midnight to 12:45 AM, a critical delay given the frequency and timing of security rounds. In other words, the burglars wanted to get in and get out between the security guard rounds, and this delay would prove costly.

Russell, likely to establish a late-night alibi, had been waiting in the area, but then had departed from the Watergate vicinity, went to his daughter's house in Benedict, Maryland, and was late driving back, causing McCord to delay the break-in. This would explain McCord's frequent, unexplained absences before the break-in—likely to confer with Russell—leading Liddy to compare McCord to the fictional Shadow, Lamont Cranston, the main character in a popular radio show, *The Shadow*.

Finally, of course, it would all but confirm the so-called "call girl theory" of motive, since Russell had been prior to the break-in, per Bailley, seemingly immersed in taping and protecting a certain Columbia Plaza prostitution ring. If Russell was in the Watergate building that night, he was likely present operationally for the CIA.

While there was much circumstantial evidence of Russell's involvement in the burglary at the time of Watergate, an intriguing fact pattern emerged years later. The case of *Dean vs. St. Martin's Press*, you will recall, John Dean brought against *Silent Coup* author Len Colodny and his publisher for defamation. As a result of the suit, Dean's finances were examined for any scent of the call girl narrative. In this defamation case, lawyers explored an interesting set of seemingly corresponding financial transactions involving Dean and Russell.

Russell was, as always, needful of cash after the burglary. Yet, without any apparent meaningful employment that could justify it, he deposited amounts of $4,570 and $20,895 on November 15, 1972, and in March 1973, respectively. Likely not coincidentally, Dean withdrew $4,850 shortly before November 15, 1972, and approximately $22,000 from the White House safe around the time of the second Russell deposit. These amounts, of course, neatly match up with Russell's unexplained receipts.

Accounting records show that the withdrawals from the White House safe were unaccounted for, and Haldeman has pointed toward Dean as the culprit, who has explained weakly that at least the first withdrawal was for his honeymoon, which apparently cannot be corroborated, while he denied the second withdrawal. In any case, the comparison of dates and amounts makes a compelling circumstantial case that Dean quietly paid hush money to Russell while as a cover-up counsel, he was also making payments to the known burglars from the hush money that the White House conspirators had raised.

There is no record that anyone in the Oval Office knew of hush money payments to Russell, or, for that matter, knew of Russell at all. If, of course, Dean was paying Russell, that would be a clear verdict in favor of the burglaries' call girl/CIA-related motivation, as well as Dean's agency in the break-ins. Russell would likely be involved in Watergate if call girls were also involved, and Dean would personally pay Russell only if he was hushing up this aspect of the case. This would damn Dean as well as the CIA, but perhaps also mitigate the guilt of the unwitting Nixon higher-ups, which would be an asset to Dean as a cooperating witness. But we admit that this evidence, while intriguing, is not ironclad.

Hougan documents Russell's work with an attractive blonde madam who appears, per Colodny's work, to have been Heidi/Cathy. If true, this would explain Russell's interest in the DNC wiretapping, which would have monitored the call girl operation he had been taping for the CIA with the girls' consent. Recall that from *White House Call Girl*, we know that Cathy told Bailley that the CIA had been protecting her. We are not certain how Russell's possible involvement first came to the attention of the FBI, but it did so quite early on.

In his initial July 9, 1972, FBI interview, Russell stated to agents that he ate at the Howard Johnson restaurant on the night before the burglary and had visited the Watergate area that night only because he was nostalgic for an old girlfriend, a prostitute, who used a hairdresser in the area. However, in his interview with the FBI of October 10, 1972, he admitted that he had eaten at the HoJo on the night of the burglary but continued to deny that he had entered the office building that night. After it appeared that the FBI agents did not buy his story, Russell reportedly told them to "shove off."

On October 11, 1972, a young reporter for the *Washington Star-News*, Patrick Collins, wrote a blockbuster article on Russell, albeit one that, similarly to the scintillating *Chicago Today* stories about Stevens, did not gain any appreciable recirculation. Collins, with concise, logical prose, linked Russell to the mysterious "sixth burglar." One of the keen revelations in the Collins article was Russell's postarrest living situation. No longer living in a fifteen-dollar-a-week room on down-and-out Q Street, he was now housed in relative luxury in a $185-per-month—that was a high rent in 1972—apartment in Silver Springs, Maryland. His benefactor, Russell revealed, often took him out for expensive meals. From other sources, we know that the benefactor was a CIA-connected stockbroker by the name of William Birely.

Other research shows him living in his Silver Springs digs with a prostitute. All of this suggests that the CIA was making sure this potential alcohol-fueled bomb did not go off.

Things were getting a bit hot for our burly investigator when Watergate Committee Minority Counsel Fred Thompson (he later became a TV star, then, briefly a presidential candidate), the assistant to Senator Howard Baker of Tennessee, issued a subpoena to Russell on May 9, 1973, seeking Russell's phone and banking records in advance of the hearings. Russell replied on May 11 that he had none. This was perhaps true since Russell did not maintain a bank account. But Thompson was certain to follow up and question Russell.

The CIA would therefore have known that this erratic man may soon be called to testify, and Russell may have unintentionally given his benefactors an even more dire warning. He confided, to the extent that this loud raconteur was capable of confiding at all, that he planned to write a tell-all book on Watergate. But he made the mistake of telling that to individuals with wide connections to the intelligence community, which likely included his own prostitute girlfriend, who may have had her own contacts in the intelligence world.

We do not know if Russell was planning to reveal Stevens's real name and role, or if he had even contacted Stevens. But as McCord's right-hand man, Russell in May 1973 certainly would have known of the CIA's and Stevens's roles in the burglary operations. He also likely knew of the satellite-linking bugs McCord had on order, which in turn would give away a broader CIA prostitute taping program. Russell would clearly have known of this if he was involved, as he had bragged, in taping of prostitutes. But whether Russell had made contact with Stevens or not, Russell knew plenty and was almost certainly the sixth burglar, a direct witness to the CIA's secret agenda. Russell's loose talk would likely have drawn CIA attention to Stevens, leading to the threatening calls he reported in May 1973.

On May 18, 1973, one day after the dire May 16–17 garage warnings of the disturbed Deep Throat, Russell fell violently ill, claiming someone had switched his heart medicine with poison. He died shortly thereafter from a compromised cardiac system.

When Howard Hunt earlier had dragooned the credulous Liddy to a meeting to discuss with the CIA poisons doctor, Edward Gunn, ways of disabling troublesome reporter Jack Anderson, one of the murderous methods discussed was what was known as "aspirin roulette." A poison pill would be substituted for aspirin in the aspirin bottle and sooner or later, the victim would swallow it. While the group ultimately dismissed this technique for use on Anderson, it is eerily similar to the method apparently used on Russell and is consistent with CIA involvement.

Russell's presence as the sixth burglar of lore does more than suggest a hidden agenda pursued by the CIA. It explains the continuing taping of the locks after all the burglars had entered. This taping would, of course, allow Russell to enter. Russell's role also explains McCord's delay in pronouncing the DNC office as clear, while inferentially waiting Russell's return from Benedict, Maryland. It would also explain the identifiable McCord's presence on the team (which, contrary to normal tradecraft, would identify the CRP if caught), and his frequent absences on the night of the burglary. Finally, we posit that Russell's involvement shows the need to curate what McCord feared would be documents that, if transmitted to Dean and others without curation, would reveal too much about the CIA's programs.

The Russell tableau is one of the most significant pieces of evidence that explain Watergate mysteries. If the Watergate burglaries were solely a Nixon administration project, would there have been any need to poison Lou Russell? Would there have been any need for his presence during the burglary? His death certificate, then, should be Exhibit A in the case against the CIA.

By the same reasoning, the October 11, 1972 *Washington Star-News* article about Russell should be Exhibit B in that same case against the CIA, documenting Russell's admission that he was in the vicinity of the Watergate office building on the night of the burglary. Russell's participation, a reasonable observer can conclude, is evidence about as powerful as one could find proving covert CIA involvement in the burglary. Or is it? Believe it or not, there is even stronger proof, which must be considered the key to Watergate. To that evidence we will turn in our next chapter.

Image of notebook and key recovered from Watergate
burglar Eugenio Martinez, public domain.

CHAPTER 17

MARTINEZ AND THE KEY

TODAY, FIFTY YEARS AFTER THE burglary, there are still lingering questions about the true target of the burglary. According to the proponents of the conventional view, the burglaries were designed to help Nixon's political interests. But this view is purposely vague because there is no clear-cut political purpose. Was it to spy on DNC Director Lawrence O'Brien? He was not in town. Was it otherwise to ferret out Democratic campaign strategies? There were none in June to be had, prior to the Democratic Convention. Were they looking for illegal donations from Cuban dictator Fidel Castro? If so, why would the burglars need to wiretap Oliver? All anyone had was the very sketchy testimony of Jeb Magruder implicating, likely falsely, John Mitchell, and even that dubious evidence does not identify a specific target within the DNC.

Although the *Washington Post* could never identify the specific political purpose of the burglary, it often in scolding tones told the public what it *was not*. It was not, readers were often told by the *Post*, about the CIA. That was just a Nixonian deflection of blame, the paper would claim. In later years, it rejected out of hand any connection of the burglary to prostitution.

However, Gordon Liddy, years after his arrest, came to believe that he was deceived about the true target, which Liddy felt was the monitoring of prostitution calls to a service protected by the Agency. Liddy was sued by Spencer Oliver Jr. and his secretary, Maxie Wells, on this very issue after Liddy spoke up about it on a radio show in the 1990s. Liddy won two defamation trials, the first by a seven-to-two vote, and the second by nine to zero.

Jeb Magruder had protected both himself and Dean, and vice versa, in his Senate testimony, as he implicated Mitchell. Much evidence we have thus far presented points to the knowledge of Dean of the burglaries' target. So, with these thoughts in mind, we reprise a memorable scene at Lewisburg Federal Prison in 1974, when White House hatchet man Charles Colson approached fellow prisoner, John Dean. Quoting from Dean's book, *Blind Ambition*, Colson articulates well the very subject of this book—that is, the mystery surrounding the purpose of the burglary:

> *It's incredible. Millions of dollars have been spent investigating Watergate. A president has been forced out of office. Dozens of lives have been ruined. We're sitting in the can. And still nobody can explain why they bugged the place to begin with.*[12]

Hearing Colson's inquiry, to which Dean, we assert, knew the answer, Dean cleverly suggested that Colson and he visit fellow prisoner Jeb Magruder to ask him:

> *"Jeb, we've been trying to put some pieces together about why we're here,"* [Dean] *began. "One of the questions we can't answer is why Larry O'Brien*

---

12   John Dean, *Blind Ambition* (New York: Simon & Schuster, 1976), 391.

was targeted. I guess you and Mitchell agreed to that in Florida but why O'Brien?"

Jeb froze. His pallid face flushed crimson. He tried to find words but only stuttered. The question had more than caught him off guard; it had overwhelmed him. "Why do you want to know?" he asked haltingly.

"Just curiosity," Chuck said.

"Well, it just seemed like a good idea," Jeb said evasively.

"Well, then. Why was Spencer Oliver's phone bugged?" Chuck pressed. Chuck was implying that the testimony that Oliver, another official of the DNC, had been bugged by accident was not true. That there had been deeper motives.

Jeb looked at me, then at Colson. "Why? Who wants to know?" he asked, as his confusion turn to suspicion. "I don't think we ought to talk about that stuff," he said sharply. Jeb turned on his heel and walked out, leaving Chuck and me staring at each other in dismay.

Chuck broke our silence. "You know, I think I know why Jeb is so damned depressed. I think he's still holding back on what he knows."[13]

Clearly, in this blackly comical scene, Magruder knows that Dean knows very well the purpose, and, of course, was some-

13   Ibid.

what confounded as to whether or not Dean really wanted him to spill the beans.

There is no better evidence of a hidden agenda within the Nixon administration, separate and apart from the CIA's, than these scenes from Lewisburg prison. After all, why couldn't Magruder in a straightforward fashion state to Colson why the burglary had occurred?

It has been widely speculated that Hunt used the supposed search for Fidelista (supporters of Castro) campaign contributions as a false flag to lure the Cubans into the operation. But just as importantly, this may well have been a claimed national security cover story also used to fool other sectors of the CIA. Put differently, not everyone in the CIA knew what the OS was doing through Hunt and McCord, since the OS was the only section of the CIA that reported straight to the director. It may very well be that while Hunt told Martinez that this was a national security CIA operation, he may not have originally told him the truth about what the national security operation was, or alternatively may have told Martinez to convey the false Fidelista story. In any event, the more we can prove overt deceit of Nixon aides by the CIA, especially lying to moneyman Liddy, the more conclusively we can prove the CIA had a secret agenda.

To demonstrate the Agency's modus operandi, we note that Liddy and the Plumbers were demonstrably defrauded by the Fielding burglary team, which had seized and copied Ellsberg psychiatric records, while lying to Liddy by telling him that they had come up empty. The burglars knew that the records had been found and copied, so we can conclude that all of them lied on behalf of the CIA to Liddy, representing the White House.

Within the Watergate burglary team, we can document clear acts of deceit. One obvious lie, unremarked by Watergate authors, was McCord's representation to Liddy that he had spent $30,000 of Liddy's budget on a state-of-the-art room bug (a microphone), which could be hidden inside furniture in O'Brien's office and could transmit while virtually undetectable. We know from Stevens that no such bug had been ordered. And we also know from McCord's Senate testimony that the team did not during the first burglary enter O'Brien's office.

After the first burglary, McCord told Liddy that the O'Brien room bug had been shielded by concrete and steel, and therefore was not transmitting. Clearly, McCord lied to Liddy, suggesting, again, a hidden CIA agenda. Both Baldwin and McCord made a big point of testifying that Baldwin's preburglary visit to the DNC headquarters was to locate O'Brien's office, itself a silly claim, because the burglars already had an office diagram. In any case, the director's corner office was readily identifiable. What the diagram would not show, however, was Maxie Wells's desk, the location of which was likely the real goal of Baldwin's casing mission.

Another clear fraud on Liddy was McCord's purchase of an additional $18,000 in satellite-linking bugs from Stevens, still on order as of June 17, clearly having nothing to do with the original burglary mission. Since a second burglary was not planned at the time of the first, the bugs on order from Stevens were likely not intended for the DNC, in any case a relatively small part of the CIA's operation.

In yet another lie, McCord earlier had told the credulous Liddy that he could not tape the overheard calls, using technobabble to explain why not. For that reason, Baldwin and McCord were not recording the calls, but simply writing notes about them, which were later typed. There was plenty of fraud practiced by McCord for the CIA on Liddy, the CRP, and ultimately the White House.

On top of this mound of deceptive behavior, there is a crowning jewel of CIA deceit. Before we get to it, let's focus on the burglar who possessed it. The Cubans on the burglary team have been conventionally depicted as well-meaning, anti-Castro fools. While there is likely truth in the notion that they gullibly thought helping Hunt would pave the way for new anti-Castro actions, this belief would make sense only if they thought Hunt was acting for the CIA. Obviously, they did, which is some proof that Hunt was in fact still acting on behalf of the CIA. This view is buttressed by the timing of Hunt's first renewed contact with the Cubans in April 1971, before he had joined the White House and, therefore, before he could say he was a White House agent. In short, Hunt would have led them to believe he was, as years before, acting for the CIA.

But wait, an observer may argue, couldn't they be fooled into thinking Hunt was CIA? Not really, because one of the members of the team was Eugenio Martinez, who himself was a CIA agent, having stayed on with the Agency following the Bay of Pigs in 1961. An eleven-year Agency veteran, Martinez would likely know if Hunt was a fellow agent working on an Agency mission. To be sure, when Martinez's agent status was reported by Seymour Hersh of the *New York Times* in January of 1973, the Agency was quick to note that Martinez was only a monitor of the Cuban community in Miami, paid one hundred dollars per month, and that the CIA fired him when it learned of his Watergate escapades.

That low salary was meant to connote Martinez's minor status, but whether or not it was true at the time, he had been a full-time salaried agent for most of those eleven years. Around the same time as his Agency employment was becoming public, the *Washington Post*, through reporter Martin Schram, published a curious article days before the Hersh exposé. Martinez, Schram wrote on January 7, 1973, was "monitoring" for the CIA what the CRP team of operatives was doing, which is why, according to Schram, he kept a diary. This article, by the way, was probably meant to blunt the impact of what Hersh was about to report. This monitoring was part of what Schram called a "widespread project," which included spying on Democratic Senators Frank Church, Mike Mansfield, and William Fulbright, and breaking into the Chilean embassy. Schram was clearly implying that these missions, just as the *Post* was characterizing Watergate, were all White House operations.

Let us stop and reflect on Schram's story, which in hindsight the *Post* would like to have back. Certainly, there was intuitively a competitive political relationship between the DNC and the Nixon administration. But there was no reason for the Nixon campaign to spy on Chile, which would be of concern to the CIA, especially in 1973, when socialist Salvador Allende held office. And the Nixon campaign would not care a whit about these three Democratic senators, certainly not for the upcoming presidential campaign (they had nothing to do with the campaign), but the CIA would, since each was a powerful player on committees overseeing or funding the Agency. Schram's article was thus unintentionally revelatory.

More to the point, an agent keeps a diary for only CIA operations, not for any other entity's operations. Martinez was keeping a diary. Are we to believe, then, that the CIA operation was merely to monitor what the Nixon administration was doing? Schram is awkwardly downplaying Martinez's role as a CIA agent in the Watergate burglary. In fact, in so attempting, he defeats his purpose by describing operations by this team that clearly had nothing to do with the White House. If this team had been carrying operations other than Watergate that had no evident White House purpose, perhaps that same team while working on Watergate was working for the CIA, unknown even to White House lieutenant Dean and the CRP's Magruder.

Shortly before the first Watergate break-in, a worried Martinez had inquired of his case officer in Miami whether CIA headquarters was aware of what Hunt was doing. He did so in a way that suggested that he, Martinez, was deeply concerned. Eventually, an alarmed station chief in Miami inquired of Langley (CIA headquarters in Virginia) about Hunt and was told to "cool it," that Hunt was on White House business. The response infuriated the station chief. Martinez, his case officer, and the station chief would be concerned only if they thought that Hunt was operating as a CIA undercover agent, and if they thought he was bringing their men into roguish acts, seemingly illegal domestic operations. In short, these worries expressed by these three agents confirm that Hunt was a CIA agent and also that he was involved in what seemed like illegal domestic CIA operations. The response of "White House business," per our theory, was a way of communicating that the operations were thereby legal.

This is all-but-necessary prelude to the most telling proof of our nation's most impactful scandal. It is relevant because it is irrefutable proof both of the Agency's deceit of Nixon and also of the true target of the burglary. On the subject of deceit, Liddy had been told that there were two purposes for the second burglary. First, to fix the original bug, which Liddy understood to be a room bug in O'Brien's office. The second purpose, per Magruder's dramatic desk slam, was to find what dirt the Democrats had on the Republicans, which Liddy thought, without having been told, was aimed at O'Brien's desk.

To be sure, when the burglars were arrested, McCord had a cheap room bug he was inserting into a smoke detector in the ceiling of O'Brien's office, which would help him cover for his earlier lie about having previously planted an inoperable room bug. After he planted this bug, supervisors could listen to talk in O'Brien's office. McCord could claim he had fixed the inoperable bug inserted during the first burglary.

That heavy lift, though, of the second burglary was the planned copying of documents, which Hunt had calculated would take several hours. We know that a copying operation was being set up the time of the arrest, but also that it was not located in the vicinity of O'Brien's office. Two drawers had been opened at the time of the arrests and, according to one witness, camera clamps had been affixed to one desk. Since the main purpose, as forcefully explained by Magruder, was copying oppo documents, the target of the world's most important political scandal can be revealed by the location of this camera equipment.

But both in the *Post* reporting and in the Woodstein book, *All the President's Men*, the location of this copying activity was not described, whereas one would think there would have been such a description by Pulitzer Prize-winning journalists. And there was no testimony offered about the location of the photography's setup in the criminal trial, which, after all, was geared to prove wiretapping, not document copying. What was this location?

When the burglars were arrested and told to assume a spread-eagle position with hands on the wall, one burglar came dangerously close to being shot when he reached into his breast pocket, where the arresting officers instinctively thought he might retrieve a weapon. Arresting Officer Carl Shoffler yelled loudly at the burglar to cease, to no avail. A wrestling match ensued, and Shoffler finally wrested from the burglar a key that had been attached to the cover of a pocket notebook by tape. What was this key which the burglar risked his life to hide?

Nothing about this dramatic struggle was printed in the *Post*, disclosed at trial, or mentioned in *All the President's Men*. As a result, there was no public question as to what the key opened. Wouldn't the destination of the key be *the key to Watergate*? The answer is, of course, it would point to the burglary's true target.

After trying the key on numerous desks and filing cabinets, the FBI finally determined that it fit the desk of one Maxie Wells. You may recall her as Spencer Oliver's secretary, and as a plaintiff who later sued Gordon Liddy for claiming her desk was connected to prostitution referrals.

It is some weak corroboration that Wells, within two weeks of the arrests, resigned her position to return to her hometown in rural Mississippi. This resignation suggests that her bosses found things that may not have been favorable to her. Parenthetically and perhaps amusingly, she eventually made her way back to Washington as a secretary for President Jimmy Carter, elected as a reaction to Nixonian skullduggery in Watergate. Wells and her sometime replacement, Barbara Kennedy Rhoden, had the only two keys to the desk, and had not lent them out, deepening the mystery of Martinez's possession of yet another desk key.

Wells had a predecessor who set up the referral program, whom Bailley called Champagne. Could Champagne have given a key to the team? Unlikely, especially because the timing does not fit. Intriguingly, Lou Russell had been a security guard with GSS, monitoring offices in the Watergate building and not resigning until April 1972, with plenty of opportunity to make a key mold.

We refer you back to Baldwin's seemingly sincere statements to the FBI, and later to the Senate, that he saw McCord from his monitoring room entering the DNC offices on May 26, long before the first break-in. In other words, McCord likely had a key to the DNC offices. The key to Wells's desk, then, easily could have been made as well before the break-in, likely courtesy of Russell.

It was revealed by Hersh in January 1973 that Martinez had kept an operational notebook, or diary, and was keeping one at the time of Watergate, but that it went missing after his car was belatedly located at the Miami Airport and his notebook seized. The notebook seemed so potentially incriminating that the special prosecutor later appointed a senior attorney, Henry Ruth, to investigate the disappearance of the Martinez diary notebook, to no avail. The CIA appears to have been the only logical suspect.

Martinez was silent throughout the criminal proceeding, finally pleading guilty along with the other Cubans. As Hunt wrote in his book *Undercover*, it was expected that the Agency would take care of blown agents. Indeed, later Martinez and Virgilio Gonzalez tried to withdraw their guilty pleas, an effort spurred by Dean's confession that Dean had destroyed Hunt's CIA operational diaries. According to Hunt, this destroyed his national security presidential authorization defense, and according to Martinez and Gonzalez, they should be allowed to withdraw their guilty pleas and proceed to trial on their defense that they thought this had been a legitimate CIA operation.

Liddy did not have prior knowledge about the Wells desk key or that her desk was the burglary target. The oppo dirt to be sought (that the Democrats had on the Republicans) we thus can conclude was not political dirt, but personal dirt on Republicans, perhaps certain lower-level lieutenants. But if this was the dirt sought, Liddy was not so informed. The vignette told by Dean about Colson's prison confrontation of Magruder shows that the target was not one shared with higher White House officials.

The key, in short, is proof positive of the secret agenda of Watergate, a CIA operation designed originally to legitimate the Agency's prostitution blackmailing schemes, with the second burglary ordered for Dean's purposes, while the CIA hoped to hide its own program in exploring Wells's desk.

Watergate is inarguably a highly important set of historical events. Yet our history of it does not incorporate Martinez and his key. Why has this remained concealed?

Both the DC police and the FBI knew that there was a struggle for what was eventually determined to be Maxie Wells's desk key, such that the evidence of this for the *Post* should have been abundant. But it is enough to say for now that the Watergate burglary has remained a mystery precisely because facts such as these have never widely known.

Image of Lee Pennington walking with FBI Director J. Edgar Hoover, public domain.

CHAPTER 18

PENNINGTON

FOR OUR PRESENT PURPOSES, IT suffices to say that if there was any foreknowledge in the Nixon White House of the Watergate burglaries, it would have resided in the persons of undercover CIA agent Howard Hunt and minor White House aide John Dean, falsely elevated in status by the pretentious title of White House counsel. And, of course, on the CRP side, Jeb Magruder and Gordon Liddy would have known in advance of both burglaries, although a puzzled Liddy could not understand their value or true purpose.

In contrast to the revisionist historical treatment by Colodny and Hougan of Hunt, McCord and Dean, Lou Russell and Michael Stevens have received only a smattering of treatment by even the revisionists. But almost no sustained attention has been given to one Lee Pennington. Oddly enough, the only significant mention of him is to be found in the little-read, quickly remaindered,1979 book by Mark Felt, *The FBI Pyramid*.

What is the significance of Lee Pennington? He fills any theoretical gaps in proof, to the point of metaphysical certainty, of the direct and moving involvement of the CIA in the Watergate break-in. How so?

McCord made bail over a week after arrest. When he did so, he was picked up at the jail, the FBI soon learned, by a man known only as "Pennington." Felt and his FBI agents immediately theorized that Pennington may be McCord's CIA case agent. The FBI had no independent hint as to Pennington's employer but inferred a possible CIA connection given McCord's status as a recent retiree—often, Felt knew, an undercover ruse. Recall that the FBI already knew by this point that Mullen was a cover company, likely concealing Hunt's Agency role. Accordingly, after some unsuccessful attempts to learn Pennington's status with the Agency through informal means, on August 18, 1972, the FBI issued a formal request of the Agency for the identity of any CIA agent named Pennington.

The CIA then provided the FBI in response only the name of Agent Cecil Pennington. It took months for the CIA to locate this Cecil Pennington through his foreign postings. When the FBI agents finally found him, Cecil affirmed in convincing fashion, to the FBI's satisfaction, that he could not have been the Pennington who picked up McCord.

Felt had left the Bureau after his agents ultimately located the uninvolved Cecil Pennington, and thus had been stymied on his quest for the identity of the Pennington sought when he reached retirement. But as we detailed in earlier chapters, the CIA was threatening lives while Felt was still employed in May 1973. So, the question of CIA participation was very much alive.

When Felt wrote *The FBI Pyramid* in 1979, he made a point of noting that the CIA had sent the FBI on a wild goose chase for Cecil while hiding one Lee Pennington from the Bureau. Lee Pennington, Felt wrote pointedly, was clearly a CIA contractor. Many learning of this deception would not be shocked that the CIA lied to the FBI. But lying to the FBI is a crime, the same crime that destroyed Nixon—obstruction of justice—and also the crime of making a false statement to a government agency.

The question arises: why would CIA officials risk criminal liability to protect Lee Pennington's identity? Certainly, the inference is that a truthful response would have suggested even worse criminality. One does not commit a crime of concealment unless the fact concealed (Lee Pennington's status) has more profoundly negative consequences than being caught in a lie. What was it about Lee Pennington that drove the CIA to lie so blatantly and riskily?

How did Lee Pennington finally surface? Two honest CIA security officers, responding to a renewed request to gather all Watergate evidence made by the new CIA director, William Colby, as a matter of conscience, stepped forward in early 1974 to tell Colby of Pennington's identity, not previously disclosed. Yes, the Agency had not been straight with the FBI. What the agents added, though, was more chilling than this admission.

While McCord was still in jail, Lee Pennington visited the McCord home to help Mrs. McCord burn in her fireplace all evidence of McCord's ongoing Agency connection. Yes, not past CIA employment postings, which were known to the FBI, but his continuing connection. In or around February of 1974, this information was relayed by the CIA both to the FBI and to the Nedzi House Committee,[14] eventually routed to the Senate Watergate Committee. It was then discovered that, in addition to Pennington's pickup of McCord and his home visit, Pennington had been provided by McCord for Agency consumption his research report on Jack Anderson, in the spring of 1972, as Operation Mudhen was winding down.

---

14   The House Select Committee, chaired by Rep. Lucien Nedzi (D-MI), explored the alleged involvement of the CIA in the Watergate and Ellsberg matters. Hearings were held before the House Special Subcommittee on Intelligence from 1973 to 1974, producing a 1,100-page report in 1975.

In the weeks leading up to the criminal trial in December 1972 and January 1973, McCord had sent five status letters to the Agency through Pennington, mainly dealing with Hunt's possible CIA defense and the statement of Garey Bittenbender, which would also expose the Agency. Thus, it appeared that Pennington, as a CIA contractor, was McCord's case agent before, during, and after Watergate.

Accordingly, risking criminal liability was rational because, as a frightened Deep Throat told Woodward in May of 1973, the CIA was deeply concerned about what other CIA activities might be discovered as a result of Watergate, worry so strong that the Agency was threatening murder.

After the CIA sent to the Senate its belatedly produced materials, they were described bluntly later by Texas Republican Senator Howard Baker in the Senate minority report on Watergate, often referred to as the Baker report:

> *The results of our investigation clearly show that the CIA had in its possession as of early July of 1972 information that one of their paid operatives, Lee R. Pennington Jr., had entered the James McCord residence shortly after the Watergate break-in and destroyed documents which might show a link between McCord and the CIA.*[15]

This quote by Baker is almost a verbatim quote of a statement the CIA forwarded to the Senate. Certainly, all knew of McCord's *past* employment with the CIA, so the only meaning of this admission was that the CIA was deliberately covering up McCord's *present* role with the Agency. And, of course, if

---

15   United States Senate Watergate Committee, "Senate Minority Report on Watergate," June 27, 1974.

Pennington picked up McCord at the jail as his Agency handler, McCord was necessarily acting as a CIA agent in Watergate.

While Stevens, Russell, and Martinez form a triple play to prove an airtight case against the CIA, Pennington's involvement is a guilty plea. That is precisely why the Agency risked so much to hide his involvement. Pennington's presence catches the CIA in the act of undercover work. And it is the Agency's almost successful attempt to conceal Pennington's identity that shows the Agency's consciousness of guilt.

Pennington was a contractor, it was finally revealed, with the highly secretive security research staff within the secretive OS. Pennington's identity was so sensitive that even the CIA director did not know of Pennington. He was paid by sterile check and was known, outside of his clandestine charges such as McCord, only by SRS Chief Paul Gaynor and two case officers to whom he was assigned over his fifteen years with the CIA.

Was Pennington the cutout to illegal undercover agents such as McCord? If any agency was to inquire, there would be no record of Pennington on the payroll. When the FBI requested information on a Pennington on August 18, 1972, Security Officer No. 1 was told by the head of personnel security that Lee Pennington was too sensitive to be given up. By this time several within the Agency had heard through Gaynor of Pennington's burning of documents at McCord's home which, to Gaynor's amusement, had caused smoke damage to the McCord living room. Gaynor's need to share this amusing anecdote beyond those who needed to know should have, but did not, cook the Agency's goose.

Following the directives of the head of personnel security, Security Officer No. 1 wrote a memo for his file about this decision not to reveal Lee Pennington's identity, as well as his secondhand knowledge that Pennington had burned documents in McCord's home showing McCord's connection to the Agency.

A year later, in August 1973, during the Ervin Committee hearings, new CIA Director William Colby (Richard Helms's replacement) asked that a package of Watergate materials be prepared for him. Security Officer No. 1 was told not to include his memo about Pennington in these materials. Disturbed by this, he nonetheless complied.

However, in January 1974, the CIA's inspector general asked to review the full Watergate file of the OS. After Security Officer No. 1 was asked again to remove Pennington materials from the file, he and another security officer both agreed to resign if forced to continue concealing Pennington.

With both houses of Congress pressing the CIA for its documents, the CIA's Office of Legislative Counsel asked all concerned to sign a memo attesting that all Watergate documents had been produced. It was then that the two security officers brought forth the earlier August 1972 memo about the destruction of materials by Pennington at McCord's home. Belatedly, the Pennington materials went to the Senate long after public hearings had been concluded.

Other than works by Jim Hougan, Mark Felt, and my recent book, *Postgate*, none of the hundreds of Watergate books and thousands of articles and documentaries have investigated these highly probative facts. It is clear that evidence of Pennington's connection with McCord, combined with the Agency attempts to suppress it, is sufficient by itself to convict the CIA of Watergate participation. And it is also proof beyond a reasonable doubt that if the *Washington Post* knew of this information and did not report it, that paper is guilty of a Watergate cover-up far more reprehensible than any Nixonian act of obstruction.

There was one Washington figure who, because he steadfastly had remained silent throughout the key years of the affair, could explain much once he chose to open up. That figure was G.

Gordon Liddy, a burglary supervisor and CRP moneyman who chose to accept a sentence for contempt of court rather than be forced to talk about anyone else, at least so long as the statute of limitations was running. In the next chapter, we will talk of this intriguing character and further explore the mysteries of Watergate.

Image of G. Gordon Liddy standing between his defense attorney Peter Maroulis (L) and reporter Sam Donaldson (R), public domain.

CHAPTER 19

LIDDY, WATERGATE'S UNGUIDED MISSILE

THROUGHOUT THIS WORK, WE HAVE confirmed solidly proven facts that never became part of the broadly accepted public narrative as exemplified by the *Post* reporting. But we have shown in previous chapters that everyone who spoke from personal knowledge about the burglary and cover-up had a motive to lie. And, with the exception of John Mitchell, lie they did. These falsehoods were not minor, mere shadings of the truth; instead, they were, to use John Mitchell's memorable phrase uttered during the Senate hearings, "palpable, damnable lies."

Many, if not most, understandable public misconceptions could have been clarified had Gordon Liddy chosen to speak up while national attention was riveted on Watergate. But he chose instead to be what he perceived to be a stand-up guy and rat out no one. So, Liddy determined that he would not tell his story until all applicable statutes of limitation had lapsed.

Since testimony about Watergate continued into 1974, to which potential criminal exposure attached, the applicable six-year statute of limitations for cover-up liability and conspiracy would not occur until 1980. In that year, Liddy published his candid account of Watergate, *Will*, and was the last of the scandal's main actors to do so. He waited so long to ensure that all statutes of limitation, as well as his term of probation, had expired. He set out to be brutally honest about both his criminality and his stupidity. The work has generally been acknowledged as the most honest of the Watergate memoirs.

The salience of his book flows from his centrality to the scandal. On the one hand, Liddy was a direct eyewitness to both burglary operations, while there had been no other book offering candid firsthand observations of either of them. Of the other burglary team members, McCord wrote an odd, inscrutable work, *A Piece of Tape*, that cannot even be called an account. Hunt's book was only a feint at revelation, with little attempt to describe what actually happened during the night of the burglary. After Hunt's CIA defense failed, Hunt would have a motive to be unified in his tale with his past employer, the CIA, with his pension at risk.

On the other end of the operation, the Nixon administration, Liddy had direct contact with the political figures alleged to be behind the burglary and the cover-up: Mitchell, Dean, Magruder, Colson, Mitchell's successor Attorney General Richard Kleindienst, and White House Communications Director Herbert Klein. He also dealt with the financial functionaries such as Maurice Stans and Hugh Sloan of the CRP, and Nixon campaign aide Herbert "Bart" Porter. Liddy also briefly monitored Donald Segretti, whose "dirty tricks" operation Deep Throat thought was a possible key to understanding Watergate. He also had contact with a number of CIA functionaries who supported Libby and Hunt with disguises, false credentials, charts, weapons, and cameras. Hunt brought Liddy to meet with the CIA poisons doctor Edward Gunn to discuss disabling columnist Jack Anderson.

Liddy was in the middle of the first awkward cover-up discussions, including his approach, along with Klein, to Attorney General Richard Kleindienst at the Burning Tree Country Club on the morning of the arrests. The purpose of this visit was to buttonhole Attorney General Kleindienst in an unsuccessful effort to enlist him to gain the release of the burglars from custody, claiming, per Dean, authorization from John Mitchell.

Not finally, Liddy was a member of the White House Plumbers team headed by David Young and Egil Krogh. He participated, along with Hunt and a Cuban team, in the burglary of the office of Ellsberg psychiatrist Dr. Lewis Fielding, an operation that appears to be a template for CIA infiltration of the White House, and, indeed, for Watergate. In short, Liddy had some connection to all of the unanswered questions of Watergate, even if he himself has been appropriately cast in the role of an unguided missile, and, in our view a dupe of Hunt and Dean.

While Liddy did earn much grudging public admiration for his stout, stand-up refusal to turn on any of his associates, in so doing he deprived the public and the various Watergate juries of important firsthand information: Dean's sponsorship of the GEMSTONE plan (and likely the subsequent burglaries), Dean's architecture of the cover-up, McCord's treachery during the burglary, Hunt's dealings that revealed his status as an agent for the CIA, his access to Baldwin's overhearings as reported by McCord, and Magruder's directions before the second burglary.

As a result of his silence, Liddy unwittingly deprived Nixon's White House of potentially exculpating or mitigating information, such as the identity of the key potential burglary conspirator Dean. Liddy thus could have warned the White House of facts suggesting that Dean was a Quisling, protecting himself to the detriment of his clients.

Liddy's silence, which unintentionally protected Dean, allowed Dean, according to Colodny, not only to lead Nixon into the ill-conceived attempt of obstruction using the CIA, but also later allowed Magruder to peddle a false story to the public by testifying to former attorney general John Mitchell's responsibility for the burglary.

Liddy also unintentionally deprived the public of details showing CIA involvement in the White House CRP operations that was deep and wide. The conventional Watergate story, which excluded the centrality of Dean, the targeted desk drawer, and the CIA, was firmly embedded in the conventional narrative by the time that his book, *Will*, was released in 1980. Thus, Liddy's desire during the scandal to help the White House actually damaged it in the eyes of history, and certainly hampered the public's ability to obtain relevant information.

One of the liars most nakedly exposed by Liddy is McCord, especially when Liddy's insight is paired with our knowledge of Michael Stevens. Liddy describes in detail McCord's touted state-of-the-art room bug, which could be hidden in furniture in O'Brien's office, virtually undetectable. The cost of the bug, according to McCord, was $30,000, which Liddy in his book verifies he gave to McCord for this purpose.

Liddy tells us of McCord's report after the first burglary about the O'Brien room bug, to wit; the bug was not transmitting, apparently because it was shielded by concrete and steel. Liddy, of course, was upset that this huge dent in his budget had come to naught. Indeed, Liddy understood that at least one of the tasks to be performed in the second burglary was adjustment of the faultily placed bug. But from McCord's testimony before the Senate, we know that he and others did not enter O'Brien's office during that first burglary. McCord even claimed, likely falsely, not to know where O'Brien's office was prior to the second burglary, supposedly tasking Baldwin with finding out during the week of June 12, causing Baldwin to visit the DNC and get a walkthrough of the premises.

We know that there was never any entry into O'Brien's office during the first burglary. Furthermore, McCord never claimed in his testimony to have planted a room bug anywhere during the first burglary, much less in O'Brien's office. What about McCord's story to Liddy that he was to repair the O'Brien room bug during the second burglary? We know this was not true, not only because of McCord's testimony, but also because he was caught with a crude, simple room bug, seemingly to be implanted in a smoke detector in the ceiling of O'Brien's office.

The FBI, in its intensive sweep of O'Brien's office, found no other room bug and indeed the presence of the crude microphone, one about to be placed in an opened smoke detector, appears to be an admission that no prior room bug had been placed.

Intelligent analysis of Liddy's book therefore demonstrates that Liddy had been a CIA chump. The conclusion thereby easily reached was that the target of the first break-in was not O'Brien's office, and from this conclusion, we also infer quite confidently that McCord and the CIA were pursuing a secret agenda, hidden from the only team member not part of the CIA, Liddy. Liddy, of course, was a necessary team member both because he con- trolled CRP money and because he constituted proof of White House approval of the CIA's operation.

This discussion also yields further proof of CIA deception. You may recall our earlier offhanded description of photos the burglars claimed to have taken during the first burglary, which were developed, somewhat belatedly, by Rich's Photos in Miami via burglar Bernard Barker. The pictures, seemingly meant as trophy shots, show letters on DNC director stationery pinned to a shag carpet by gloved hands, presumably meant to show the penetration of O'Brien's office by the burglars. But, as we noted, the DNC offices did not feature shag carpeting, while the Howard Johnson rooms of the burglars did have such carpeting. Clearly, the photos were meant to fool Liddy and other White House officials who might learn of the burglary into believing that O'Brien was the true target of the first break-in. The staged photos are merely corroboration of the obvious inference that the burglars never intended during the first burglary to enter O'Brien's office, and that at least Liddy and possibly Magruder were fooled into thinking so.

Another small, but nonetheless telling, observation in Liddy's book was of McCord's frequent, unexplained absences from the scene in the hours before the burglary, while the team waited for DNC offices to clear. The DNC offices had been occupied late by a young man using the Wide Area Telephone Service (WATS) line that allowed free long-distance calls throughout the United States, often found in government or large corporate offices.

While these discrepancies between Liddy's book and McCord's testimony may seem minor, they are hugely important. They prove that at the very least, McCord and Hunt were lying to Liddy about the purpose of the first burglary, in which the O'Brien room bug was to be implanted. Liddy describes Magruder's emphatic gesture, prior to the second burglary on June 12, when he ordered Liddy to reenter the DNC offices, much to Liddy's chagrin, over a valueless, costly mission. Liddy wrote that Magruder had slammed his palm into the lower-left-side desk drawer where the Nixonites always kept their oppo dirt on opponents. He quotes Magruder, "'we want what they have in there," which Liddy immediately understood was the dirt that the Democrats had on the Republicans. While this command does not seem like much at first blush, Liddy's revelation is the first time any of the protagonists has suggested the true purpose of the second burglary.

But if there is a primary ox that Liddy unintentionally gores in his book, it is most assuredly that of Dean. Dean has always professed to be a Clean Gene. However, Liddy describes Dean's strenuous efforts to convince him to leave a good White House job to become general counsel of the CRP, a temporary and obscure post. Dean accomplished this by promising Liddy a huge intelligence operation, according to Liddy's account, with a budget of "half a million for openers," in Dean's words. By so convincing Liddy, without any power of Dean over this budget, Dean got a vehicle to fulfill the blind ambition he describes in his bestseller, that is, his own intelligence portfolio. Liddy would do anything he was asked, legal or otherwise, while Dean knew that there would be plentiful CRP campaign cash for Liddy to spend on Dean's schemes. And he would deal with a weakling Magruder, who likely would fear displeasing Dean, who Magruder felt was close to Haldeman's group.

Liddy's book also puts the lie to Dean's faux ethical pose that he withdrew from supporting Liddy after Liddy's amended February 4, 1972, presentation to Mitchell. Liddy describes no revulsion by Dean at Liddy's plans, which were scaled down from the first presentation of a week earlier, but, rather, describes Dean's continuing encouragement as he characterized Mitchell's second negative reaction as being financially motivated. Dean was clearly a strong continuing supporter of Liddy's covert intelligence schemes, contrary to all that Dean has said postarrest.

Why do Dean's motivations matter? Dean's encouragement of Liddy now puts in focus Dean's seeming fascination with escort services. In short, Liddy does much unwittingly to puncture Dean's balloon of hypocrisy and help us understand the motives for the burglaries.

A final grouping of observations by Liddy unveils much about Hunt and the CIA. Liddy details a cooperative agencywide support for their ventures, with disguises, weapons, fake identification, and safe houses supplied on demand. Even the impressive GEMSTONE charts for the January 27, 1972, presentation to Mitchell were professionally prepared by the CIA graphics department. We have earlier discussed the false preemptive claim of CIA official General Robert Cushman that Ehrlichman had asked him for carte blanche assistance from the CIA when hiring Hunt, a claim that never made sense. Ehrlichman was not intending to supervise Hunt and had no idea what tasks Hunt would be assigned, nor what help he would need from the CIA.

But the death knell for the CIA claims of innocence is Liddy's description of the lunch meeting to which Hunt had invited Liddy on March 24, 1972, with the supposedly retired CIA poisons doctor, Edward Gunn. Even in 1980, Liddy believed that the ensuing discussion of disabling or assassinating columnist Jack Anderson was for Hunt's vaguely described "principal," which Liddy assumed was the White House. As we noted, at the conclusion of the meeting, Hunt had Liddy provide a $100 bill to Gunn, which the ingenuous Liddy thought to be appropriate spy craft protocol.

As of the writing of his book, Liddy had no reason to suspect that Hunt's true principal was the CIA. In the 20/20 vision of hindsight, we can see that the discussion of disabling Anderson came at the same time that the CIA was openly intimidating Anderson via Operation Mudhen, while McCord was preparing his research paper on Anderson, which he transmitted to the Agency through Pennington. Liddy's lunch with Gunn, then, follows our theme that the CIA was using the White House as cover for its otherwise illegal domestic operations, the Anderson operation being one. By describing this meeting, Liddy stumbles into proof of a secret CIA agenda.

We note, parenthetically, that this episode inspired the 2010 book by reporter Mark Feldstein, *Poisoning the Press*, based on the very sophomoric theme that Nixon's troubles stemmed from his churlish distrust of the vigorous, investigatory press, which Feldstein posits led Nixon to plan Anderson's poisoning. For Feldstein, the book may have won him a tenure as a journalist turned professor, but any metanalysis of his book is that of a media that reports the narrative of what it *wishes* had occurred, an aspirational version of reality, not what *actually* occurred.

To conclude this chapter, we must ask why, nearly fifty years after Watergate, do the well-educated sectors of the public not yet know of the matters we have discussed? Watergate was a scandal causing a tumultuous political upheaval, the only time in our country's history that a president has been removed from office. It had largely accomplished this by aggressive press coverage thought to have been bull's eye correct at the time. We must now ask whether the facts we have discussed in these pages were simply unknown to the *Washington Post*.

Image of FBI Deputy Director W. Mark Felt (aka Deep Throat), public domain.

CHAPTER 20

DEEP THROAT: LAW BREAKER OR LAW ENFORCER?

IN THIS BOOK, WE HAVE not treated Deep Throat's work in depth, except for his last garage meeting with Woodward in May 1973. We have not delved into the earlier meetings, especially the first and the longest, occurring in the early morning of October 9, 1972. In that meeting, which lasted until 6:00 AM, Deep Throat explained at great length and depth for Woodward the narrative of a White House campaign of "spying and sabotage."

The sensational story of October 10, 1972, was the most important *Post* article, radically changing public assessment of the scandal. As a result, Walter Cronkite, the revered anchor of *CBS Evening News*, began covering Watergate in earnest. Ted Kennedy, because of this article, formed a committee eventually headed by North Carolina Senator Sam Ervin that became known as the Senate Watergate Committee. It was this committee that convened dramatic televised hearings that transfixed a nation. In short, the Deep Throat/Bob Woodward garage meeting of October 9, 1972, was the pivotal journalistic episode of Watergate.

Because the meeting is common knowledge, along with the *Post* article flowing from it and the resultant sensational hearings, it is counterintuitive to include it as a major mystery of Watergate. Wasn't this meeting, featured in the bestselling book and major motion picture, the key to busting the White House Watergate cover-up? The short answer is that this meeting is truly of critical importance, but not for the reasons that history has postulated, and which books and movies have portrayed.

The *Washington Post* collaboration with Deep Throat is crucial to our understanding of Watergate because it helps explain how the mysteries of Watergate have so long gone unsolved, and worse, unlamented in their lack of solution. In a sense, this well-known meeting, enshrined in history, is itself a mystery that must be deconstructed to fully understand Watergate.

What was the genesis of this meeting? It did not occur until the scandal had been simmering for four months, with but tepid public reaction over this odd, puzzling burglary. If in fact this meeting caused, through the reporting following it, an explosion of interest in the scandal, why didn't Mark Felt (aka Deep Throat) meet with Woodward earlier? If the public had been uninterested for the four months previously, why wait?

Up until this meeting, Deep Throat did give Woodward bits and pieces of information. For instance, he informed Woodward immediately following the arrest that the burglars had Hunt's White House phone number, whereupon Woodward confirmed Hunt's White House consultancy in an exciting article. Soon, Deep Throat also told Woodward that Hunt's safe contained a loaded handgun, also causing a minor sensation.

But, by and large, Deep Throat's help to Woodward consisted of these tidbits, as opposed to the sweeping narrative that Deep Throat later detailed in October, in a session lasting seven hours. Why this substantial increase in the assistance that Deep

Throat was giving to Woodward? Let us first focus on what Mark Felt's motives were as he became Deep Throat. To explore Deep Throat's purposes, we should analyze the effect of these two early scandalous bits that he provided Woodward. Woodward had covered the burglary arraignment just hours after the arrests because he was on the low-level local crime beat. Normally, given that the story soon was shown to have national implication, the national reporters would be assigned the story and Woodward removed. But these titillating scoops from his secret source kept Woodward on the case, assisted by Carl Bernstein, a superior copywriter. For Mark Felt, he understood the benefits of having a megaphone that could not be traced back to him, since Felt had made Woodward to pledge not to reveal their friendship, developed when Woodward was in the Navy.

These early leaks would also benefit the FBI. With a clear White House connection now publicized, the Bureau had the basis for the all-out investigation which Felt wanted. By September 15, 1972, the FBI, using over three hundred agents, conducted over fifteen hundred interviews. In short, the *Post* reporting gave Felt the cover for the exhaustive probe he wanted. There was therefore mutual benefit in the relationship.

Why, we should ask, did Felt care so much about doing such a thorough job? Professional pride is one easy answer. But there is more. In his first postarrest meeting with FBI Director Patrick Gray, Felt fervently proclaimed to the director, "The reputation of the FBI is at stake!" Felt understood that the Bureau's widely known integrity was its greatest strength because of the citizens' trust of the FBI. As one agent who worked with Felt told me, "Half of our work was already done before we got out of the car to conduct the interview." And when the FBI reached a conclusion, the citizenry believed it was the result of unbiased professionalism.

If, as a result of this early *Post* reporting, the FBI was allowed to conduct fifteen hundred interviews, what changed so much to make Felt become Deep Throat and go to the risky extreme of the garage meetings? The answer, which all should have seen, but did not, came on September 15, 1972, about twenty-five days before the garage meeting, when the Department of Justice announced the indictments of the seven original defendants— the five burglars and their two supervisors, Hunt and Liddy. The spokesman for the Department of Justice also offered, "No more indictments are expected to be forthcoming."

What no member of the public had been told at the time was that the grand jury had been limited to consideration of the burglary only. Put differently, no member of the public had been told that there may be crimes *other than* the burglary. Certainly, if the FBI developed solid evidence that a higher-up had authorized the burglary, that would be fair game to bring to the grand jury.

The Justice Department has authority to convene and conduct grand juries, and in most cases, nothing keeps the FBI from investigating any federal crime and bringing it to any one of the many U.S. attorneys throughout the country. Any U.S. attorney, in normal situations, can bring any the case before the district's grand jury. However, there are exceptions. If the case is one of election crime or public corruption, because of fear of local politically influenced prosecutions, only "Main Justice" in DC can authorize an investigation into these two categories of crimes. But ironically, this power gives Main Justice the ability to obstruct investigations throughout the country.

In what we call the "silent obstruction," Main Justice was refusing any investigation other than of the burglary, no matter what crime or potential crime was uncovered in the investigation, and no matter how the crime might help prove the burglary to be part of a larger program of skullduggery. We call this a "silent" obstruction for two reasons. First, no member of the public knew about this restriction. Second, while there was nothing illegal about restricting such investigations, if the restriction was publicly known, the public outcry would be loud. But in Watergate, unlike the case of, say, publicized corruption, there would be no reason for the public to know of potential crimes other than the burglary. For this reason, we call the obstruction silent.

Mark Felt knew about a variety of potential crimes other than the burglary that had been uncovered in his investigation, and yet his FBI was not given permission to investigate using the grand jury. Why was this failure so important? Why did it matter that crimes other than the burglary were not being investigated? Because Felt knew that proof of these other crimes could possibly help prove higher authorization, going to the White House, for the burglary itself.

If there were other election crimes authorized by the Oval Office, by inference they might show that the Nixon inner circle also had likely authorized the Watergate burglaries, which would be somewhat similar in intended effect to these other crimes, assuming Watergate was meant to spy on or sabotage electoral opponents.

Felt's FBI had found that one Donald Segretti, recently a second lieutenant in the Army, a lawyer and University of Southern California graduate, had been recruited by President Nixon's close aide, fellow USC graduate Dwight Chapin. He was paid by Nixon's private estate lawyer, Herbert Kalmbach. The FBI had learned that Segretti had crisscrossed the country, recruiting other young conservative lawyers, mainly for the purpose of pulling destructive pranks on the opposition, beginning with Nixon's primary opponents. These became known as "dirty tricks" or the "Segretti dirty tricks." At USC, dirty tricks in campus political campaigns were traditional, indeed widely known as "ratfucking." An example might be posting signs changing the time of a campaign rally.

We hasten to add that the John F. Kennedy 1960 campaign featured the well-known trickster Dick Tuck, who became the darling of the media. To give just one example of Tuck's pranks, as Richard Nixon had begun speaking from the rear of a train on a "whistle stop" campaign tour, the train began slowly pulling away, to Nixon's befuddlement. Apparently, Tuck had given a bit of cash to the train engineer to "mistake" the time of departure. This type of prank had been considered standard fare and, in a sense, recognized fair play. To be sure, Segretti's program was perhaps an extreme and excessively efficient version of these tactics, taken, it could be argued, to a new level. Although Segretti was not supervised by Liddy and Hunt, the two sometimes looked in on Segretti, ironically in hindsight, to make certain Segretti did not prove to be an embarrassment to the White House.

Because the Segretti operations seemingly had approvals of, and perhaps supervision by, Oval Office personnel per Chapin and Kalmbach, Felt thought that the burglary might be part of a larger program of spying and sabotage leading to the Oval Office. In short, Felt hypothesized that investigating the Segretti operation might be a side door, so to speak, into finding higher-level approvals of the burglary program.

Felt knew that Segretti's tricks were small potatoes, and they were not his ultimate target. And he also knew that if the burglary investigation were to cease as of September 15, it would not look good for the FBI, since the Bureau might be viewed as being party to a seeming whitewash of Watergate. Felt always thought that one or two lower-level lieutenants in the White House were behind the burglaries, and told Gray that on June 23, 1972, imploring him to urge the president to give up the young lieutenants who Felt hypothesized were behind this foolish caper.

By publicizing the Segretti dirty tricks as a potential template for the Watergate burglary, Felt, now becoming an engaged Deep Throat, thought the ensuing public pressure would force the White House to permit continuation of his investigation before the grand jury, now folding in the Segretti program for inquiry. His goal was not to seek revenge on his boss Patrick Gray, or to harm Nixon for not naming him Director, as many have ignorantly postulated. As Felt told us years later, "I was not out to get Nixon. I was just trying to do my job."

Before the indictments were announced on September 15, 1972, Felt had sent several gracious, insightful memos up the chain of command through Gray to Main Justice, while seeking this broadened investigation. In the weeks following the indictments, he continued his campaign to seek investigative authority directed toward the Segretti dirty tricks, but he was continually rebuffed. As a result, he had no choice but to use the *Post* to be his megaphone for raising public awareness.

But why did he need to risk lengthy garage meetings with Woodward? The first meeting, the most significant one, tells us much about the true capabilities of modern journalism, at odds with the modern image of awesome capability. Felt did not want simply to give Woodward his written FBI interview reports. This would be unethical, would endanger any future prosecutions and would, if discovered, point back to Felt and his FBI as the source. So, he determined that he would teach the reporters to fish rather than giving them fish. If the reporters were good critical thinkers, interviewing the right witnesses would give them all they needed to know. But critical thinkers Woodward and Bernstein were not.

Posing as a volunteer source, Felt, I believe, (and this is subject to some debate between the author and Carl Bernstein) was the self-identified "government lawyer" who called Bernstein in late September 1972, to give him the name of one of Segretti's attempted recruits, Alex Shipley, an assistant state attorney general in Tennessee. Segretti had explained his operation to Shipley in detail as he recruited him, such that a *Post* story about the dirty tricks would be sensational and verified directly out of Segretti's mouth to Shipley.

Alas, despite interviewing Shipley, Woodstein did not understand the narrative or its connection to Watergate, which to Felt was obvious, nor were they sure about its accuracy. According to Barry Sussman, the reporters' editor, the *Post* was not going to publish the Shipley/Segretti story at least until Deep Throat met Woodward in the garage, after which they understood the story and were comfortable it was true. Put differently, had Deep Throat not met with Woodward in the garage on October 9, there never would have been the "spying and sabotage" story that was so crucial in exploding the Watergate cover-up. Also, had not Felt made his (we infer) anonymous call, they would not have revisited the Segretti story.

The October 10, 1972, story was indeed explosive, perhaps more so than Felt had predicted. The story as intended kept the investigation open in the face of public pressure. It was also likely a factor in Patrick Gray's infamous implosion at his confirmation hearings beginning February 27, 1973. These confirmation hearings constituted an inflection point, which many observers view as being the first significant crack in the dam for the Nixon White House. Gray was so flustered that he promised to allow the questioning senators to rummage through all his FBI investigatory files, a gaffe which immediately caused the loss of confidence in Gray by the White House. As John Ehrlichman intoned famously to John Dean about Gray's performance, "Let him twist slowly, slowly in the wind." Our point here is that implosion would never have transpired had not it been for the sensational October 10, 1972, *Post* article.

Let us examine the effects of the October 10, 1972, article. The story gave rise two days following it to the formation of what became the Senate Watergate Committee, formed originally by Senator Ted Kennedy, who wisely, given his own ethical lapses, handed off the investigation to North Carolina Senator Sam Ervin. What was crucial about the *Post* story was the strong public pressure it invoked. Senate Republicans could not deny subpoena power to the Committee, as Congress had done just weeks before in denying Representative Wright Patman his request for subpoena power for a congressional investigation.

But the article was most useful as a continued narrative framework to be used by the *Post* throughout its reporting, especially through the time that McCord railed to Sirica in March of 1973, and Dean and Magruder were turning state's evidence. The president and his former attorney general, among others, had been put permanently by the *Post* in the crosshairs using the Deep Throat-inspired spying and sabotage narrative. And as dangers of revelations about the CIA and escort referrals loomed, the narrative was highly useful to the *Post* in selling its version of sole White House guilt, while steering attention away from the Agency.

For instance, as Earl Silbert approached the burglary trial in January 1973, he filed his pared-down witness list. The *Post* none too subtly upbraided him by repeating again and again that he had taken Segretti off the witness list. The *Post* used this observation to suggest that the prosecution was covering up for the true authors of the burglaries, which per the *Post* were White House and CRP officials. The *Post*, likely knowing that it had wrongly named William Timmons of the White House and Glenn Sedam and Robert Odle of the CRP as recipients of wiretap summaries

(Woodstein apologized to the three in their later book), nonetheless, without any sense of shame, ominously noted their absence from the witness list as well. All of this was to suggest a cover-up by the prosecution.

Judge Sirica, known to study the *Post* on the bus on his way to court, had the White House in mind as he upbraided the prosecution and witnesses for not revealing the higher-level movers of the pawns before him. Of course, Sirica never seemed to have a clue that Silbert, if allowed to try this case without restriction, would have pointed to a CIA theme, that is, Hunt and his aspirations for control of Mullen, a CIA cover company. This, of course, would have pointed to the CIA as being the source of authorization for the burglary, or at least part of the motive and intent behind it.

So, the *Post*'s coverage, combined with the appellate court's restrictions, Hunt's plea, and Silbert's necessary change in strategy, served to continue the implication of White House authorization of the burglary as part of the "spying and sabotage" narrative so sensationally established in October of 1972. Felt, of course, had put forth this theme as an investigative hypothesis, not as proven fact. But as time passed and evidence was put forth in the Senate and later the cover-up trial, the Segretti program was all but forgotten while the "spying and sabotage" theme lived on. The Segretti program, in short, had nothing to do with the burglary. But it had served its purpose in deflecting attention from facts the *Post* knew to be a big part of the truth, but which the paper had concealed.

As the investigation moved from September 1972 to May 1973, it had become abundantly clear that there was a large component of CIA involvement in the burglary operation. The irony, of course, is rich. (We confess to using the words "ironic" and "ironically" frequently in this book, but our defense is that everything about this scandal reeks with irony.) The first garage meeting, and the reporting based upon it, had turned Watergate into the country's most significant historical scandal. However, it did so based on an investigative hypothesis which was ultimately proven inapplicable.

The last in a series of garage meetings between Deep Throat and Woodward occurred on May 16–17, 1973. It was this meeting that should have resulted in the public's learning the real essence of the scandal, replacing the now discredited spying and sabotage hypothesis. What would have happened had Woodward and the *Post* done what they claimed to do—tell the truth without fear or favor? The public would have learned about its main intelligence agency's roguish, illegal adventures, including threatened murder. It would have been told of swampish prostitution referrals by a major political party. Also, significantly, questions would have been asked as to who in the White House, if not high-level officials such as Nixon and Mitchell, approved this extremely silly venture. A lesson perhaps would have been learned about the inability of the White House to control its own sprawling bureaucracy, starting with its White House staff and extending to its intelligence agencies.

Nothing at all was reported about the sensational garage meeting of May 1973, in which Deep Throat revealed that the CIA was involved in Watergate, and, more importantly, wished to cover up other activities to which an investigation of Watergate and its role might lead. It suffices to say that history's most heralded, revered, and iconic source was not used to solve Watergate's mysteries, but rather to shroud them further. This was not Mark Felt's wish.

As we leave our discussion of these mysteries and look forward to more fully discussing Watergate journalism, we should begin to ask about the use of anonymous sources. Yes, as many observers have noted, these sources may lie under the shroud of anonymity. But it is also the case that the reporter can lie about what the anonymous sources said, or, more likely, can conceal salient facts that the source revealed, a form of fraud. A source wishing to remain anonymous cannot correct or supplement the record. We believe, based on the evidence, that this happened not only with Mark Felt, but with MPD Lieutenant Carl Shoffler, to name just one other witness with salient information. These suppressions of truth from these known witnesses are extremely troubling. The question we raise as we conclude is not about Watergate itself but about Watergate journalism: why has it taken over fifty years to clarify these mysteries? And why are they being explained, at long last, by a nonjournalist?

SECTION 2

WATERGATE JOURNALISM

Image of *Washington Post* building in Washington, DC, public domain.

CHAPTER 21

BIG QUESTIONS ABOUT BIG JOURNALISM

IN THE FIRST TWENTY CHAPTERS, we have outlined what we posit was the true narrative of Watergate. Many of the facts, particularly the most pertinent ones, had not been widely published or known to anyone outside a small circle of *Washington Post* reporters, law enforcement, and a few key actors in the scandal. But if our narrative is correct, then something was likely amiss with what has been touted as the greatest feat of investigative journalism the world has ever known. Could it be that the *Post* reporting was either wildly incompetent or spectacularly fraudulent? Certainly, even if there might be quibbles about some of the details and inferences we present, the *Post* has much explaining to do. In our view, the delta between *actual* truth and the *Post's* *reported* truth cannot be innocently explained.

There are at the least a number of large questions about Watergate journalism raised by our treatment of the scandal. In this chapter, we will frame these questions and seeming contraventions of the truth, and then attempt to address them in subsequent chapters.

The initial argument against our narrative that will leap to mind for many is simply the argument of authority. That is, just as the Catholic Church fathers say there are three persons in one God, the very fact that this doctrine comes from designated authority makes it inarguably true for believing Catholics like the author. By this reasoning, the *Post* is recognized as the leading authority on Watergate and therefore if the *Post* claims our narrative is substantially false, and that its narrative is substantially true, it must be so. But the authority the *Post* wields, unlike that of any religious institution, should be grounded in earthly fact, not religious doctrine, which is agreed by the faithful to be unassailable in its major tenants, by virtue of its authority springing from a higher power. But for some, this argument, circular that it is, carries weight. We would suggest that an argument based on the supposed infallibility of the *Post*, especially given the facts explicated in our first twenty chapters, has been soundly disproven.

But what about the argument that a Pulitzer Prize board had examined its reporting, and by virtue of awarding that prestigious prize, implicitly verified its accuracy? That argument, in short, is a nonstarter. There is nothing to suggest the Pulitzer judges vetted the accuracy of the reporting, which, to be fair, was loudly and wildly praised at the time. And a number of Pulitzer Prizes have been given out in the past for what turned out to be falsely favorable reporting on the two most murderous regimes in world history—those of Joseph Stalin and of Adolf Hitler. So, the award of a Pulitzer Prize to the *Post* means very little about the accuracy of its reporting.

But unlike the Pulitzer Prize board, there actually were juries that did consider a number of facts in our frankly revisionist treatment. These two juries are those which rendered verdicts in the case of *Wells v. Liddy*. Both verdicts were rendered in favor of Liddy, the first by a seven-to-two vote, the second (on retrial after appeal) by a nine-to-zero vote. In essence, after lengthy trials with excellent trial counsel, with the lowest burden of proof cognizable in our system, that is, preponderance of the evidence, plaintiffs Maxie Wells and Spencer Oliver Jr. could not prove it false that they had been running a call girl referral system.

Following the first verdict, the *Post* published a bizarre anti-verdict editorial, claiming that a trial is no place to determine historical truth, an astounding claim:

> *Courts are a capricious venue for arguments about history. Sometimes, as when a British Court last year resoundingly rejected the holocaust denial of historian David Irving, litigation can help protect established history from those who would maliciously rewrite it. But conspiracy theorizing generally is better addressed to the public arena by rigorous confrontation with facts. That's true both out of respect for freedom of speech, even wrongheaded speech, and because historical truth does not always fare so well in court. A jury in Tennessee in 1999 embraced the looniest of conspiracy theories concerning the assassination of Martin Luther King Jr. And this week in a Federal Court in Baltimore, the commonly understood and well-founded history of the Watergate scandal took a hit as well.*

> *The forum was the defamation case of G. Gordon Liddy, the Watergate felon and radio talk show host who has promoted in speeches a "revisionist" (false would be a better description) account of the scandal. Mr. Liddy has argued that the burglary was not an attempt to collect political intelligence*

*on President Nixon's enemies, but an effort master-
minded by then White House counsel John Dean
to steal pictures of prostitutes, including Mr. Dean's
then-girlfriend and current wife, from the desk of a
secretary at the Democratic headquarters.*

*The secretary, Ida Wells, is now a community col-
lege teacher in Louisiana and was understandably
offended by the implication that she was somehow
involved in a call girl ring. She sued Mr. Liddy and
the battle had dragged on for four years. The jury
failed to reach a unanimous verdict, but it split
overwhelmingly in favor of Mr. Liddy. The majority of jurors felt that Ms. Wells' lawyers had failed
to prove his theory wrong. They found this in spite
of the fact that Mr. Liddy relies for his theory on a
disbarred attorney with a history of mental illness.
The call girl theory "is possible" one jury told Post
staff writer Manuel Roig-Franzia, "it sure makes
me more curious." "We'll never know what happened," said another.*

*The danger of such outcomes as this one is that
this sort of thinking spreads, for whether or not Mr.
Liddy's comments legally defamed Miss Wells, we
do know what happened at Watergate and it had
nothing to do with prostitutes.*[16]

As any experienced trial lawyer will tell you, there is no engine
that is better for the determination of truth than cross-examination. The very good lawyers on both sides in *Wells v. Liddy* had
many months of opportunity for full disclosure through written

---

16   Editorial Board, "The Courts and History," *Washington Post*, February 4, 2001.

discovery, document production, and weeks of deposition and trial cross-examination. It is therefore reasonably inferred that the *Wells* verdicts were thumping rejections of the conventional story of Watergate as written almost exclusively by the *Post*.

To be fair, the newspaper business has its own imperatives, with daily deadlines to be met while hurriedly attempting to get to the readers the most relevant available facts. Certainly, some rapid selection, some quick curation, some on-the-spot discretion must be exercised determining what was fact for the reader. In doing so, with a healthy skepticism toward all things Nixon, the *Post* understandably may have discounted facts veering away from pure Nixon venality. Certainly, by the late 1990s and early 2000s, after years of sleuthing by researchers like Jim Hougan, Len Colodny, and others, after Freedom of Information Act (FOIA) documents were garnered, and, yes, after Liddy finally published his memoirs, new facts might have emerged that in good faith were either not encountered by the *Post* in the early 1970s or received in such a way that they did not appear reliable at the time. As we recount in *Postgate*, this had been my working assumption as we read the two engrossing books by Hougan and Colodny.

The *Post*'s editors' *Wells v. Liddy* reaction could have just been one of wounded pride for having negligently missed key facts, or so we thought. Thus, to be fair, we here present the possibility that the *Post* may have missed a part of the story in good faith while telling a major part very well. We will leave that to you, the jury, as we proceed through our proof in following chapters. In addition to the *Wells v. Liddy* verdict, we have previously presented a wealth of information comprising both direct and circumstantial evidence in support of the revisionist story. That said, it is one thing to say that our narrative is the best interpretation of the evidence, but quite another to contend that the *Post* should have sussed out the truth during the scandal.

This complex web of deceit known as Watergate had been proven mainly by lengthy, close examination of circumstantial evidence, while discounting much direct evidence. For instance, both John Mitchell and John Ehrlichman denied certain crimes under oath, Mitchell in authorizing the burglaries, and Ehrlichman for knowing that Fielding would be burglarized to obtain Ellsberg's records, and yet both were convicted. On the other hand, Dean and McCord, we contend, likely lied about certain aspects of the scandal, but were believed. It could be viewed as an undue burden to place on the *Post* reporters and editors to be as skilled as an experienced trial judge in ferreting out the truth. Indeed, this is the view we held until 2010, when we began researching *Postgate*.

Why is the question of the *Post*'s intent to deceive so important today? Didn't this scandal begin fifty years ago? We respond that the question is quite central to the most important issues roiling society today, and is especially important in the writing of history, as Watergate has become history and no longer a current event. A majority of Americans, we venture to say, do not trust the honesty of the major media. If that's true, the distrust may have its roots in the scandal that lionized "investigative journalism."

During the Watergate years, the great majority of Americans, conservative and liberal, trusted the media. If they had not, the country would never have reached consensus on Nixon's removal. Let's pause and reflect on the demonstrated reality that a media perceived to be fair can broker democratic compromise and consensus. But after our review herein, can we conclude that consensus was fraudulently obtained in Watergate? Did this journalism, even though credited at the time, ultimately begin the draining of the reservoir of public trust in the media? If we can now confidently decide that the country was in fact journalistically defrauded in Watergate, such is a strong argument militating against reliance by our divided country on what appears to be a partisan, untruthful media.

But secondly, and more importantly, such deceit would suggest that a major cause of our current societal division is untruth promulgated by that same partisan media birthed in Watergate journalism. The *Post* has long boasted, with great credibility, and virtually all sectors of society have long agreed, that Watergate was a journalistically impelled scandal. The *Post's* Watergate reporting profoundly affected the course of our country's history. It not only knocked out of office the politically popular, if personally unlikable, President Nixon, but it also greatly influenced the election of Jimmy Carter over Gerald Ford.

According to pollsters, Watergate was a key issue in favor of Carter, who constantly promised, in a clear insult of the Republicans of Watergate, "a government as good as the American people." Carter begat Reagan, an avowedly conservative leader, hammered by the media for the same, while Democrats reacted by becoming more openly leftist. These widening divisions, it would appear, began as a result of Watergate.

The Reagan presidency set in stone the media's cheerleading, begun with Watergate, for all things "liberal," the modern term "progressive" being more apt, and against all things "conservative," the term "classic liberal" more fitting. But the point here is that a new form of media resulted from Watergate, one openly partisan, attempting to influence political outcomes, not merely to report on them. In short, the paper encouraged the factionalism that the founding fathers hoped to cure through a free press.

Well-regarded former *Rolling Stone* reporter Matt Taibbi is a good authority to cite on this subject because he acknowledges that he is quite far Left politically, and, indeed, criticizes the media from a radical leftist standpoint. Taibbi has noted, and we agree, that post-Watergate, a new crop of so-called "investigative journalists" aspire to be on the other side of the velvet rope, that is, part of the powerful elite controlling society. This new brand of post-Watergate journalist is far from the likes of the H. L. Mencken, Damon Runyon, and Jimmy Breslin, who were separate and apart from, and skeptical of, the elites of both Left and Right.

In this regard, if a journalist wishes to be part of the political power structure, as this new breed does, one must pick a team. It is only natural that the team in most cases would be Democratic and Left, since that is the natural home of those challenging authority and/or wishing to change the status quo. And if the journalist wishes power, she should slant the facts toward one side, rather than striving for the best attempt at objectivity. In recent years, for example, it was frequently forewarned that Donald Trump should not be "normalized" by journalists. If he did one good thing, for example, getting vaccines developed quickly, thus saving lives, the partisan press should not be seen to rate that achievement positively, for fear, again, of "normalizing" Trump. This is not journalism. It is advocacy, shilling, marketing. If these reporters were all conservative advocates, that would be of equal concern.

This all being so, of what significance would it be if the *Post* deliberately misreported Watergate? Better put, of what significance would it be if our society, as a whole, were to adopt a newly formed consensus view that Watergate journalism was a deliberate fraud?

Such would confirm the growing suspicion that journalists are not approaching stories from a position of truthfulness. The press would thus be exposed as doing something other than speaking truth to power. Indeed, in many cases, the truth speaker and the truth seeker just might be those persons or groups the media seeks to skewer.

Therefore, a judgment of *Post* fraud in its reporting on Watergate would be a powerful weapon for society's conventional thinkers, targeted by journalists today. After all, it is difficult for a mafia don to be credibly indignant when accusing another of extortion. A judgment of fraud against the *Post* for its Watergate reporting would, in our view, encourage humility and balance, and give the country much better reporting of its democratic issues and skirmishes.

It is of great historical note whether a president was removed from office by willfully practiced journalistic deceit. Watergate would take on an entirely different historical meaning, dramatically reversing the narrative of good and evil, white hat and black. Shades of gray that would include the media would again be introduced. The idea that all humans are by their very nature flawed, regardless of party or politics, might be a better way of brokering and assuaging modern society's arguments.

How in coming chapters can we determine the question of the *Post*'s willfulness in its Watergate reporting? Let us look at whether the *Post* reported the facts surrounding the burglary arrests as fully and accurately as it could have, knowing what its reporters *likely* knew. For instance, did the *Post* know the location of the open drawers and camera clamps while failing to inform the reader of these important facts? And did the *Post* know of the existence of the key held by Martinez and his struggle with Officer Shoffler to keep from him the key? Did the *Post* have reason to know of Mullen's cover contract? What about Hunt's planned CIA defense? If it learned of a possibility of such a defense, wouldn't a logical next step be for the paper to determine the facts on which such a defense would be based?

Indeed, is there any evidence that the *Post* reporting was distorted to give the reader the view that the CIA was most certainly *not* involved in Watergate? Another issue: did the *Post* reporters likely know of the prosecutors' plans to question Baldwin on his meretricious overhearings? What effect would that story have been on the public's view of this puzzling story? What about the prosecution's plans to prove Hunt's purported blackmail motive? Did the *Post* know of this intent and conceal it? If there was in fact a possible blackmail motive for the burglaries, shouldn't the *Post* have reported by whom, of whom, about what? Wouldn't this have a bearing upon our most important political scandal?

Wouldn't the foregoing have a bearing on whether Richard Nixon should have been removed from office? Democracies thrive on discussion and debate. Was our discussion and debate short-circuited by the failure of the *Post* to bring up these issues for debate in this very important scandal?

What did the *Post* learn about Pennington? Is there any proof of deliberate failure to write of his role as McCord's apparent handler? Wasn't his role secret, even within the CIA? Did the *Post* learn of Pennington's pickup of McCord at the jail, or could it have easily done so through its police contacts? What about his burning of documents at McCord's home?

We have gone over evidence pointing to McCord's undercover status. To paraphrase the words of Senator Howard Baker about President Nixon's guilt, shouldn't we ask: what did the *Post* know and when did it know it? One application of this inquiry is to ask whether and to what extent confounding facts were within the grasp of the paper during Watergate, but yet were never reported.

There is also another test of intent to defraud, often the key to proving intent in criminal trials. After the potentially criminal act has been committed, did the suspect acknowledge mistakes honestly, or did he lie or conceal evidence? Prosecutors' best method of proving criminal intent is by evidence of false exculpatory statements. People who are innocent normally don't lie about the events that occurred earlier. People who are guilty cover up. That was a truism that led to Nixon's demise. "The cover-up is worse than the crime" was a common refrain during Watergate. In accord, we ask: did the paper cover up?

Therefore, we should examine how the Pulitzer Prize-winning paper reacted when seemingly new evidence became clearly available. Did it conceal the evidence? Did it lie about what the nature and effect of the evidence was? In short, did it honestly admit overlooking a key fact, or did it make false exculpatory statements?

In the following chapters, we will examine whether the *Washington Post* covered up Watergate, and whether it did so more reprehensibly than its favorite target, President Richard M. Nixon. Did the *Post* profoundly affect our history through practiced deceit? Let us now examine that important question.

Image of Watergate burglar Bernard Barker's address book, public domain.

CHAPTER 22

BURGLARY INFO
GONE MISSING

THERE IS NO DOUBT ABOUT the intensity of the *Washington Post* reporting from the very outset of the burglary of the Watergate offices of the DNC. It was the *Post* that quickly announced the burglary, the arrests, and the possible ties to the White House and the president's reelection committee. The *Post* had two reporters immediately assigned to this story early that morning. Local crime reporter Bob Woodward was called to duty that Saturday morning, along with legendary jailhouse reporter Alfred Lewis, who knew the DC police well and had insider access. By the following Monday morning, the *Post* had assigned ten reporters to the case. It is undisputed that the nation's attention was immediately drawn to the burglary arrests as a result of the *Post* reporting, which quickly pointed out the White House and CRP employment of some team members, as well as the Bay of Pigs connections of all the burglars and one supervisor, Howard Hunt.

We also know that scandal did not explode for months, and that the public's initial take, while accepting the apparent involvement of CRP and White House employees, was *ho-hum, no big deal.* In short, the country would not have exploded in shock if a CIA connection or a noncampaign purpose would have been exposed at the outset. If that is so, what would it matter if the *Post* had reported more fully the intriguing facts we have here revealed about the burglary and its immediate aftermath? In fact, it would have mattered plenty. As the saying goes, "One never gets a second chance to make a first impression." But even if so, the first impressions of Watergate were not scandalous.

However true it may be that the country showed little excitement in the initial stages, when the scandal finally exploded, first impressions returned to focus, now magnified. The Deep Throat/Woodward garage collaboration of October 1972 was the key journalism that ignited the scandal, but that ignition was based in part on early impressions that the burglars were working for Nixon. This series of stories, especially the key October 10, 1972, story after the first Deep Throat garage meeting, relied heavily on the resurrected narrative that the burglary was seemingly a campaign-inspired event. Such was the soil that nurtured Deep Throat's hypothesis that the Segretti dirty tricks program, clearly a campaign initiative, was related to the spying and sabotage of Watergate.

To be sure, as we have explained, this Deep Throat "overall" was only a *hypothesis* proffered as a way to achieve expansion of the FBI's burglary investigation into other areas that may or may not be related. In so connecting this burglary to the campaign, the sensational reporting necessarily ignored the other evidence the FBI was then exploring of CIA involvement and its monitoring of meretricious conversations. In spite of Deep Throat's belief that White House involvement was likely limited to a couple of foolish young lieutenants (which it was), as a dedicated public servant he needed a full and fair investigation, on which he now felt stymied.

What we will call the "Deep Throat garage reporting" set the scandal and its journalism on its sensational path to the removal of a president, while this journalism won a Pulitzer Prize, best-selling books, an award-winning movie, and glory for all *Post* participants. Why would better initial reporting have changed any of that?

When the October reporting broke, the "spying and sabotage" narrative fit snugly with the initial journalism. But let's say that the initial burglary stories would have had the cumulative effect of casting doubt on a campaign intelligence target. If so, the October stories may not have provided the inference that the Oval Office ordered the burglary, even though it sponsored Segretti. In short, the initial burglary reporting was far more critical than appreciated at the time.

With this introduction, what can we say about the *Post* reporting on the burglary, the arrests, and the immediate aftermath? The *Post* reporting, including Woodstein's bestseller, *All the President's Men*, has proudly emphasized how much it and its reporters enjoyed the inside track on the arrests and the evidence seized at arrest. Both in the *Post*'s ongoing reporting, and Woodstein's book two years later, the reporters took pains to list in minute detail each item seized. For instance, one of the first reports of the burglary by the *Post* listed the following items seized in an article bylined with the name of Alfred E. Lewis, likely written by Woodward and Bernstein on oral report from Lewis. This first article describes what was found on the burglars:

> *All wearing rubber surgical gloves, the five suspects were captured inside a small office within the committee's headquarters suite.*
>
> *Police said the men had with them at least two sophisticated devices capable of picking up and*

transmitting all talk, including telephone conversa-
tions. In addition, police found lock-picks and door
jimmies, almost $2,300 in cash, most of it in $100
bills with the serial numbers in sequence.

The men also had with them one walkie-talkie, a
short-wave receiver that could pick up police calls,
40 rolls of unexposed film, two 35 millimeter cam-
eras and three pen-sized tear gas guns.[17]

In their book, at pages fifteen and sixteen, Woodward and
Bernstein also described those items taken from the burglars:

The five men arrested at 2:30 A.M. had been dressed
in business suits and had all worn Playtex rubber
surgical gloves. Police had seized a walkie-talkie,
40 rolls of unexposed film, two 35-millimeter cam-
eras, lock picks, pen-size tear-gas guns, and bug-
ging devices that apparently were capable of pick-
ing up both telephone and room conversations.[18]

Their book then quotes part of Lewis's oral report, verbatim,
albeit with the ellipses left out of the oral report:

"One of the men had $814, one $800, one $215,
one $234, one $230," Lewis had dictated. "Most of
it was in $100 bills, in sequence....They seemed to
know their way around; at least one of them must
have been familiar with the layout..."[19]

---

17 Alfred E. Lewis, "5 Held in Plot to Bug Democrats' Office Here," *Washington Post*, June 18,
    1972, A01.
18 Bernstein and Woodward, *All the President's Men*, 15–16.
19 Ibid., 16.

And the reporters go on to say Lewis also noted in his dictation, "One wore a suit bought at Raleigh's. Somebody got a look at the breast pocket."

Note in these quotes how Woodward and Bernstein inserted ellipses when relaying Lewis's report. Were there items of evidence listed by Lewis that they did not report? It seems likely at least *something* was left out in those ellipses. That, after all, is what ellipses are for.

In the book, the reporters proudly note their jailhouse reporters with inside access, the most prominent being Alfred Lewis, described by the reporters as "half cop, half reporter." Lewis, they boast, had immediate access to the evidence and its inventory. They also cite jailhouse reporter Eugene Bachinski, an inside-track reporter.

Let me quote from *Washington Post* editor Barry Sussman's book, *The Great Cover-Up*:

> *Also that Sunday, Larry Fox, our night city editor, told me that D.C. cops might let a Post reporter look over some of the burglars' possessions. They did, and E.J. Bachinski, a police reporter, found two address books with the name Howard Hunt in them, and the notation "WH" in one and "W. House" in the other. He also found a check for $6.36 from Hunt to a local country club. So it was that the Post, hardly 48 hours after the arrests—and through the work of its White House correspondent and a night police reporter—was able to tie the break-in to both the Nixon re-election campaign and the White House.[20]*

---

20   Barry Sussman, *The Great Cover-Up: Nixon and the Scandal of Watergate* (New York: Catapulter Books, 2010).

We know that the reporter Alfred E. Lewis had a special status among the police in Washington, DC, and that he was allowed in the DNC suite postarrest, while other reporters were not. Lewis clearly got a look at all the evidence, as indicative of his quotes. Wouldn't Lewis have seen, or perhaps held in his hand, the desk key? And Sussman tells us about Bachinski examining the items subsequently found in the burglars' hotel room. It appears that *Post* reporters had in their hands, or at least were able to personally view, all of the items seized in the arrests and in the immediate aftermath from the hotel rooms. In the most important criminal case in United States history, a *Post* reporter saw, and perhaps held in his hand, the most important piece of evidence in that case. But that piece of evidence was never reported, not in three thousand *Post* articles, not in Woodstein's bestseller, not in Sussman's lengthy book.

Okay, one might respond. The *Post* examined each piece of evidence, or at least Lewis and Bachinski had access to what was seized. So what? Well, you may have noticed that there was an item not mentioned in the above descriptions. Yes, it was the key. This key would be legitimately claimed, without hyperbole, to be the single most important piece of evidence in our country's history. Simply noting that the burglars possessed a key, a key that did not appear to be door key or a car key, but rather a desk, drawer, or cabinet key (obvious from its design) would have aroused in the public an obvious question in this curious drama: a key to what desk, what drawer, what cabinet? Wouldn't this key reflect the intended target?

Yes, this key, as we have discussed, would have eventually pointed to the burglary target, the desk of Maxie Wells. Yet, fifty years after the fact, very few people know of the key's existence, while the vast majority do not, including many erudite professors and historians.

Now, to be sure, the key was taped to the outside cover of a small pocket-sized notebook that had been in Martinez's suit coat breast pocket. Perhaps it was simply overlooked, and the item was listed simply in its entirety as a "notebook." But it appears the initial reports do not mention any notebook. In Woodstein's book, the authors mention that two notebooks were seized. I previously had thought that these two notebooks included the Martinez pocket notebook, but in reviewing Sussman's book, *The Great Cover-Up*, I note that these two notebooks were seized in the hotel rooms of the burglars the day after arrest. So, the only item which we know to have been seized but *not* mentioned in any *Post* report or book is the Martinez pocket notebook with a key attached, perhaps reattached after it was grabbed from Martinez. To be sure, camera clamps were not mentioned, but they could be considered to be attachments to the cameras described.

Therefore, while it may well be that one could understand why the key would not be separately mentioned, it is interesting that even the pocket notebook was not separately mentioned. Still and yet, all of us can imagine circumstances in which perhaps it was understandably negligent that the notebook was overlooked. After all, there were some items, like the camera clamps, that were not mentioned. We hasten to add the possibility that camera clamps were not mentioned precisely because they would point, like the key, to Maxie Wells' desk, since later evidence in the defamation trials established that the clamps had already been affixed. Perhaps we have not yet made our case that it was more likely than not that the *Post* intentionally failed to disclose the existence of the key. However, there was a dramatic event during the arrest that was also not reported, bearing directly upon the *Post*'s failure to report the key.

After the arresting officers told the burglars to assume a spread-eagle position, one of them, Eugenio Martinez, reached into his suit coat breast pocket to grab something. Arresting Officer Carl Shoffler yelled at Martinez, to no avail, and as Martinez persisted, Shoffler grabbed him while the burglar had an object his hand, trying to rid himself of it. Martinez was trying to rid himself of the key, separated from the notebook. Shoffler finally wrestled the key from the wiry Martinez, nicknamed, "Musculito" for his strong, compact build. Shoffler said later he almost broke Martinez's arm. He offered later to author Len Colodny that it was clear Martinez was ridding himself of the key because, "It would've identified the target" of the burglary. This dramatic encounter, including and involving an officer who was never shy about talking to the press, should have warranted a separate front-page story. But neither this incident nor the key was mentioned anytime, anywhere in the *Post* reporting or in two comprehensive books to follow, one by Woodward and Bernstein, one by Sussman.

We cannot say what Shoffler or his companion, Officer John Barrett, told the *Post* at the time but we have some indication that they spoke. How so? One of the *Post* articles noted that the police were able to observe "a suit bought at Raleigh's." As Lewis dictated, "Somebody got a look at the breast pocket."

Since it is not customary for arresting officers to examine clothing labels during an arrest, unless something is felt on pat-down, the observation likely came in a spontaneous way during the arrest. All burglars were wearing suit coats. Only one seller's tag was mentioned. It only makes sense it would have been that of Martinez and his suit coat, and that the observation would have been made during the struggle with Shoffler as Martinez was reaching into his suit coat pocket and pulling out, but not ridding himself of, the key.

We infer that Shoffler likely made the observation and was the source of the Raleigh's breast pocket mentioned in the article. Wouldn't he, common sense suggests, have told reporters how he came to see it? Did he simply tell Lewis he saw a Raleigh's label without mentioning the dramatic struggle of how he saw it? Such contravenes common sense. I have included a verbatim transcript of Shoffler's interview years later with Colodny in our book *Postgate*. This was a memorable, dramatic struggle between Shoffler and Martinez. As Shoffler told Colodny, Martinez was attempting to rid himself of the key because it "identified the target."

But there's more to support this common sense. Shoffler was known to be talkative and had given scoops to reporter Maxine Cheshire of the *Post*, a good friend, on numerous occasions. But even more indicative, it was Shoffler who himself "dimed"[21] the *Post* to alert it to the arrests because he said the suspects would not identify themselves.

The *Post* had Shoffler's name and presumably would know to call him or interview him at the station. And, of course, as we have noted before, Alfred Lewis and Eugene Bachinski, as jailhouse insiders, knew Shoffler and his colleagues well. It is difficult to believe that in the hubbub of the arrests, some *Post* reporter did not get wind of this dramatic struggle between Shoffler and Martinez. We note that Sussman has said he had ten reporters on the case that weekend. Yet, regarding the key and the dramatic struggle with Martinez, *Post* reporting was crickets, nada, nothing.

What else do we know about the *Post*'s access to facts about the arrests? We know that the *Post* became close with the head

---

21   The word "dime" refers to the old phrase of "dropping the dime" on a suspect, which means taking a dime and putting it in a pay phone to make a phone call, presumably to law enforcement. This was a phrase commonly used in 1972 and is still somewhat in use today.

of the FBI's street investigation, Special Agent Angelo Lano. Certainly, Lano had provided information that *Post* reporters later in the investigation misreported as Haldeman being an identified (in the grand jury) signatory to the slush fund, a dramatic event in the book and movie. Indeed, in *All the President's Men*, Woodward and Bernstein note their wealth of contacts with a wide swath of FBI agents. So even if one of these reporters did not learn of the Shoffler/Martinez wrestling match from police at the time of the arrest, this should have been an item clearly available to the reporters from the FBI in the days following the arrests. So, while we have no proof positive that the *Post* knew of the key and intentionally failed to report it, at least by a preponderance of the evidence, we must conclude that to be so.

As we noted in earlier chapters, on June 20, Woodward and Bernstein published a cryptic reference to the sixth person involved in the burglary. This June 20 reference must have involved information learned from the FBI or police on June 18 or 19, days immediately following the arrests. We note this reference only to suggest that these reporters had some access to investigators shortly after the arrests to obtain this information about the sixth burglar. Wouldn't those same investigators mention the curiosity of the key and the struggle for it?

We know that in the days following the arrest, the FBI tried the key on each desk in the DNC offices until it was found to open the desk of Maxie Wells. Common experience tells us that, with many desks, often only one drawer, the lower file-sized drawer, has a locking mechanism. So, it may well be that the key was for that one desk drawer. It appears that the FBI quickly determined to whom the desk drawer key was connected, as the Bureau interviewed both Maxie Wells and her incoming replacement, Barbara Kennedy Rhoden, on June 27, 1972. It was a Tuesday, about one work week after the weekend arrests.

In these interviews, the FBI inquired about who else would have been given a copy of the key, about which neither had any knowledge. As far as these two ladies knew, they had the only two copies that were in existence. These interviews are memorialized in three FBI reports of June 27, 1972. Not only should Woodward and Bernstein have known of these interviews through their FBI contacts, but also, the *Post* was very close with the DNC, which would have known well of this scenario. If the reporters did not learn of the key from the arrest interviews, they knew from the FBI that it was searching for who had the key. That the *Post* was tight with the DNC points to the paper's possible motive to conceal.

Post reporters also had connections with the local police, who knew of the key seizure. Moreover, one of its FBI contacts with which it inarguably had a strong connection was that of Woodward and the head of the investigation, Mark Felt. The key was obviously an important issue for the FBI, and yet there is no mention in the *Post* of the FBI's interest in the key or its interviews of Wells and Rhoden.

Is it possible that the *Post* did not know about any of this intense investigative activity? Yes, it is *possible*, but it is not *probable*. Remember, Deep Throat (Mark Felt) was speaking to Woodward starting shortly after the arrests, where he mentioned the address book referring to Howard Hunt, as Woodward explains in *All the President's Men*.

Throughout the Watergate investigation, the *Post* appeared to tailgate the FBI, following the FBI's leads and interviewing the same witnesses. This parallelism is documented by many observers, who have shrewdly noted that most of the *Post* interviews followed closely upon FBI interviews of these same witnesses, with very similar statements given.

Did Woodward and Bernstein, and the many other *Post* reporters on this case, fail to learn of the FBI's interviews of Wells and Rhoden and the intense search for the desk to which the key belonged? It is inconceivable that this would be so.

Now let us go to a subject we have brought up previously: the sixth burglar who might have been involved. Here's that brief blurb from Woodward and Bernstein on June 20, 1972, just days after the June 17 arrests. The article was titled, "Bug Suspects White House Tie Hinted." But in that article, here is a curious reference:

> *Police sources say they were still looking for a sixth person believed to have been involved in the incident.*[22]

Wouldn't it have been of great interest to *Post* readers to report how and why this person attracted interest? Clearly, whoever informed the reporters of this sixth person would have known, or they would have learned through follow-up interview, that this sixth person was not dressed like the other burglars, who were wearing suits. And with the *Post* reporters' close relationships with the arresting officers, they knew that no one else was in the DNC suite at the time of the arrests, and they also would have learned that this fellow strolled into the lobby from the staircase, obviously having been lurking somewhere in the building. Wouldn't most legitimate occupants, if any there would be at 2:30 in the morning, have used the elevator to access the lobby?

A participant not caught in the DNC offices, casually dressed, and using the stairway would reasonably raise—as one possible inference—that some entity may have been involved other than

---

22   Bernstein and Woodward, "Bug Suspects' White House Tie Hinted," *Washington Post*, June 20, 1972, A4.

the White House or CRP, perhaps for purposes other than that of the five arrested burglars. Why wouldn't this episode merit sensational headlines?

One other fact that the police and security officers knew, and the FBI likely knew as well, was the presence of tape on the eighth-floor locks, of no apparent utility to the sixth-floor burglars. So, perhaps a lurking individual on the eighth floor could, either known or unknown to the others, be connected to this operation. But if so, what would be his role? In any case, the *Post* did not report this taping, negligently or intentionally.

The reports did say that "two file drawers" were opened at the time of the arrests. The reader would not know at that point that the location of the drawers might be a critical fact, but the *Post* likely did and did not mention the location of these open drawers. If the drawers were revealed to be those of Maxie Wells, Spencer Oliver Jr., or the Association of State Democratic Chairmen, this would argue against a campaign dirty trick. The court of appeals opinion in *Wells v. Liddy* noted, "a drawer in Wells' desk was opened during the break-in." They were looking, it would seem to one with full knowledge of these facts, for something other than campaign information, which this peripheral group, the Association of State Democratic Chairmen, presumably would not have had.

While a drawer in Wells's desk may have been opened, we suggest that it may not have been the locked drawer. In any case, we note in Sussman's book a curious avoidance of mentioning the location of the camera equipment:

> As they entered the Democrats' offices, the GEMSTONE team immediately went to work. They began removing the ceiling tiles above

O'Brien's office and setting up camera equipment
to photograph more documents.[23]

Most reading this would think that the drawers were near or in O'Brien's office, where the burglars were about to photograph documents. So, it appears to us that when Sussman wrote this in 1974, after all the evidence was in, he was intentionally avoiding revealing the location of the equipment or the desk drawers. You will look in vain for such information in *Post* reporting or subsequent books by its editors and reporters.

Finally, we come to the issue of the camera clamps. There is a question as to whether some camera clamps had already been placed on a desk at the time of the arrest. Author Shane O'Sullivan suggested that they were not yet on the desk because in testimony in the trial of January 1973, Officer Barrett introduced a written log showing camera clamps in a gym bag after the arrest. But, notwithstanding this note, we can infer from other evidence that some clamps had been placed. The Sussman quote above speaks of "setting up camera equipment."

Buttressing Sussman's book, Martinez testified to the Ervin Committee that the group had already begun copying documents. Shoffler told Colodny that camera equipment was on the desk at the time of arrest. In any event, nothing was ever reported about the clamps having been placed at their location. If the location of the drawers was presented, perhaps the location of the clamps would have been redundant, or vice versa. But mentioning the clamps, even without their location, would have given the public an interesting implication that the main purpose of the burglary was not wiretapping but document copying. How many historically knowledgeable citizens know that today? Probably very few, especially since with Hunt's later plea and

---

23   Sussman, *The Great Cover-Up*, 7.

Judge Bazelon's appellate court ruling, there was no motive for the prosecution to do so, since its case was charging wiretapping, not document copying.

Another unreported fact was that Maxie Wells was about to leave her job as of her FBI interview of her and her replacement Barbara Kennedy Rhoden on June 27, to return home to Mississippi. Wasn't this resignation extremely sudden, or at least of coincidental timing? Was her abrupt departure related to what the DNC found in her desk drawer before the FBI got to it? If the *Post* knew that Wells was leaving her position almost immediately after a burglar was arrested with her desk key, wouldn't a report of this invite the logical reader to infer something negative, noninnocent about what was in her desk that these CIA-connected burglars wanted?

Our point here supplements the queries we have regarding the sixth person. Were the antennae of the DNC and its close ally, the *Washington Post*, already sensing early on that the double issues of prostitute referrals and CIA involvement were already in danger of discovery? Luckily for the DNC, only one paper was reporting in any depth on the scandal in those early days, and that paper was deeply compromised by its close relationship with the DNC and also by its admitted loathing of Richard Nixon.

Let us put aside the *Post*'s failures regarding the sixth burglar, the open drawer, the camera clamps, and focus on the most important failure: the key and the struggle for it. The failure of the *Post* to report the key or its location is perhaps the most significant mystery of Watergate journalism. We here propose a solution to that mystery: the *Post* concealed highly relevant facts *intentionally*. Those facts would have pointed us to its ally, the DNC, and away from its enemy, Richard Nixon.

Image of Howard Hunt testifying at the Ervin Committee Hearings, public domain.

CHAPTER 23

MULLEN'S COVERED-UP COVER CONTRACT

THROUGHOUT THIS BOOK, WE HAVE spoken about the status of PR firm Mullen and Company as an entity providing cover for covert CIA agents. Needless to say, an undercover agent must have a cover under which to work. Mullen provided that cover in Watergate by hiring Howard Hunt as a purported copywriter. As we note in an earlier chapter, the American public never learned from the *Washington Post* during Watergate of Mullen's status as a cover company, which, to be sure, was by its very nature intended to be kept under tight wraps. How important was it that the public learn of Mullen's potential covert role as a cover for a CIA agent who had infiltrated the White House?

The public learned soon after the arrests that both Hunt and McCord were ostensibly retired CIA agents, and that the Cubans had worked with them and the CIA during the abortive Bay of Pigs operation. It also knew that Hunt worked as a full-time copywriter for Mullen. Wouldn't adding Mullen's status as a cover contractor be only a trivial additional layer for public consumption? As a *Post* acolyte might argue, this is only a bit of new information. But, on the other hand, while it may have been but a small factual fillip, it could well have been a huge tipping point in society's view of the scandal. How so?

Let's say that it was revealed shortly after the arrests that Mullen, Hunt's employer, was a CIA cover company. Immediately, the possibility that Hunt may have been acting as an undercover CIA agent would have been ineluctable. And if he was so acting, one leading question to be asked, given five other Bay of Pigs veterans on the team, would have been, doesn't this look like a CIA undercover operation?

If this cover status were also known in the White House, Richard Nixon would immediately have latched onto it as an explanation of his private brooding thought: *I understand that someone could think I'm crooked, but how could they say I would be so stupid as to order this silly burglary?* The CIA's participation would show, in Nixon's view, that he was more a victim that a victimizer, and his inner circle was not the moving force behind the silly escapade.

With some credibility, Nixon could have portrayed Liddy, clearly part of his administration as a former White House aide and now CRP counsel, as a wild man who was swept up in Hunt's fatuous spy schemes, thinking he was promoting the public interest. So, yes, the simple fact of Mullen's cover contract would have been a huge advance on the story. It would have significantly shifted the focus of the Watergate story. The public examination of the CIA's role would have been ardently sought by a curious populace.

Was this a domestic CIA operation? Would this involvement affect parties other than Hunt, McCord, Mullen, and the CIA? Most certainly, because the CIA would not have been interested in campaign strategies. So, the Agency's indifference to Democratic strategies would tend to militate against a campaign

THE MYSTERIES OF WATERGATE

target, and thus against involvement of higher-ups in the White House. Another way of saying this is that Nixon would not go to great lengths to support a CIA operation of any kind, much less a fatuous one.

In addition to the burglars' presumptive CIA status, the focus of the burglary on the domains of Maxie Wells and Spencer Oliver Jr. would also have added a significant piece to the puzzle. The immediate story would have been what was so interesting to the CIA about the contents of the Maxie Wells desk.

It is not a leap too far to say that the entire emerging theme of the Watergate narrative would have been radically altered, from a bungled campaign operation to a bungled CIA intrusion on the Democrats. A corollary result of focus on the CIA would raise the interesting questions of what exactly the Democrats were doing that would interest the CIA. How many citizens today understand what in the DNC the CIA was examining?

Given that, with the *Washington Post* acting, as always, as the blood brother of the DNC, we can posit a motive for the *Post not* wanting to uncover the Mullen cover contract for fear of exposing Democratic secrets. But is it fair to the *Post* to assume its reporters could have uncovered or did uncover Mullen's cover contract that the *Post* subsequently hid what it knew? Put differently, we cannot fault the *Post* if the CIA successfully did what it is paid to do, that is, keep its covert operations covert.

What did the *Post* miss or misstate? We know that a Mullen-associated lawyer, Douglas Caddy, appeared at the arraignment, having hired, seemingly in the middle of the night, lawyer Joseph Rafferty to represent five defendants. So, the question immediately arose as to how it came to be that a Mullen lawyer was involved in the affair. The first *Post* story on him quoted Caddy's explanation that a year earlier, he had had a "sympathetic conversation" with the wife of one of the Cuban burglars, Bernard

Barker. She, a Miami resident, became worried that her husband had not called her late that night, as he promised to do, and, therefore, she called Caddy. Of course, the story was so much patent poppycock that it is difficult to believe that this tale would be critically accepted even by a junior-high newspaper.

After all, did Bernard Barker always call his wife early in the morning when he was out on assignment? Why would she assume he was arrested? How did Caddy learn that Barker was arrested if his wife did not? Why would she expect Caddy to get involved, giving that her husband had nothing ostensibly to do with Mullen or Caddy? And why would he then scramble in the middle of the night to seek counsel, paying Rafferty out of his own pocket? Because, we were asked by the *Post* to believe, the two somehow had a nice conversation a year earlier. The story strained credulity, yet the *Post* published it without a trace of skepticism. The story was quickly superseded, but we question why a major newspaper would publish it unless it was part of a program of conscious deception. Hasn't the *Post* reminded us for fifty years how fearless and indefatigable their reporters are at finding the truth?

Soon after the burglary, when Woodward with Deep Throat's help discovered Hunt's participation, the paper was forced to explain why, if a Mullen lawyer hired a criminal lawyer for the defendants at the request of a Mullen employee, that is, Hunt, who supervised the burglars, this burglary really had nothing to do with Mullen. But Woodstein simply quoted Robert Bennett as saying that Hunt and Caddy formerly shared an office at Mullen, became close personal friends and, therefore, Hunt called Caddy early that morning. Given Bennett's explanation, what is so irresponsible about this story?

Caddy was a young, stylish man, easily identified as part of the gay, urban demimonde. Hunt was a middle-aged, rumpled scuff-shoe Ivy Leaguer who enjoyed a country club lifestyle in suburban Maryland with his wife and four children. In short, they were not social friends. Moreover, Caddy was not anywhere close to being a criminal lawyer or even a litigator. Yes, it is possible that Hunt and Caddy had been professionally close. And it's possible that Hunt knew no other lawyers, in spite of working in the lawyer-infested DC area for years and belonging to a fashionable country club. But, on balance, and on the whole, this new story was also hard to swallow. The *Post* printed the story anyway, which seemed designed to take any spotlight off Mullen. The patina of credibility this explanation did have would have been lost if the public knew that Mullen was a cover company. If that fact were known, then Bennett himself would not be taken at face value in vouching for the odd friendship of the two. It is far more likely, as we say, that the relationship was professional, and Hunt called Caddy precisely because this was a Mullen operation for which it provided CIA cover, and Caddy would have access to Mullen/CIA cash to do what was needed.

It is this question that loomed large when prosecutors in open court, seeking to force Caddy to respond to certain questions before the grand jury, told the court that Caddy had said he had "intimations" that Mullen was connected to the CIA. This little item should have, with analysis and exploration, raised significant questions. After all, the burglary operation and arrests had Mullen written all over them, and Mullen's president, Robert Bennett, seemed compelled to enter the fray to explain away Mullen's participation.

Did the *Post* raise the obvious possibility that if Caddy's "intimations" were correct about Mullen's CIA connections, and six suspects of seven had CIA connections, ergo, Hunt ran the burglary as a CIA operation undercover? No. Instead, the *Post* quashed any such inquiry, again, using the ubiquitous quote machine, Bennett. "Caddy," Bennett was quoted by Woodward and Bernstein, "must have been referring to the work of Mullen for Radio Free Cuban in the 1960s."

Let's think about this one. Caddy spoke of his *present* intimations that Mullen had CIA connections. Was he really referring solely to a job, one publicly known, that Mullen did for the CIA many years earlier? After all, this was 1972 and the anti-Castro broadcasts had begun by order of President Eisenhower in March 1960, continued by President-Elect John Kennedy. But as of 1972, the CIA program had not been a hot project for years, nor had Mullen been recently involved, as Bennett implicitly acknowledges. Even with these articles, seemingly written to exculpate Mullen, it was still difficult for a curious reader to erase all questions about Mullen.

Of course, with Bennett now front and center, doing spin for Mullen, and with questions about Mullen's participation difficult to erase, the *Post* needed to explain not only Mullen, but also Bennett. It quickly did so, announcing in a headline story by Woodstein that Bennett was a Nixon campaign fundraiser. The story now seemed to explain Mullen's wide presence, that is, as a political crony and supporter of the president. The *Post* reported that Bennett put together "dummy" organizations through which he made for certain donors contributions to the Nixon campaign. In present parlance, Bennett appeared to have been a campaign donation "bundler," although that term was not used at the time. Financial and political ties to Nixon now were used by the *Post* to explain Mullen's ubiquity.

What's wrong with this story? Well, it's missing a key fact known to the *Post*: Bennett did not perform this fundraising function for a wide swath of Nixon donors, as is typical of a "fundraiser." Rather, Bennett did this for one big donor only. That one donor was one Howard Hughes, the reclusive billionaire, widely known throughout America. But the *Post* never disclosed Mullen or Bennett as connected to Hughes, especially in regard to fundraising. Why is this nondisclosure significant? Because by 1972, the strong association of Howard Hughes with the CIA was an open secret among the cognoscenti, especially those in Washington, DC. His longtime aide from 1955 to 1970 was Robert Maheu, who was simultaneously associated quite publicly and quite strongly with the CIA, mainly through Maheu's detective agency. Clearly, Hughes had strong, well-known, long-lasting CIA connections. In other words, if Bennett was a fundraiser, he was the bag man for Hughes, a major CIA asset. But the *Post* did not tell the public that.

Please recall in addition to being involved in funding anti-Castro operations after the dictator came to power, Hughes also helped the CIA raise the sunken Soviet ship, the *Glomar Explorer*, beginning in 1968, a project we hasten to point out which would not have been publicly known and perhaps not known to the *Post* in 1972. The listener might conclude that the foregoing is merely a weak circumstantial indictment of a paper that won a Pulitzer Prize for this very reporting.

This case would be much better if at least one set-in-stone marker of Mullen's CIA connection was shown beyond the circumstantial suggestions we have thus far been making. In response, we will provide one such marker. On June 21, 1972, in response to the astute query from the FBI as to whether Mullen was connected to the CIA, the Agency detailed the cover contract it had with Mullen. This meant that Mullen hired CIA agents, giving them ostensible cover as Mullen PR employees. This arrangement would certainly suggest that Howard Hunt was such an agent under Mullen cover as a copywriter.

Because of that sensitivity, it was difficult to believe that the top FBI brass would share this information with its street agents, or at least not all of them. So Woodstein could not reliably use their many special agent connections at the lower levels of the Bureau to ferret out this cover contract. But wait. Hasn't Woodward for fifty years ballyhooed his close, significant relationship with one Deep Throat?

Until the world discovered Deep Throat's identity in 2005, most speculated that this gold-plated source was a disillusioned, conscience-stricken White House official. But now that we know that Deep Throat was the FBI's number two, Mark Felt, in charge of the Watergate investigation, wouldn't it be obvious that Felt have been a ready source for Woodward of Mullen's cover status, which Felt clearly knew by June 21, 1972, if not earlier? In other words, because Woodward was so close to Mark Felt, wouldn't Woodward have learned early on that Mullen was a cover contractor?

Let us emphasize that Deep Throat would never steer the reporter wrong, as Woodward has avowed. So certainly if, after Caddy's "intimations" were publicized, Woodward asked Felt about Mullen's relationship to CIA, it is hard to believe that Felt would not have at least encouraged Woodward on that question, or simply confirmed Mullen's status. So, Woodward would have had Felt's confirmation if he asked for it, as Woodward made abundantly clear in *All the President's Men*.

Astute observers might quibble with our suggestion in two ways. First, the matter involved national security, and therefore perhaps Deep Throat would not have been as readily willing as he otherwise might be to convey that information. Secondly, such a tip would point to the FBI as a source, since the White House would not have had this memo from the CIA, but the FBI would have. Since Deep Throat was wary of pointing to the FBI, perhaps prudence would have dictated him keeping this information from Woodward. But, to answer this point, if Woodward had reported Mullen's connection, he would not have had to reveal that the ultimate source was the memo. The reported "source" could have been left vague, as anonymous sources often are.

In any case, both of the above objections are overcome by CIA documents reflecting inquiries to Mullen from *Time Magazine* reporter Sandy Smith, a close friend of Felt's, and a frequent recipient of his tips. Smith called Robert Mullen on February 21, 1973, and then visited the Mullen offices to talk to Mullen on February 22, 1973, asking whether there was in fact a cover contract. Mullen's report to the Agency on Smith's overtures led the CIA to conclude that someone in the Bureau had disclosed the essence of its memo, and perhaps read at least some of it to Smith. We know this from Agency documents produced years later through FOIA requests.

Clearly, the Agency concluded, after debriefing Mullen, Smith had been told by someone in the FBI of the Agency's disclosure, but, just as clearly, Smith had not been given a copy of the document and had not been told of everything in it. This wise restraint by Smith's FBI source had Felt's MO written all over it.

Mullen refused to confirm to Smith, and *Time Magazine* published nothing about the cover contract. So, both objections we raised are overcome by the Agency's own analysis. The Agency had concluded quite rationally that Smith had been told by someone in the FBI of the memo, because only the FBI, and at that, only its top officials, would have seen the memo from Mullen. The leaker, then, was not worried about the FBI being fingered. More significantly, we can point to Felt as a leaker because he is the only top official that survived Patrick Gray's earlier purge of officials suspected of leaking in the fall of 1972, in the wake of Woodstein's sensational "garage" reporting.

Felt had given several other key tips to Smith, a longtime friend, several right around the end of February 1973, when

Smith was making inquiries of Mullen. Is it reasonable to con-clude by circumstantial evidence that Woodward had the same information as Smith had, or would have had it if he sought it from Mark Felt? We think so. But, of course, it appears that Woodstein stayed far away from this issue, so much so that we can now conclude that there was an intentional suppression of this information by the purportedly dogged Woodstein, perhaps, we might conclude, on orders from their superiors. Put differ-ently, this was spectacular stuff, and headline-seeking reporters would have published stories about it if their superiors permit-ted. And if the reporters wanted to keep this confidential, and their editors did not, the paper would have published the stories. In short, we cannot blame Woodstein for this and many other suppressions of truth.

This imputed scenario is very close to being as ironclad as circumstantial knowledge can go. Woodward had a close contact who knew all about Mullen's cover contract in an ironclad way, a source that told Woodward he would never be untrue to him. But we have an even stronger piece of evidence.

This is a CIA memorandum from CIA case agent Eric Eisenstadt to the deputy director of plans for the CIA, summariz-ing reports to the Agency from Bennett. This memo of March 1, 1973, recounts a July 10, 1972, debriefing of Bennett, just twen-ty-three days after the arrests. In this report, Bennett is summa-rized as saying that he made a deal with Woodward, whereby in exchange Bennett's "feeding stories to Bob Woodward", the reporter "is suitably grateful…and protects Bennett (and the Mullen Company)."

Bennett later, after July 10, did source two very lame pieces for Woodward. But what items would Bennett have been referring to as having been sourced *before* July 10? Only the lame cover-up articles where Woodstein quotes Bennett, those we have already referenced, pointing to the White House and away from Mullen. So, the logical conclusion is that Woodward and the *Post* covered up Mullen's status, not to protect Mullen *per se*, but rather for its own purposes, that is, to protect the DNC. In other words, the *Post* was covering up the story for its own anti-Nixon purposes and for pro-DNC motives, and not for the benefit of the CIA.

As a former criminal prosecutor, I view the CIA memos of March 1, 1973, and the debriefing of July 10, 1972, as detailing a conspiracy of obstruction between Mullen and the *Washington Post*, where the *Post* agreed to keep Mullen's CIA connections under wraps. CIA documents also, quoting Bennett again, detail a "back door" approach to Joseph Califano's law firm, Williams, Connolly and Califano, which was handling the litigation brought by the DNC against the CRP. This approach to the law firm, by attorney Hobart Taylor, was admittedly to "kill off" any revelations about Mullen that might come up in the DNC/ CRP litigation. The firm could kill off such revelations arising from litigation, but only with certainty if the *Post*, its stepbrother, agreed as well.

This back door entry to the DNC law firm necessarily involved Joseph Califano, a partner in Williams, Connolly and Califano. Since Joseph Califano was also the *Post*'s general counsel, we can fairly conclude that the *Post* was a witting participant in the efforts to kill off any revelations about Mullen. Again, the primary motivation in the *Post*'s shielding of Mullen was likely to protect the DNC, not the CIA. Here is a question which the *Post* would not want answered: did the paper ever inform its readership that it was acting in conflict of interest in reporting about a scandal involving the DNC, with whom it shared a general counsel? Doesn't the *Post* constantly remind us how gosh darn ethical it is? All of this would prove a solid case of *Post* dishonesty if we let it rest here.

In a subsequent chapter, we will analyze what should have been an explosive report by the minority of the Watergate Committee, whose ranking member was the well-respected Senator Howard Baker of Tennessee. We will confine our remarks about this "Baker report" to its findings that Mullen was in fact a cover company for the CIA. But rather than report truthfully about the implications of what was objectively a stunning revelation, bearing directly on the question of whether the CIA was involved in Watergate, the *Post* did its level best to mute the effect of the Report, which, in preinternet days, most citizens could not access.

Here is a portion of the *Post's* "News Analysis" by Laurence Stern of July 3, 1974, detailing the key findings of the Baker report about Mullen's cover contract:

> *Among other things, the report describes how the CIA used a Washington public relations firm as a cover for agents operating abroad...*[24]

What this treatment did was deliberately bury the obvious conclusion that Mullen was providing cover for *domestic* agents like, say, Hunt. So, if we combine the *Post's* seeming suppression of the facts showing first, the Wells/Oliver burglary target with, secondly, suppression that the burglary supervisor was likely an undercover CIA agent, or at least working for a company that had a cover contract, then we can safely conclude that these two instances of fraud by concealment had a materially deceitful impact on an important American historical narrative.

The *Post* could not even bring itself to mention Mullen's name as the agency that had the cover contract, nor did it mention that Hunt had worked for Mullen while burglary supervisor.

---

24   Laurence Stern, "Few Conclusions Given by Baker on CIA, Watergate Tie," *Washington Post,* July 3, 1974, A10.

If these were the only instances of fraud that the *Post* committed, they would suffice to convict the paper of a substantial cover-up of Watergate. But as we will show, there is much, much more.

Image of President Richard Nixon, H. R. Haldeman, John Ehrlichman, and John Mitchell in Oval Office, public domain.

CHAPTER 24

COVERING UP THE CIA DEFENSE

WE HAVE WRITTEN SO FAR about various aspects of Watergate that never made their way into the public domain. One very important subject not broached at the time of the burglary trial was the possible status of Howard Hunt as a CIA agent. But if he was planning to present a CIA defense, and the *Post* discussed this issue, Watergate would have taken a dramatic turn in the eyes of the citizenry.

A key feature of our democratic system has traditionally been public trials, where absent some extremely rare circumstances, all the facts, testimony, and exhibits are available to the public. An important function of our press, encouraged by the First Amendment, is full reporting on trials where issues of public importance are aired. Certainly, Watergate was such a matter of public interest and education about the workings of the administration in power. When we examine the *Washington Post*'s Watergate reporting, there is no better measure of it than its reporting of the burglary trial proceedings. As noted earlier, the reporting should involve filed motions, in-court hearings (outside the jury's presence), and the trial itself. As noted, this journalism should include both pretrial and trial stages. So, if the *Post* learned of Howard Hunt's planned CIA defense during discovery proceedings, this would be a significant matter to report.

We have already discussed elements of this CIA defense in previous chapters. Part of the defense was that he was a falsely retired CIA agent, while, of course, working for Mullen undercover as a supposed copywriter. Also, we know that this defense was weakened when John Dean withheld the Hermès operational notebooks from the materials garnered from Hunt's White House safe. One of them would have shown him journaling his approvals, those into which he had inveigled from the White House. A notebook would also show his reports to CIA superiors, likely through his high-level CIA contact, Thomas Karamessines, with whom he had bimonthly tennis dates.

We cannot say for sure what Hunt's lawyer, William Bittman, told the *Post*, co-counsel, or prosecutors when he came up empty on this request for the notebooks Hunt had kept in his White House safe. Did Bittman complain to the prosecutors that this failure to produce these notebooks had hurt his defense? It makes logical sense that he would have. I do this for a living, and lawyers usually scream bloody murder when important evidence is not produced by the other side. Had Bittman told the *Post* or other *Post* sources about his need for the notebooks to buttress the CIA defense? It seems probable and likely, but we cannot say anything beyond that.

But let's fast-forward. Earl Silbert's confirmation hearings for his nomination to United States attorney for DC began in April of 1974. Silbert, an assistant U.S. attorney, and his trial assistant Seymour Glanzer, who were assigned the burglary trial, both testified that they were preparing in the fall of 1972 for Hunt's "CIA defense." Now, to be sure, both Silbert and Glanzer were careful always to refer to the defense as "spurious" or "phony," but there was no doubt but that these prosecutors knew with certainty of the planned defense by Hunt.

There was at the time no formal requirement that the defense give the prosecutors formal notice of this defense. If there were such a requirement, the planned defense surely would have been made public. But if the prosecutors knew of the defense to such a certainty that they spent considerable time preparing for it, they must have heard of the defense either directly or indirectly from Hunt's defense camp. Both Silbert and Glanzer confirmed that the likelihood of this defense was known. Wouldn't our supposed superhuman Watergate reporters at the *Post* have heard of this defense as well? In answering this question, we should be reminded that FBI agents were the prosecutors' investigators, and the CIA defense would require vigorous investigation. The reporters' FBI contacts, we confidently infer, surely knew of the defense.

Post reporters, as Woodstein admits in *All the President's Men,* had many close relationships with lower-level FBI agents who were on the ground as DC Watergate investigators. We suppose we need not remind the audience that *Post* reporter Bob Woodward had a very close relationship with the head of the investigation, who had access to *all* information, Mark Felt. So, we ask, if the prosecution knew of the defense, if the FBI agents who were helping the prosecutors knew of the defense, is it likely that the many *Post* reporters, with all of their sources, had never heard of the defense? In any case, Silbert's confirmation hearing testimony in April and May 1974 cements this issue.

Let's assume that the *Washington Post* was innocently ignorant of this defense in the fall of 1972. And let's assume that the *Post* was not trying to hide the defense from the public. If so, when Silbert made his dramatic testimony about the CIA defense, shouldn't the *Post* have shouted this from the rafters? Wouldn't this have been a sensational story? *Hunt had been planning a CIA defense*, the headline should have said. But oddly the *Post* wrote nothing about this key public revelation of Silbert.

This was the first time that in a public record the CIA defense was bruited about. And, even at that, the public was not getting regular *Post* reports of Silbert's testimony. The *Post* was likewise silent when the ostensibly retired James McCord testified before the Ervin Committee early that summer, beginning May 24, 1973, explaining how his lawyer, Gerald Alch, was approached by Hunt's lawyer, Bittman, to corroborate this defense. McCord's testimony was in turn confirmed by his lawyer Gerald Alch. While the *New York Times* published a transcript of this testimony, without comment, along with the entirety of McCord's statements, the *Post* stayed far away, publishing neither the testimony nor a comment on McCord's stunning revelation. To be sure, McCord adamantly denied in this testimony that the CIA was involved in Watergate and blasted the substance of the CIA defense proposed by Hunt. But reporting this denial would have raised questions since, after all, it confirms that Hunt was contemplating this defense.

To be sure, Hunt would not have proposed such a defense if it did not reflect reality or at least approach reality. In undercover work, skillful efforts are made to make it appear that the agent is not working for the intelligence agency actually employing him. Hunt likely had no idea that the CIA had given the FBI early on, that is, on June 21, 1972, a memo admitting a cover relationship with Mullen. Ironically, per the past chapters, had the *Post* published the existence of this document, which it knew about, but which it did not publish, Hunt would have known to seek it in his discovery from the prosecutors. Such a document would have helped immeasurably in his defense. Certainly, the government could not have denied the cover relationship with impunity. The

Post's cover-up of the Mullen cover contract, admitted in a CIA memo, thus helped its subsequent cover-up of Hunt's potential CIA defense. In addition to depriving Hunt of information that would have assisted his defense, the *Post* also withheld information that would have helped Richard Nixon understand the episode, including the treachery of an intelligence agency that is supposed to truthfully report to the commander in chief.

We should ask whether Hunt or his attorney, Bittman, ever revealed their reason for seeking the two Hermès notebooks in discovery, which would have broached the CIA defense planned. Bittman did put up a stink to the prosecutors in early December when they did not produce the notebooks in response to Bittman's discovery requests. Did *Post* reporters, ostensibly all over the case, know of Bittman's disappointment and further discussions with the prosecutors about the missing notebooks? We can only say, from this remove, that an alert reporter could have learned of this, one with his ear to the ground of courthouse gossip. There is, in our view, a high degree of likelihood that a *Post* reporter did learn this by December 1972.

But for our present purposes, this question is not momentous because the *Post* did learn of this nonproduction by early March 1973, as revealed by a March 3, 1973, article by Woodstein about the missing notebooks. Bittman was likely a progenitor of the article because his client was then being evaluated for sentencing by the Probation Department, where extenuating and mitigating circumstances are material, in this case apparent foul play by the government in withholding crucial defense information. Bittman is in fact quoted in the article, which revealed Hunt's requests for the notebooks and the failure of the prosecution to produce. Bittman is portrayed in the article as wanting the notebooks because they would support his claim of an "illegal search" of Hunt's safe, and this was certainly one of his purposes.

The theory of the illegal search was that the notebooks, with recent entries, would have shown continued occupancy by Hunt of his assigned White House office, and thus an expectation of privacy, a basis for a Fourth Amendment illegal search claim, which would not have existed had he abandoned the office. Clearly, the *Post*'s major purpose in publishing this article was to use the missing notebooks to suggest that they would have revealed administration "topsiders" who had authorized the operation. In other words, the *Post* printed the story in a way to suggest Oval Office guilt. And in doing so, did the reporters conceal the proposed CIA defense? This seems highly likely. Moreover, the paper concealed the significance of the notebooks, one of which was an operational diary used only when a CIA agent is actively engaged in operations.

A successful challenge to the searches of Hunt's office, after all, would likely not have allowed Hunt to walk free. The government could prove Hunt's participation in the burglary seven ways to Sunday without any of the safe's contents. In other words, a ruling that the search was illegal would not have prohibited most of the evidence against Hunt, and thus would not have resulted in a successful defense. The burglars possessed a country club check of Hunt's in the amount of $6.36. His address and phone numbers were in their address book, and Baldwin could finger Hunt as running the operation on site. It is therefore a realistic inference to say that a freely cooperative Bittman, speaking of his defenses to the reporters, would, yes, have mentioned the illegal search defense, but would likely have mentioned much more harmful effect of the missing notebooks as harming the CIA defense, which would be based upon Hunt's claim of being an undercover CIA operative, and which would have, if believed by the jury, resulted in his full acquittal.

Do we have any other evidence that Bittman would have told the *Post* of this defense? We do. The first tranche of Oval Office tapes were produced in late October 1973. On them, Dean discusses with Ehrlichman having withheld the notebooks from Hunt's safe. Because Dean realized that the court would soon in early November 1973, learn of his withholding of the notebooks, he quickly "remembered" that he had sequestered them and later destroyed them. His lawyers then duly informed the court of same. What would Hunt's lawyer tell the *Post* about Dean's confession?

To be sure, there has been no suggestion that Dean actually showed the notebooks to Ehrlichman, since they would have nailed Dean—the true reason Dean withheld them. Dean likely had let Ehrlichman know that the notebooks implicated Ehrlichman in the Fielding burglary, such that Dean was supposedly protecting Ehrlichman by withholding the notebooks. Up to this point in November 1973, Dean had denied knowing anything about Hunt's claim of missing notebooks. In December 1972, he denied to the prosecutors ever seeing them, claiming he had no idea what a Hermès notebook was. After ostensibly coming clean to the prosecutors for many months before November 1973, he still had concealed his concealment of the notebooks.

It certainly comports with common sense, in summary, that the paper's eager reporters would have heard of the CIA defense, but never wrote about it, corroborated by their failure to report this defense when Earl Silbert later affirmed that the CIA defense had been forthcoming. This failure is redoubled by the absence of reporting on the true importance of the missing Hermès notebooks when the subject arose in March 1973. In the next chapter we will analyze whether the *Post* aided and abetted in concealing the implications of Dean's admitted concealment of evidence. Was "Watergate's paper of record" guilty of a cover-up far more significant than Nixon's?

Image of Judge John Sirica, public domain.

CHAPTER 25

BLACKING OUT BLACKMAIL

IN THIS CHAPTER, WE WILL be continuing our analysis of the CIA defense explored by Watergate burglary supervisor Howard Hunt, who was simultaneously working part-time at the White House and full-time for the CIA cover company, Mullen and Company. We will also be looking at the national security defense offered after trial by two of the four Cuban Watergate burglars, Eugenio Martinez and Virgilio Gonzalez, who believed they were working on a legitimate CIA mission when breaking into the Watergate building, but who also understood that they were required to plead guilty as part of their CIA work. We discussed the involvement of the Cuban burglars in Chapters 17 and 18. We will as well be digging into the wrangling over the admissibility of evidence before Judge Sirica. With that prologue, let us discuss Blacking Out Blackmail.

With the production of the first set of Oval Office tapes in late 1973, Dean was forced to admit having kept Howard Hunt's operational notebooks, which Dean pulled out of Hunt's White House safe, and not giving them to the FBI but instead destroying them later. His defense for not telling the prosecutors about this destruction after he turned prosecution witness: he forgot.

The *Post* overlooked this incredible claim, failing to ask what Dean was hiding. In any case, he fessed up to Sirica to sequestering the notebooks, as he had to, given his admission on the White House tapes. Of course, he portrayed the sequestering as protecting his bosses.

Interestingly, the *Post* editors assigned this November 1973 story to reporter Timothy Robinson, rather than Woodstein, who had written the deceptive March 1973 story. Please recall that in the March 3, 1973, article, Woodstein depicted Hunt's wish for the notebooks to support his defense of illegal search, ignoring his intent to prove his CIA defense. In this story, Robinson paraphrases Hunt as having wanted the notebooks in order to support his defense that "he thought the Watergate operation was legal because it had been approved by high government officials." This certainly is a different motive than proof of an illegal search. But the article did not explain how such approval would be a defense. This approval, of course, as we have explained in earlier chapters, would have been a defense only if the operation was a national security operation with presidential approval. So, what is missing from Robinson's rendition is the idea of national security. National security, in turn, would lead one to look at the CIA.

Of course, the CIA defense had been referenced by McCord in his testimony of May 1973, about the approach he rejected from Hunt's lawyer to corroborate it. Interestingly, while McCord had rejected the CIA defense angrily, saying that the CIA was not involved, he had told both the *Post* in March of 1973, and later the Senate, that he thought that this was a legitimate national security operation approved by the attorney general. He simply did not admit that the CIA was involved.

While we don't know what Robinson asked Hunt or Bittman in November 1973, a reporter with the slightest curiosity would have asked how such high-level approval was a defense, and in any case was likely told that by Bittman. Certainly, there was no reason in November 1973 that Bittman would have held back to Robinson, and he apparently did not do so as to the idea of high-level approval. This would seem to buttress the notion that in March 1973, he would have told Woodstein the same thing. That is to say that the notebooks would have buttressed Hunt's defense of high-level presidential approval for a national security operation.

We can thus infer, from the limited exposé of Robinson in November 1973, that that same information was available to Woodstein in March of 1973, but that it was not published. In the same November 6, 1973, article, Robinson notes that Gonzalez and Martinez wished to be "allowed to withdraw their pleas because they thought the break-in was a legitimate government intelligence operation." What Robinson did not hook up in the article was that the two Cubans considered the destroyed note-books—of the man they thought their CIA leader—to be evidence of this legitimate intelligence operation. Wouldn't this connection have helped the reader?

So, in talking about Gonzalez's and Martinez's defense, Robinson conceals, or at least omits, the connection of their resurrected defenses to the notebooks and to high-level presidential approval. And in talking about Hunt's defense, he omits the assertion of the national security intelligence operation about which Gonzalez said Martinez are complaining. Of course, had Robinson done so, he would have given the reader a clue as to why Hunt thought high-level official approval would be a defense. Without this connection, many readers would view this defense of Hunt as a curious stretch, a weak, desperate claim. So what, an intelligent reader may have asked, if there was presidential approval? Viewing this article from the vantage point of this book, this rendition of Hunt's defense is obvious, but it was not then, and that was because the *Post* refused to make the connection, and did not explain the defense, not obvious to a normal reader.

Martinez and Gonzalez had said publicly, long before November 1973, that they thought they were on a CIA mission. This claim was widely explained, especially by the *Post*, as being a result of Hunt's deceit of the Cubans. We note that Robinson here refrained in his November 6, 1973, article from naming the Agency as part of the Cubans' defense. So, while we give credit to Robinson for writing a piece more helpful than the earlier Woodstein article, we cannot help but discern a reluctance by the *Post* to suggest the obvious: Hunt, Martinez, and Gonzalez considered that Watergate was a legitimate CIA operation. Yes, the article's headline that "Dean admits to destroying evidence" is instructive, but it is not as important as the *implications* of that destruction.

With Hunt's plea and the *Post*'s covering up of the CIA defense, did that quash all hopes that the public trial would reveal CIA participation? And, of course, its corollary, the targeting of escort referral conversations? No, it did not.

As we noted above, the prosecution had long been preparing for Hunt's CIA defense, which apparently escaped all reporting by the supposedly vigilant *Post*. Perhaps to counter this defense, but certainly to explain motive, the prosecutors were preparing a case which co-opted much evidence that Hunt would likely have offered. But whether Hunt or the prosecution would get the better of this dispute, both CIA participation and the overhearing of naughty girls and boys would have come to the fore in the trial, along with the sensational claim that the burglary was in part a CIA operation.

When an experienced litigator, in preparation for trial, runs across clearly provable facts which seem inconsistent with his originally planned case, he is wise to incorporate such provable facts into his own narrative. This would be the situation facing the prosecutors as they prepared to counter Hunt's defense. Hunt was planning to show a CIA defense, in part by pointing to the Mullen CIA cover contract.

The prosecution, of course, knew that Mullen had a cover contract. It also knew that the burglars were tapping the phone of Spencer Oliver Jr. and they also knew that the fruits of the calls were embarrassing sexual assignations. These embarrassing sexual assignations were testified to at length by both Silbert and Glanzer in Silbert's confirmation hearings in the spring of 1974. So, there is no doubt but that the overhearings were primarily sexual and salacious. The prosecution, putting these elements together in a competent but perhaps imperfect way, seized upon a strangely coincidental fact. Spencer Oliver Sr. was in competition with Hunt for future control of the CIA's lucrative cover contract with Mullen.

Senior himself was apparently hooked up with the CIA and had unsuccessfully sought to bring Oliver Jr. into Mullen employment, successfully fought by Hunt. So, the prosecution was planning to portray Hunt as seeking sexual dirt on Oliver Jr. as part of his campaign against Oliver Sr. for future control of Mullen. In short, the prosecution theory was that Hunt was seeking blackmail dirt on Oliver Sr. Accordingly, the prosecution planned on arguing a blackmail motive for Hunt, using provable elements of Hunt's defense to preempt his claims, as experience litigators do.

This prosecution narrative, when sensationally revealed to the public at trial, would have disclosed all of the elements we accused the *Post* of covering up—Hunt's CIA connections through Mullen, his CIA-based motives to burglarize and eavesdrop, and the salacious nature of the overhearings. Had Hunt been pursuing his CIA defense at trial, these same elements would have been in play, but with legitimate intelligence motives as a basis, not blackmail. In short, Hunt and the prosecution would be using the same facts, arguing them to different ends.

Let's focus for a moment on the term "blackmail." Had it been publicized that "blackmail" was a possible motive, the first question which would arise in public discourse would have been, what was the compromising material sought? Campaign information would not be compromising blackmail information. In short, the term "blackmail" would have led to call girl talk and the CIA, and certainly the evidence in support of that theory would have loudly spoken to those issues.

In spite of the sensational effect of *Post* reporting in the fall of 1972 to portray the burglary as part of the campaign of spying and sabotage in support of an election campaign, all of that would have flown out the window with the case that the prosecution was intending to put in evidence. The prosecution was tight-lipped and did not seek pretrial publicity about its blackmail theme. So, we do not contend that the *Post* could have learned of this plan from the prosecutor's office. But local FBI agents would have helped prepare the prosecutor's case and would have been able to inform the *Post* reporters with whom many were very close. So, as we have noted above, the CIA defense was well known, and at least to reporters familiar with FBI investigators, the blackmail counter to the CIA defense also should have been easily discoverable.

In determining whether the *Post* knew at some point of the prosecutor's blackmail theme, let's first note that in the summer of 1972, the *Post*, the DNC, and a Mullen lawyer, Hobart Taylor, all met to discuss plans to keep Mullen and the CIA out of the public eye. By this time the FBI had determined that the key fit

Maxie Wells's desk and that Maxie Wells had quickly resigned. It is likely that all involved knew what had been in the desk.

We also refer back to an earlier chapter wherein DNC outside lawyer Charles O. Morgan asked for a luncheon with Silbert and Glanzer in December 1972. This invitation, we infer, was not casual. The DNC had already known that the prosecution planned to have Baldwin testify to lurid overhearings, one purpose of the lunch to obtain such confirmation. This is an obvious conclusion, not only from the lunch invitation, but also the Democrats had an inside line to Baldwin's lawyers, and Baldwin was being questioned at length by the prosecution. So, the DNC would know what the prosecution was up to, and we know that the law firm had completed its noninterview with Baldwin in late August 1973. The young lawyer interacting with Baldwin's team, Alan Galbraith of Williams, Connolly and Califano, prepared a lengthy memo about Baldwin's expected testimony. He gave it to his senior partner Edward Bennett Williams on August 31, 1972, whereupon Williams instructed him to share it with the *Post*. In any case, with Cassidento and Califano tight, the girlie evidence was clearly known to the DNC as well as Califano's client the *Post*. Thus, the hiring of Charles Morgan to try to stop the planned testimony about it.

It is also possible that even before the luncheon, in addition to knowing about the naughty talk evidence, the Democrats knew of the blackmail theme, which Morgan skillfully drew out of Silbert's mouth when they spoke. Did Morgan know of the blackmail theme before the lunch? We think that is likely. But whether the Democrats knew this before, they certainly knew it *at* the lunch, and prepared to have Morgan try his "desperation pass play," seeking to quash such testimony at trial.

In any case, given the *Post*'s relationship with the Democrats, it is likely that the paper knew of the blackmail theme (at least by

December when Morgan had lunch with Silbert and Glanzer), knew of the girlie overhearings far earlier, and knew of Morgan's plans. It also knew that the Democrats deeply wished, as shown by Morgan's hiring, to keep it all hidden. In short, it is logical to infer that the *Post* sought to protect its political sibling, the DNC, and had the motive to hide the girlie talk from the public. Hiding this talk would also involve hiding participation of the CIA, since the CIA was not interested in campaign strategies.

With Hunt's plea, the chance of the public's learning of the CIA defense at trial was gone by the beginning of the January. But the dangers posed by the prosecution's case still loomed. Given its close relationship with the DNC which had hired Morgan, the *Post* probably knew of plans of the prosecutors to involve the CIA and call girls in its case. We do not have proof positive that the *Post* knew of the "blackmail" theme so stated, which is why Morgan's planned motion was so important, that is, to quash Baldwin's testimony about what he overheard, central to the blackmail theme.

On January 5, 1973, in open court, Morgan and Sirica had a memorable exchange. Morgan told the court that the prosecution intended to show "the motive in this case was blackmail, not politics." Sirica then asked, "you say the motive the government expects to show is blackmail?" Morgan answered, "yes."

Sirica, taken aback, said, "that is the first time I heard that." As Morgan quipped in his book, "actually it was the second time in 10 minutes he had heard that" since Gerald Alch, James McCord's attorney, had just said hypothetically the government might do just that.

Our point here is that this colloquy should have yielded a stunning headline in the *Post*. The public then and now, approximately fifty years later, is still scratching its collective head over the motives for this senseless burglary. Yet here two defense law-yers spelled out the prosecution's putative motive in open court.

To be sure, Morgan argued that the overhearings were for a "political use rather than a blackmail use." But this argument in open court should have alerted the public that the prosecution, usually given credibility by the public, was going to prove that the surveillance was for blackmail. But the *Post* did not cover this highly significant argument, and the important word, "black-mail," was never printed on *Post* pages. Indeed, the argument about this evidence was not even summarized in the *Post*. A cov-er-up of the prosecution's blackmail theme? It sure looks like it.

After these arguments, Sirica allowed the prosecution to examine Baldwin as to a general characterization of the over-hearings, that is to say, as intimate, salacious and highly embar-rassing. But Sirica also allowed Morgan to take an emergency appeal. One week later, Morgan, in open court before the appel-late panel, repeated Silbert's luncheon claim, "Hunt was trying to blackmail Spencer and I'm going to prove it!" The prosecution did not object to this characterization, apparently corroborated by Morgan's clever reference to his associate, Hope Eastman, who was in court sitting next to Morgan, as a corroborator of the statement.

Appellate Judge David Bazelon, likely not understanding the full case that the tight-lipped Silbert was to present, wondered aloud why anyone would wish to blackmail Spencer Oliver Jr., a man of presumed modest means. So Bazelon himself discussed blackmail in open court. Bazelon's panel then reversed Sirica and quashed Baldwin's testimony characterizing the salacious conversations monitored. But it is of great significance that the *Post* published not a word of the blackmail theme nor, of course, of the intimate nature of the conversations overheard, also dis-cussed in general terms in open court.

Why is it that after fifty years of speculation as to motive, mostly about the red herrings put forth by the *Post*, we are talking about "blackmail" now, and that it is a novel discussion? It is because this potential prosecution theme was covered up by Watergate's paper of record, and this in one of our country's most important trials. We ask our readers: have you ever before heard of the blackmail theme that was proposed by the prosecution in this case?

Even if we hypothesize that the *Post* innocently missed Hunt's CIA defense and the blackmail prosecution theme at or before trial, these issues were explored indulgently at Silbert's confirmation hearing in the spring of 1974. The *Post* published nothing of these key points in Silbert's testimony.

Covering up Silbert's testimony at this stage of the scandal was easily accomplished because the *Washington Post* was filling its paper daily with an avalanche of Watergate stories and other scandalous bits used to sink Nixon. The *Post* now hyped not just Watergate, but the Fielding burglary, milk lobby contributions in exchange for price supports, and the alleged ITT antitrust fix. The *Post* as well exposed shady Nixon administration dealings with one Robert Vesco, and other bits too numerous to mention. So, it was very effective for the *Post* to point to shiny objects outside Silbert's bailiwick.

What is it about these Silbert hearings that should have excited notice in the *Post*, in turn revealing sensational previously unreported stories? First, there was abundant inquiry into the potentially embarrassing, sexually charged phone calls overheard. Notably, there were also in connection with the sexual talk extended discussions of blackmail as a planned motive in the burglary trial. And a great amount of the questioning revolved around what Silbert and his assistant, Seymour Glanzer called the "spurious" or "phony" CIA defense Hunt was planning.

To quote all of the colloquy in these hearings about sex, black-mail, and the CIA defense would require a several chapters. Let us quote just a few examples to show that there was plenty from which the *Post* could have written sensational stories, informing the public what it had omitted previously. Recall that these hearings occurred when Nixon was still hanging on by a thread and was desperately looking for a way to shine the light away from him and his White House. Polls showed that 42 percent of the public around this time believed Nixon ordered, or at least was aware of, the burglaries before they happened, of course untrue.

If the public knew that the material sought in the Watergate burglaries was not campaign information, but sex talk, and that the CIA or Mullen were somehow involved, Nixon's fate may have been avoided. He may have looked to some degree like a victim, even if, to be sure, he covered up exploration of the involvement of his underlings. Let us quote from a few excerpts from the hearings of April and May 1974, about Silbert's trial plans in November and December 1972, and ask you if any of this should have resulted in an article.

> SENATOR HART: *You indicated that he became concerned that a spurious defense based on CIA sponsorship might be raised, and, again, you contacted the CIA. What was your inquiry of them at that time?*
>
> MR. SILBERT: *Well, Senator, as I indicated in the report, we were trying to anticipate at the trial which way the defendants might go. It was Mr. Glanzer's thought, one of my colleague's thoughts, that one of the defenses they might raise would be, as you indicated, the spurious CIA defense.*

Later, Silbert talked about his investigation in the fall of 1972 as to what motivated this burglary.

> MR. SILBERT: We were never able to determine the precise motivation for the burglary and wire-tapping, particularly on the telephone of a comparative unknown, Spencer Oliver. Baldwin had told us that McCord wanted all telephone calls recorded, including personal calls. There were many of them being extremely personal, intimate and potentially embarrassing.

Then Silbert testified:

> MR. SILBERT: Now with respect to the blackmail, possible blackmail, Baldwin told us McCord was interested in having him listen to all of the conversations on the wiretaps, not only those relating to political intelligence, but those related to personal matters. And a number of those conversations were personal, and for that matter, why would he want that kind of information? And a logical inference that we drew, Senator, was that there might be some attempt to compromise, blackmail, compromise either the participants in those conversations and that is why we suggested that not as the motive, but as one of the possible variety of motives, that might have impelled the conduct of these defendants, particularly Hunt and Liddy.

Now there was plenty more about sex, blackmail, and the CIA defense, but it suffices to say that these hearings went on for several days on these matters.

Let's assume against all evidence that the *Post* innocently missed these matters even during the Silbert hearings. It certainly refused to take notice of them when we published *Postgate* in November 2019. Its silence on damning, strongly documented allegations speaks volumes about the *Post*'s guilty mind. We have already seen the *Post*'s guilty, overheated negative reaction to the first *Wells v. Liddy* verdict, a reaction which the *Post* knows in hindsight was not a good way to proceed if it wished to hide its faulty reporting. Deplatforming is far more effective than histrionic rhetoric, which draws attention.

Democracy Dies in Darkness, the *Post* states proudly every day on its masthead. Its reporting on the CIA defense and the blackmail theme, or we should say its *nonreporting*, bear the earmarks of deliberate concealment and suppression, seeking not to inform the public, but to deceive it.

Image of James McCord at the time of the burglary arrest, public domain.

CHAPTER 26

MISREPRESENTING MCCORD'S MISCONDUCT

JAMES MCCORD SHOULD HAVE BEEN, from the outset, a truly engrossing character, even if he himself did not have a personally engaging manner. The characteristically tight-lipped, supposedly retired CIA veteran stayed far under the public's radar before his dramatic letter to Judge Sirica, read aloud by the court at his sentencing hearing on March 23, 1973. What should have previously interested the media, led by the *Washington Post*, in McCord? Woodward answers this question partially when he tells us in *All the President's Men* that he audibly gasped when McCord, after telling the court at his June 17, 1972, arraignment that he was retired from the government, then softly whispered to the court, almost as if in confidence, "C-I-A."

Now let's fast-forward to McCord's public statements following his written March 1973 rant to Judge Sirica. He soon explained to the *Post* that he thought the Watergate operation was legal, as a presidentially approved national security mission. He told the *Post* that John Mitchell, then Attorney General, had approved it. McCord did not say that this was a *CIA* national security operation, but, again, let's think about this. We have six former CIA operatives employed on a national security operation, at least as posited by McCord. Wouldn't it also make sense it was likely a *CIA* national security operation?

Wouldn't a veteran CIA man have asked what about this operation made it a seeming national security operation? Of course, he would have, for otherwise he would be engaged as a common burglar. And if, as McCord testified later, he was to tap DNC Director Larry O'Brien's phone and another undescribed Democrat at the team's discretion, exactly how did this seem to be about national security?

One piece of evidence that the *Post* should have considered and reported is the statement of MPD Intelligence Officer Garey Bittenbender, who questioned McCord at the jailhouse before arraignment, later questioning him further in his jail cell. McCord told Bittenbender, according to Bittenbender, that he, McCord, had been on a CIA mission. This is consistent with McCord's whispered response to the court, believing, as Hunt later wrote in his book, in the CIA's normal assistance of extricating its blown agents from prosecution. It is also consistent with McCord's otherwise head-scratching claim that he understood this to have been a national security operation.

Since McCord likely thought at the time that this would be claimed to be a legal CIA operation, not having talked to the Agency after his arrest, his statement to Bittenbender would have corroborated his defense of lack of criminal intent, that is, his statement to Bittenbender that this was a CIA operation. It was not at the time an admission against McCord's interests, but rather a statement to corroborate McCord's defense of a national security operation. Now, of course, as we have noted, the CIA chose not to go that route.

After McCord testified to the Senate about the existence of Bittenbender's statement, the paper felt compelled to add its two cents so as to negate the force of a clear statement by an intelligence officer, one provided to the defense, including McCord's lawyer Gerald Alch. So, Bittenbender's statement was clearly one provided to McCord by Alch within the discovery process. How would the *Post* support McCord's claim that Bittenbender must have been mistaken? All it ever said about this devastating statement by Bittenbender was this brief blurb of May 23, 1973, placed on page twelve:

> *McCord testified that Alch mentioned during the December 21 lunch that Metropolitan Police Intelligence Officer, Garey Bittenbender, had 'purportedly claimed' that McCord told him the break-in was a CIA operation. Inspector Albert Ferguson, Chief of Intelligence for the Metropolitan Police said yesterday that Bittenbender's notes indicate only that he knew McCord was a former CIA agent, not that he had been told the break-in was a CIA operation.*[25]

You will glean from this article that neither Captain Ferguson nor the *Post* dispute that Bittenbender provided the interview report we here describe, but only that Ferguson claimed Bittenbender's notes don't reflect the officer's subsequent written statement. Nothing was said about Bittenbender's written MPD report, which of course detailed the CIA admission by McCord. Clearly, the *Post* is trying to assist what we know to be McCord's deceit as between an honest Bittenbender, who considered himself a friend of McCord, and McCord, who was covering for his Agency. We will take Bittenbender on this dispute all day.

---

25   Paul G. Edwards, "McCord Disputed on Idea of Linking Burglary to CIA," *Washington Post,* May 23, 1973, A12.

Still and yet, is it possible for the *Post* to claim innocence about McCord, if all we have is their kerfuffle about Bittenbender's statement? That becomes impossible once we focus on the mysterious Lee Pennington.

We should remind you that it was one Lee Pennington who picked up McCord at jail after the arrestee made bail. Why is this significant for our purposes of examining *Post* journalism? Well, first, with the *Post*'s highly touted, bragged-about jailhouse reporters and police sources, the *Post* knew about this pickup immediately. The FBI, we know, learned of this man known as Pennington, his name noted in police records.

While the FBI was doing its job of finding out who Pennington was, wouldn't the *Post* have performed its basic function of simply reporting the fact of McCord's pickup by Pennington? But it did not do that.

The FBI, as we note, was intensely interested in Pennington's identity, and given Woodward's close relationship with Mark Felt, wouldn't Felt have disclosed the FBI's investigative hypothesis that Pennington was McCord's CIA handler? Felt treats Pennington in his 1979 book, *The FBI Pyramid*, as involving an important inquiry for the FBI. Wouldn't Felt have disclosed his salient suspicions to Woodward? It seems highly likely.

Several agents, in addition to Felt, knew of the August 18, 1972, memo by FBI Special Agent Donald Parham to the CIA, to identify any CIA agent name Pennington. So, again, Woodstein could and would easily have found out about this inquiry from one of their many FBI contacts, and they likely did. But nothing about Pennington was reported.

Felt concluded shortly after the burglary that this was "a White House operation, a CIA operation, or both." It is highly probable that Felt did not hide this from Woodward, especially since Felt wanted some publicity about the connections of the burglars, so as to ensure that the FBI's investigation would not be whitewashed, thus smudging his beloved Bureau. That is precisely the reason that Felt told Woodward about Hunt's apparent White House connections: it would shine a light on the FBI's investigation and make sure it stayed open. Wouldn't Felt have also given Woodward the same tip about Pennington? And, in any case, the pickup by Pennington would have been available from the police and the many sources that the *Post* had at the jailhouse, and the FBI's search for him available from several of Woodstein's many FBI agent sources.

When Felt learned that the CIA had given the FBI the name of a clearly uninvolved agent, *Cecil* Pennington, Felt was clearly angered. But throughout Felt's time in the Bureau, ending in June 1973, the *Post* published nothing about Pennington, not even the FBI's institutional frustration.

All of this makes for strong circumstantial case that the *Post* concealed all pertinent facts about Pennington. This would be a strong indictment of the *Post*, if this is all we have to offer, but there is, as in many of the other issues under our microscope, a capper, definite proof not only of the *Post*'s knowledge of Pennington's status but of intentional *Post* cover-up of this important fact of Pennington's involvement. That proof came to the *Post* at least by early July 1974.

Around July 2, 1974, as we discussed in an earlier chapter, Senator Howard Baker issued his succinct forty-nine-page minority report, pithy compared to the eleven-hundred-page monstrosity put forth by the majority in June 1974. An honest CIA security officer busted the CIA's attempted obstruction of Senate requests for Watergate documents, giving rise to the Baker report. One of them stated quite clearly that one Lee Pennington, the CIA contractor, had gone to McCord's house after arrest, while McCord was still in jail, to help Mrs. McCord burn documents showing McCord's connections to the CIA. Since McCord's *past* employment by the Agency was not in dispute, the only meaning of this tableau was concealment of McCord's *present* CIA status.

The Baker report was perfectly clear on this obvious point. This was not simply a conclusion of the Baker report but was the direct finding by the CIA itself, underlined for emphasis, in the documents it gave to the Senate. Therefore, we have another irrefutable marker of *Post* concealment. If the *Post* reported this matter fully the paper would have reported that McCord had a CIA handler who destroyed documents to hide McCord's *then-present* CIA undercover agency, and it would also have reported that the CIA had obstructed justice to hide Pennington from investigators. Did the paper do either? We will let you be the judge.

Before we quote the *Post*'s rendition of the Baker report on this matter, we note that Pennington had been an FBI agent many, many years earlier (we have published above a picture of Pennington with Hoover during his FBI tenure) leaving the Bureau in the early 1950s. With that in mind, here is how Laurence Stern reported this unambiguous finding of the Baker report, which had repeated essentially verbatim an unambiguous finding of the CIA itself. We quote from his July 2, 1974, article about Pennington's actions. Note this quote references former CIA security director Howard Osborn, published on page eight of the report:

> The former CIA Security Director provided misleading information to the FBI on the identity of a former federal investigator who helped Watergate burglar James McCord, Jr.'s wife destroy CIA records at their home immediately after her husband's arrest.[26]

---

26   Stern, "Baker to Say CIA Helped Hunt Get Job," *Washington Post*, July 2, 1974, A8.

First, Pennington is described as a "former federal investigator," not a present CIA contractor. Is the *Post* trying to hide that these records were destroyed by the CIA? Of course. Also, note that through this quote, the *Post* suppresses the real evidence of CIA Agency that the Pennington saga shows, since the "CIA records," were records of McCord's *present* connection to the Agency, not past CIA records. This was the *Post* and Stern's dishonest take on what the Baker report said. This clearly deceitful rendition of the Baker report proves far more than false reporting about Baker's strongly supported conclusion about Pennington and McCord. It also strongly corroborates, circumstantially, that the *Post* had been avoiding reporting about Pennington for two years.

The conclusions of the Baker report are in black and white, and yet the *Post* does not report honestly about them, knowing that the public in preinternet days would not have access to the Report. By so doing, the *Post* is guilty beyond a reasonable doubt of hiding evidence of McCord's CIA agency, clearly cemented by Bittenbender and Pennington. If this is so, and the *Post* also hid evidence of the Maxie Wells/Spencer Oliver target, of Hunt's cover contract, and of Baldwin's salacious overhearings, we can conclude that the *Post* knowingly, willfully, intentionally, and with premeditation and deliberation, kept its readers deceived and left in darkness.

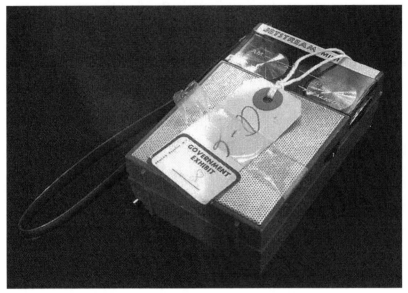

Image of recording device recovered from the Watergate burglars, public domain.

CHAPTER 27

STRANGER DANGER: HIDING STEVENS AND RUSSELL

THAT WATERGATE WAS A JOURNALISTICALLY impelled scandal, we can all agree. The *Washington Post* has long taken credit for uncovering the scandal of the Nixon administration's criminality. It has thereby taken ownership of the practical results of its journalism, and indeed has proudly claimed to have been the major actor causing Nixon's resignation, the only presidential abdication in American history.

But what if, just as the Nixon administration was accused of having done, the *Post* covered up Watergate intentionally while possessing far more information about it than the clueless, head-scratching executives in the allegedly conspiratorial Oval Office?

Granted, as a media member, the *Washington Post* is not liable criminally for any willful and intentional factual distortion in published material, as would be a government official making false representations in a proceeding of a government agency. But is the *Post* morally accountable if it failed to tell the truth to the American public? We think so and believe most Americans would, too.

Let us introduce a strand of traditional Western thought that bears upon Watergate and the *Post's* reporting of it. As Plato recounts from a debate of Socrates, if a man could make himself invisible, would he act morally? Major Western thinkers such as Cicero, Rosseau, H. G. Wells, Wagner, Tolkien, Ralph Ellison, and others have asserted that if an individual is invisible, it yields an irresistible temptation to immorality.

So, with this preface, to what extent did the *Post's* hiding of Watergate truths make the actors invisible, and thus prone to immorality? To what extent did the *Post's* unchallenged, unexamined journalism become a form of invisibility, leading to its own journalistic immorality? We have thus far spoken of various journalistic cover-ups by the *Post*, of the intriguing facts of the burglary arrests pointing to a target other than that which the *Post* postulated repeatedly in print, dealing not with campaign strategies but salacious interactions. We have described how the *Post* strained to conceal the Mullen cover contract and the seeming CIA agency of Hunt and McCord. The *Post* helped immeasurably to cover up for the CIA and McCord as McCord faced sentencing before Judge Sirica.

But for McCord to unwrap on the White House to Sirica, he had to have confidence that nothing would erupt to spoil the hard-won cover-up of the Agency. If the White House could recover strongly, prospects for the CIA would not be bright. Accordingly, in late March 1973, McCord made a strategic decision. Because the *Post* had done such a good, if dishonest, job of pointing to the White House and away from the Agency, and after Gray imploded, McCord calculated that he could rail against the White House and that the *Post* and Judge Sirica would eat it up, weakening the White House further. So, rail he did, as the *Post* and Sirica ate it up. But he knew there were still two wild cards who could destroy the Agency, forfeit pensions, and ruin Agency programs. Those wild cards were Lou Russell and Michael Stevens. As we will discuss, the emergence of either one, speaking truthfully, would be a huge body blow to the CIA, but the two together would be nuclear annihilation of the Agency.

Stevens was a danger mainly because of Russell, who could point to Stevens as corroborating proof of what Russell had to say. Dean had recognized this danger and had paid off Russell, or so it appears circumstantially from his depredations of the White House safe.

It would not at the time have been wise for Hunt to be out front on this, for fear of CIA wrath and loss of his pension. But Russell and Stevens could change Hunt's decision tree. A strengthened White House, buoyed by strong, public awareness of CIA involvement, could pardon Hunt with impunity.

All of this, again, goes to the importance of Russell and Stevens. Each of these two posed existential dangers to the CIA and Dean, while they could have, by the same token, saved Nixon.

On May 1, 1973, the Republican minority subpoenaed Russell, asking him to bring his phone and bank records, and as noted above, Russell stonewalled the subpoena.

But the *Post*, in spite of the minority's interest in Russell, and Woodward's close association with the Committee's lead investigator, Scott Armstrong, printed not a word about Russell or the Committee's interest in him. This was not a minor omission. Just mentioning in bland terms that the Minority was interested in a McCord contractor who was likely lurking in the building at the time of arrest would have raised questions that could not be answered by the discredited and jejune "spying and sabotage" narrative to which the *Post* was still clinging.

Unfortunately, both for Russell and posterity, as discussed above, he had begun ruminating about writing a bestselling tell-all book, not a great idea if the CIA was not in agreement.

We can only speculate that Russell's plans involved pointing to Michael Stevens, which Russell knew would seal the deal of a CIA Watergate operation. Stevens had seen McCord's CIA validation letter, had spoken directly to sources at the CIA, knew of the satellite-uplinking bugs, and Russell knew about Stevens. Russell stiff-armed the Committee on May 9, 1973, sure to invoke new questions from the Committee about his records, and in any case, questions about his lurking in or around the Watergate Office Building on the night of the burglary, a gift to the minority from Collins and his sterling article of October 11, 1972.

Please note that had Collins not printed this article, the minority might have been in the dark about Russell, given that the Committee did not have FBI reports, and that the *Post* had been silent.

We have talked in an earlier chapter about the spectacularly revealing nuclear bomb-reporting of *Chicago Today* on May 14 and 16, 1973, following Stevens's FBI interviews of May 12 and 14, 1973. Shortly after those FBI reports and articles in the *Chicago Today*, Deep Throat had his dramatic, brief meeting with Woodward in the garage on the late night/early morning of May 16 and 17, 1973, where he warned, "Everyone's life is in danger!"

Let us consider basic morality. The *Post* had a clear and dire warning from the head of the FBI's investigation. The warning was not meant primarily for the *Washington Post*, no matter how Woodstein and *Post* editor Ben Bradlee melodramatically took it. The lives truly in danger were those of witnesses, not reporters. When Stevens's life was in danger, *Chicago Today* printed blockbusters, as it should have.

After the *Chicago Today* articles and Deep Throat's warning, the *Post* had in its hands a twofer. It could open a new, exciting frontier in the burgeoning Watergate story of CIA participation in the burglary and other illegal operations the Agency wished to protect. And they could protect the lives of both Russell and Stevens. The articles would be solidly sourced both from *Chicago Today* and Deep Throat. But the *Post* ignored to reprint, without jeopardy, solidly sourced, important articles.

But putting aside the protection of Russell for the moment, why wouldn't a *Post* report that a federal investigation had revealed that the CIA was threatening lives to protect against being outed? Yes, eventually Woodstein wrote in their book, which they had not reported when the story was fresh, part of the story in dramatic, but muffled, implication, and then only in April 1974 as Nixon was on his way out, only for the purpose of selling books. But when the story could have done some good for society and for Russell and Stevens, the *Post* stayed silent. In short, it did not report the news. Instead, the *Post* reporters culled out of this tableau a few dramatic parts and then published them in *All the President's Men* without any real explanation of what they meant.

As we discussed in an earlier chapter, Russell was poisoned apparently through "aspirin roulette," and so the threat he posed died aborning. However, shouldn't have the *Post* written about Russell's suspicious death, which followed Deep Throat's frightened warning?

Stevens did not publicly testify, likely protected, as he should have been, by national security privileges. Because of his sensitive national security role, he could claim the right not to disclose anything and the Committee was likely to eagerly agree. In any case, we know we did not hear from Stevens in the public hearings. But the *Post* certainly knew of Stevens, not only through

Deep Throat, presumably, but also, clearly, from the *Chicago Today* articles, to which every major paper would have access.

Publishing the Stevens story, or, better put, Deep Throat's terrified warning to the reporters, would have given minority senators a basis to question McCord. But there is more. Russell's friend, detective John Leon, was badly shaken by Russell's death shortly after his poisoning on May 18, clearly, sensing its true provenance.

Leon, a veteran DC investigator with a long history in the dusky world of wiretapping, was scheduled to make a dramatic appearance on July 9, 1973, with George H. W. Bush, then head of the Republican National Committee. He was to reveal the extent to which there had been years of rampant illegal wiretapping by both the Democrats and the CIA. But Leon never made it to the press conference. He, like Russell, died of a sudden heart attack, in this case dying immediately. Bush, of course, canceled the press conference. Again, while the *Post* would have understood the context of Leon's death more than any media player, it chose to remain quiet as to its surrounding circumstances. So, yes, the *Post* stayed immorally silent for all of this.

But the *New York Times* as well was acting immorally, ridding itself of Watergate's most prized journalistic source, Deep Throat, for meaningless short-term gains. Mark Felt had leaked to John Crewdson of the *New York Times* that Daniel Ellsberg, then proceeding to his criminal Pentagon Papers trial in Los Angeles, had been overheard electronically on what came to be known as the "Kissinger wiretaps," targeting both prominent newsmen and Kissinger's own National Security Council staffers. It was an impactful story, causing the dismissal of the Ellsberg prosecution and the revelations of some highly controversial wiretaps. Oddly, Mark Felt soon admitted in print to being one of Crewdson's sources, although claiming he had confirmed only what Crewdson had already known. In turn, Director William Ruckelshaus confronted Felt and soon Felt resigned, causing a huge loss not only to the *Post*, but also to the *New York Times*, which was desperately trying to catch up to the *Post* on Watergate reporting.

The Crewdson leak by Felt reared its ugly head a year later when the special prosecutor learned in May 1974 from Donald Segretti that Crewdson had possessed a raft of FBI documents, at least one an original. And an FBI secretary, sitting outside the FBI's executive suite, had seen Crewdson emerging in May 1973, right after the Ellsberg article, with a briefcase bulging with documents. So, Felt, now retired, was investigated for rewarding Crewdson with stolen documents. Felt firmly denied all. Many, of course, suspected that Felt was guilty of this minor crime, but it was not strongly provable and the investigation soon closed.

Coincidentally, Ruckelshaus was my father's law partner in their small four-attorney firm in Indianapolis, which had at various times included Ruckelshaus's father and brother. But why Felt had confirmed the leak, I never understood, nor did anyone else until 2007. I was then in Indianapolis on another case, had some time between meetings, and visited my father's old firm, which had hired my longtime buddy, Bill Hasbrook. As I was chatting with Bill, he asked me if I wanted to see "Jack," as John Ruckelshaus Jr. was called. He was a wonderful guy and aging lawyer who came to the office only sporadically.

"You still representing that ratfink, Felt?" Jack bellowed when he saw me. "Yes, I still represent Mr. Ratfink," I laughingly replied.

"Damnedest thing I ever heard," Jack continued. "A *New York Times* guy calls Bill [William Ruckelshaus] and tells him, 'You know who leaked the Ellsberg story to me? Mark Felt.' Bill confronted Felt and told him, 'Don't let the door hit you on the ass as you leave.'" I was, of course, stunned, but did not let on to Jack, as we continued. This meant to me that Crewdson had obtained his Segretti documents from Ruckelshaus as a payoff for revealing his anonymous source, Felt. Ruckelshaus had done the right thing for the FBI, ferreting out a leaker, but for Crewdson, these documents were silver pieces of journalistic betrayal. Needless to say, I was shocked by this.

An author whom I like personally, Max Holland, had written that Crewdson really did not call Ruckelshaus, but instead, the caller must have been Felt's bête noire, William Sullivan, disguised as Crewdson. This claim in the book, *Leak*, is absurd and meant to protect Holland's source, Crewdson.

I confirmed recently in a chat with Bill Ruckelshaus before he passed away that indeed the caller claimed he was Crewdson. Bill did not remember any distinct New England accent of the caller, which would have pointed to Sullivan. Of course, Crewdson thought there was gold in the Segretti story, so his thirty pieces of silver paid in exchange were counterfeit tin. He had burned a key source for nothing, that is to say, the Segretti 302 documents, and, ironically, lost a chance to use Felt to catch up to the *Washington Post*. Woodstein's exploitation of Felt, similarly, was only for their own commercial purposes. Crewdson's exploitation of Felt's leak was for his own catch-up with Woodstein for commercial purposes. His hoped-for stardom strips all pretense from both the *Post* and the *Times* as being interested in seeking truth without fear or favor. Felt's treatment by these reporters from our most elite newspapers shows the righteous, ethical pose of these papers to be so much poppycock.

Before we leave this chapter, a couple of ironies. On May 8, 1973, the *Washington Post* was announced by a Columbia University committee to be a winner of the 1972 Pulitzer Prize for its Watergate reporting. Meanwhile, with no life raft in sight,

Nixon had begun jettisoning all unnecessary occupants from the sinking ship.

With intense heat from the *Post*, Nixon went literally overboard by throwing Attorney General Richard Kleindienst off the ship, as well as other executives who were truly criminally culpable, which Kleindienst was not. This was the biggest of all presidential blunders, perhaps an unforced error, perhaps, more accurately, an error forced by the *Post*'s dishonest reporting.

With Kleindienst gone, successor Elliot Richardson agreed with the Senate in his confirmation hearings to appoint a special prosecutor, at the time not required by law or regulation but certainly not inappropriate. With the *Post*'s hiding of the roles of Russell and Stevens, and the poisoned Russell's death, the CIA now had clear sailing. The special prosecutor's office would go on to perform sterling work prosecuting Nixon administration figures aggressively. But it showed no appetite for confounding these prosecutions with a narrative that would subtract from and harm the nailing of its White House targets. Nixon's banishment of Kleindienst was the final nail in his coffin, and by the same token, the final protective wall shielding the CIA.

The *Washington Post* was part of the CIA's obstruction of justice, even if the *Post*, as a media player, bore no criminal liability. The only development that could at this point, in May 1973, derail the CIA cover-up by the *Post* was disclosure of certain CIA documents that inculpated the Agency to its bureaucratic eyeballs. Thus far, the Agency had wrongly withheld them. If by some chance these plainly incriminating documents surfaced, surely the *Post* would report on this fully and fairly, wouldn't it?

But as we leave this chapter, it suffices to say that by hiding Russell and Stevens after concealing Mullen, the salacious DNC talk, Hunt's CIA defense, the prosecution's blackmail theme, Pennington, and Bittenbender, the *Post* was in the process of completing its self-assigned job as the chief CIA/DNC cover-up architect. But if clear evidence from a reputable source was produced showing definite proof of heavy CIA involvement in Watergate, would the *Post* report these revelations truthfully?

Let's put the question differently. Let's assume that hypothetically, there emerged from the CIA documents that were akin to Agency guilty pleas. Would the *Post* be so brazen as to mischaracterize black-and-white, unambiguous truth?

Image of G. Gordon Liddy leaving the U.S. District Court after pleading not guilty to breaking into the Democratic National Committee headquarters. © Everett Collection Historical / Alamy Stock Photo.

CHAPTER 28

KEEPING A LID ON LIDDY

WE HAVE DESCRIBED EARLIER THE honorable but ultimately harmful decision of Gordon Liddy to remain silent throughout the Watergate era. And we have also shown how this stand-up soldier was a dupe whose candid observations, if shared with White House officials other than John Dean, would have unwittingly revealed the duplicity of both James McCord and Dean. After waiting for the six-year statute of limitations to run, Liddy ended his silence to publish his bracingly candid account of Watergate, *Will*.

But whether his silence was admirable or very stupid—and it likely was both—his book amounted to a test of the bona fides of Woodward and the *Washington Post*. If Liddy in his honest account revealed facts at variance with the received narrative, would the *Post* acknowledge these newly revealed truths and revise its take on Watergate accordingly? Or would it ignore or distort *Will's* firsthand revelations? This book, as it turned out, was a test of the hypothesis that we had developed by 2010: the *Post* was deeply and intentionally dishonest in its Watergate reporting.

Luckily, the *Post* did directly address Liddy's book. Apparently realizing that Liddy's account was an inarguable part of Watergate history that could not be ignored completely by journalists and historians, the *Post* characterized it for posterity head-on by having it reviewed by the unchallenged master of all Watergate wisdom, its managing editor, Bob Woodward himself. Because of his iconic status, Woodward's analysis of Liddy's work, rather than the work itself, was more likely to become part of the received version of Liddy's story. While Woodward used this opportunity to cement selected observations of Liddy into Watergate lore, he also gave us from our present vantage point a direct view of Woodward's—and the *Post*'s—candor, or lack thereof, about Watergate. Put differently, if Woodward concealed or distorted Liddy's revelations in the book, it is likely that he and the *Post* also did so regarding the same facts during Watergate and were continuing to cover up whatever consequential falsities it had published years earlier, or what truths it had concealed.

Making this exercise meaningful is the universal acknowledgment that Liddy's account was extraordinarily candid and truthful. Woodward himself joins this chorus in praising the book's truthfulness:

> *Liddy's account of Watergate is not only believable, but some of what he reveals is front page news... Liddy is meticulous. His story rings true and balanced against the other evidence and testimony of the many Watergate investigations, it is credible. A hundred little facts and inferences convince me he has been as honest as he could be.*[27]

So with this acknowledgment, Woodward/the *Post* cannot claim that Liddy's account was knowingly false, even if, as

---

27   Woodward, "Gordon Liddy Spills His Guts," *Washington Post*, May 18, 1980.

I recounted in several instances above, he was likely fooled, as, for example, in his belief that O'Brien had been targeted and that the photos pinned to a shag carpet were taken in O'Brien's office.[28] So how faithfully Woodward recounts Liddy's observations amounts to an excellent test of good faith and of the presence or absence of intent to deceive, both on his part and that of his editors at the *Post*. Written in 1980, the review would have the added advantage of years of perspective and opportunity for reflection.

Woodward explicitly tells us what is new in Liddy's book, offering eight categories, as per the following quoted passages under each of my headings.[29] I will divide my analysis of Liddy's revelations into two segments. The first will deal with these eight categories of new insights that Woodward claims Liddy made. The second will deal with the items that Liddy revealed but Woodward did not fully address. There will necessarily be some overlap between the two because in some cases, Woodward described Liddy's insights only partially.

A. Liddy giving Kleindienst a full account of the break-in on the day of the arrests:

> Richard Kleindienst, who was attorney general on the day of the break-in (Mitchell had by then become chairman of the reelection committee), was given a full account directly by Liddy the day the burglars were arrested.

---

28 To "prove" they had penetrated O'Brien's office during the first burglary, the burglars presented Liddy with photos of purported DNC documents claimed to be taken in the office. His office did not have a shag carpet, but Baldwin's hotel room did. This is clear evidence of a secret CIA agenda necessarily duping Liddy, who never understood the targeting of the DNC and O'Brien.

29 Each of the following eight quotes are taken from Woodward's book review, "Gordon Liddy Spills His Guts."

B. The tape placed intentionally on the door lock so a guard could see it:

The much-discussed piece of tape holding open a stairwell door in the Watergate office building was put there intentionally so a guard could see it. That way, Liddy reasoned, the guard would assume it had been left innocently by a janitor whereas a clandestine and inconspicuous method of holding the lock open would arouse more suspicion

C. Liddy's lack of belief that McCord was a double agent who sabotaged the entry:

Liddy says he does not believe the speculations that James McCord, one of the burglars, was a double agent who knowingly sabotaged the illegal entry.

D. The plan to assassinate Jack Anderson:

So, when he gets down to the accounts of crucial meetings, planning sessions and the actual illegal operations themselves—the Watergate break-in of June 17, 1972, or the "entry" at the office of the psychiatrist of Pentagon Papers defendant Daniel Ellsberg, or the planned assassination of columnist Jack Anderson—Liddy is meticulous. His story rings true and balanced against the other evidence and testimony of the many Watergate investigations, it is credible.

E. Mitchell's willingness to pay organized crime for kidnapping and drugging demonstrators:

Mitchell was willing as attorney general to pay Nixon campaign funds to members of organized crime for their services in a scheme—never carried out—to kidnap, drug and ship to Mexico radical demonstration leaders. Liddy quotes Mitchell as saying in response to the proposal, "Let's not contribute any more than we have to the coffers of organized crime."

F. Liddy's telling Mitchell of the planned second break-in:

Liddy says he delivered logs of wiretapped conversations to Mitchell two days before the Watergate arrests and told him of the planned break-in by announcing that, "The problem [with one of the microphones] will be corrected this weekend, sir." Mitchell has repeatedly denied that he knew of the June 17 break-in in advance; Liddy offers convincing evidence to the contrary.

G. The motive for the break-in:

Liddy offers his explanation of why the Nixon White House wanted to break into the DNC headquarters in the first place...to find out what [Democratic National Chairman Lawrence] O'Brien had of a derogatory nature about us, not for us to get something on him or the Democrats.

H. The CIA's knowledge of the break-in:

The CIA made the expensive charts used to brief Attorney General John Mitchell in early 1972 on the planned illegal GEMSTONE break-in and bugging operations. For me, this suggests more than anything available to date that top CIA officials must have known in advance about Liddy's illegal operations. In my opinion, CIA Director Richard Helms must have been given some inkling from the men over at the CIA graphics department, but Helms has denied it.

Is Woodward being truthful in his recounting of Liddy's insights? Hardly. There is of course no defense to the claim that Liddy told all to Kleindienst on the morning of the arrest. And, yes, Woodward is mostly correct about the tape. The burglars did not intend that the guard see it, but if he did, in Liddy's view, the guard would think an innocent maintenance man placed it.

Liddy did not believe that McCord sabotaged the operation, but much of his description is consistent with a CIA agency. Liddy compared McCord to the fictional "Shadow" Lamont Cranston because he slipped away so often (consistent with Lou Russell's hidden participation), conduct Woodward wished to keep hidden from the reader.

Woodward makes the discussion of assassinating Jack Anderson sound like a White House initiative, whereas any knowledgeable observer understood this to be part of the CIA's Operation Mudhen, and that Dr. Edward Gunn, a poison specialist, was, as Liddy noted but Woodward omitted, a "retired CIA asset." So, properly understood, this meeting supports the theme of the CIA's inveigling White House dupes to legalize the Agency's otherwise illegal operations.

Woodward is directly dishonest in stating that the dry Mitchell was willing to pay organized crime. The former attorney general, rather, was wittily rejecting a fatuous scheme of Liddy, and Woodward's addition of the parenthetical microphone reference was even more deceitful, if that is even possible. A microphone was never mentioned, and Mitchell had no idea what "problem" Liddy was obliquely hinting at in a meeting attended by nonburglary team members. Mitchell did not know of the second break-in, contrary to Woodward.

By 1980, Woodward also knew that Larry O'Brien was not the true target, and that Liddy was duped on this score, lacking even in 1980 knowledge of the Wells desk key. And to suggest that "more than anything" the GEMSTONE charts showed the CIA must have known about the planned break-in and bugging operations is to praise with faint damn. I have detailed in this book a raft of far more inculpatory facts showing not only CIA knowledge but also CIA direction and participation for its own purposes.

Perhaps more significant are two Liddy revelations that would have revised the commonly believed narrative of Watergate, but which Woodward ignored precisely for that reason, because there was no good spin possible. It was Dean, Liddy documents, who was the father of GEMSTONE, pushing Liddy to the CRP with a promise of an intelligence budget of "half a million for openers." Dean's sponsorship of the Mitchell presentation meetings, where Mitchell swats away Liddy's silly plans, is a key part of Liddy's account. Dean's participation in this "blind ambition" dirt gathering is consistent with his sending of Tony Ulasewicz to Watergate for a casing trip in November 1971. In short, Mitchell was not the father of Watergate but its attempted abortionist.

Woodward also ignores the $30,000 McCord pulled from Liddy for what Woodward should have known was McCord's false representation of purchasing a sophisticated room bug for O'Brien's office. This ties in nicely with the tableau of Michael Stevens and the CIA satellite-uplinking bugs that the confirmed CIA agent McCord ordered from him, using part of the $30,000. Again, Woodward omits this discussion because it devastates the false narrative he sold the public during Watergate.

In short, Bob Woodward's dishonest review, after years of reflection and discussion, buttresses the conclusion that he was similarly dishonest during the scandal and was simply continuing his cover-up of what actually occurred.

Image of Senator Howard Baker, public domain.

CHAPTER 29

BAKING BAKER

As of June of 1974, the CIA, the DNC, Mullen, and Dean had all escaped detection masterfully, thanks to their friends at the *Washington Post*. The *Post* did not report honestly about the odd circumstances of the burglary, as we have described; reporting that would have raised great curiosity about this otherwise inexplicable burglary.

In light of the false public messaging by a Democratic-leaning paper in a country with a Democratic Congress, it looked like Nixon was on his way to certain removal in early 1974, as the House Impeachment Committee (sometimes named after Chairman Peter Rodino of New Jersey) was moving toward articles of impeachment. But there was one wild card still to turn over. From the outset of the 1973 Ervin Committee hearings, there was the distant but distinct rumble of possible CIA participation. As we have pointed out, the *Post* had hidden the most clearly damning CIA evidence.

In 1973 Minority Chairman Senator Howard Baker of Tennessee described in colloquial terms the seeming vague but persistent evidence of CIA participation. "It's like animals crashing around in the forest. You can hear them, but you can't see them," Baker said. So, it is with this background in mind that we describe the drama within the CIA, which reached its climax in early 1974.

The head of the FBI's Watergate investigation, Mark Felt had thought from the outset that a promising portal through which the FBI could view CIA engagement was the mysterious Lee Pennington. If Pennington's role became known, the CIA would be proven to have acted criminally, not only in Watergate but elsewhere in the United States for decades through Pennington as a domestic agent. Pennington was likely in contact with domestic CIA undercover agents other than McCord, each one proof of illegal Agency action in the U.S. We have elaborated at length above about the Agency's efforts to conceal the "sensitive" Pennington, led by Director of Security Howard Osborn.

Osborn, as head of the OS, reported to Colby, the CIA director, yet was withholding documents that Colby specifically requested. We now have officials at the very top of the Agency clearly obstructing justice, and very provably so, should anyone so reveal. All of this risky criminality was performed to protect against anyone even knowing about Pennington's existence, which would in turn lead to the very clear cover-up of McCord's agency with the CIA. As we discussed, eventually, honest officers forced the Agency to produce these sensitive documents, which should have been a death blow to the Agency, not only as to Watergate, but many other operations.

Meanwhile, with the Senate inquiry now winding down, Congressman Lucien Nedzi's House Select Committee was on top of this quickly, soon interrogating Osborn, Pennington, Gaynor, and the two security officers. Senator Baker became deeply interested in this testimony, and now had a raft of documents incriminating the CIA in a multitude of ways beyond just McCord and Pennington. But with Nixon barely hanging on by a thread, Baker needed to hurry, hope that the public would be informed of these spectacular developments soon, and give the Nixon forces the ability to explain the cloak-and-dagger activities for which the president was being falsely blamed.

Baker's forty-nine-page report was issued on July 3, 1974, and was itself a summary. So let us summarize the summary, hitting only its biggest points. This report would be published, but, before the internet, and with no book or pamphlet published embodying it, only a few would have access, and fewer still would actually read it. So, the *Post*, in essence, knew it was invisible, and as Plato has said, *an invisible man tends to be a dishonest man.*

The reporting on the Baker report would thus be a test of the honesty of the *Washington Post*. Administration figures had already been indicted for covering up evidence. So, if the *Post* were to do the same thing—cover up facts it learned about Watergate's criminality, including obstruction—why wouldn't the *Post*'s agents be considered morally if not legally criminal, part of the great cover-up?

In any case, the Baker report should have been a blockbuster for the *Post*. Let us now list Baker's key indictments of the CIA, which it appears the *Post* should have already published. Baker concluded, first, that there were serious credible links between the CIA and the Watergate burglary, as well as the Fielding burglary of Daniel Ellsberg's psychiatric records. More specifically, Baker documented both McCord's ongoing relationship with the CIA and Pennington's obstructive acts destroying evidence of the link. He as well detailed the CIA's other obstructive acts of hiding evidence both from Congress and the FBI.

The Baker report documented deep CIA involvement in the Fielding/Ellsberg burglary. The report also described Martinez's disturbing reports in March 1972 to his Miami station chief, in which he was deeply concerned about Hunt's activities. Recall that the Watergate and the Fielding burglaries were only *some* of the operations on which the Cuban team had assisted. Recall the break-in of the Chilean embassy and the monitoring of three prominent Democratic senators who oversaw the intelligence agencies, plus likely many more yet unknown.

Martinez had wanted assurances that these Hunt-led operations were known to and approved by Agency brass. When the station chief related this concern to Washington, the CIA's director of plans, Thomas Karamessines, told the station chief to "cool it," that Hunt was on White House business. After Martinez was arrested, the CIA assigned a new case agent for him, and ordered him to drive from Miami to DC without the use of traceable credit cards.

The Baker report was clear about the Mullen cover contract, including Bennett's involvement with the Agency. Baker noted that the CIA had refused to provide Hunt's file because it was too sensitive. The report also disclosed Bennett's reports about the cover-up agreement with Woodward, and Mullen lawyer Hobart Taylor's entreaties with DNC counsel, all to cover up Mullen's role as a cover contractor.

Finally, the report contradicted the CIA's assertion that it had quit giving assistance to Hunt in his White House role once it learned of the Fielding/Ellsberg burglary in late August, 1971. Instead, the report showed the Agency continued filling all of Hunt's requests, up through Watergate, on an agencywide basis. The report's thorough summary of Agency assistance gives rise to the strong inference that Hunt was acting as a CIA agent while at the White House.

To these solidly documented indictments, how did the *Washington Post* respond? Was it the fierce proponent of the "public's right to know" or was it part of a deliberate cover-up?

On July 2, 1974, the *Washington Post*'s Laurence Stern did a preview, based on sources who had read the report, as to what the yet unpublished Baker report would say. We suspect that Stern had a bootlegged copy. The headline for this preview, which should have trumpeted an upcoming explosive report, referenced the pedestrian item of Helms's help to get Hunt his White House job: "Baker to Say CIA Helped Hunt Get Job."

This absurdly vanilla item was clearly meant to tell the public, falsely, that the report would be ho-hum. Then Stern summarizes in the lead article the overall conclusion that will be coming: "Sources who examined the report say it proves no conclusive links between the CIA and the original Watergate break-in, such as have been hinted by former White House aide Charles Colson and by Baker."

According to Stern, the question that the report addresses was whether the CIA officials took "efforts to minimize its involvement in the Watergate investigation." So, note that Stern frames the question not as to whether the CIA was involved in the *burglary*, but whether it was involved at all in the *investigation*.

Let's stop right here. We all know the value of hyping a coming attraction—a book, a boxing match, a movie—to get a wide audience. The *Post* was doing just the opposite, in essence telling the public: *Don't ruin your 4th of July holidays for this report.*

Incidentally, the nondescript July 2 headline we just quoted appeared on the first page of the *Washington Post*, ensuring that otherwise interested citizens would not follow up on the July 3 story. On July 3, with the report now published, Stern continued his reporting, but, oddly, did so in two different articles, one on page A1, which anyone who anticipated this article would see as the main payoff from the preceding day's lead-in. The headline read, "Report Critical of CIA. Baker Hints Agency Knew of Break-In." Now, the lead paragraph:

The Central Intelligence Agency may have known in advance of the plans for break-ins of the offices of Daniel Ellsberg psychiatrist and the Democratic Committee's Watergate headquarters, a Report released yesterday by Howard H. Baker, Jr., Republican of Tennessee suggests.[30]

So, this front-page headline does not talk about the issue of McCord and Hunt being undercover CIA agents or that the break-in of both Fielding and the Watergate DNC offices were actually CIA jobs. Rather, the question posed is whether or not the CIA knew in advance of these operations, a very bland suggestion. Most readers interested in Watergate would not scour the rest this paper for any additions to this Baker report story, and they were unlikely, in any case, to do so on July 3.

But let us stop right here. We now have two front-page headline stories on consecutive days, one telling us that Richard Helms—gasp—helped Howard Hunt get a job after retirement. The other told the shocking story that because of casing photos, the Agency may have learned in advance of the Fielding burglary, and in some form or fashion may have known in advance of the Watergate break-ins. Even this underplayed story should have, but did not, raise the interesting question as to why the CIA would have kept casing photos for an operation as to which it had no part.

There was a second July 3 story starting on page A10. It was here that the *Post* finally got down to summarizing for the reader, should the reader go to page A10, where the bland story was buried. The findings and conclusions of the Baker report were, according to the article, well, nothing much. Here is the

---

30   Stern, "Report Critical of CIA. Baker Hints Agency Knew of Break-In," *Washington Post,* July 3, 1974, A1.

page A10 headline: "Few Conclusions Given by Baker on CIA-Watergate Tie."

Recall Baker's prior statement before getting these explosive documents, that animals in the forest could be heard but not seen. Here are the lead-in paragraphs to this story, supposedly summarizing the conclusions of the report:

> *Sen. Howard H. Baker Jr. (R-Tenn.) once likened the role of the Central Intelligence Agency in the Watergate scandal to "animals crashing around in the forest—you can hear them but you can't see them."*

> *This Aesopian image still fits notwithstanding Baker's release yesterday of a 43-page report which is rich in insinuation, long on footnotes but short on substantive findings.*[31]

In short, this report says there's nothing new here, whereas in fact there were incredibly explosive, incriminating allegations, solidly documented. The Baker report detailed the CIA's cover arrangements with Mullen, which should have led the paper to finger Hunt in this journalism. *Post* reporting also should have described the CIA drama described earlier, clearly criminal obstruction designed to hide both Pennington and McCord. And it detailed the unholy alliance between Mullen and the *Post*, through Woodward, to "protect" Mullen. But here is how Stern capsulized the evidence, which deliberately waters down what Baker found:

> *Among other things, the Report describes how the CIA used a Washington public relations firm as a*

---

31   Stern, "Few Conclusions Given by Baker."

*cover for agents operating abroad, asserts that the
CIA destroyed its own records in direct conflict with
the Senate request to keep them intact, asserts that
a CIA operative may have been a "domestic agent"
in violation of the Agency's charter, and recounts
how one CIA employee fought within the Agency
against withholding information from the Senate
committee and other Congressional committees.*

*The Report recites several instances in which it
says CIA personnel with whom the committee staff
sought to interview were not made available by
the CIA. In addition, the Report lists several other
instances in which it says the CIA either ignored,
resisted, or refused requests for information and
documents by the committee.*[32]

Note that this article avoids nailing Hunt, or McCord, or
even Mullen as an undercover agent. Later, when the article does
name Mullen, it does so by describing it as a cover for agents
abroad, missing the entire point. The summary of obstructive
activities makes it appear there was no obstruction at all, but
only *thoughts* of withholding information, along with clearly
stated objections to committee requests. In essence, normal, lawful document wrangling.

Baker devotes much space to Martinez's concerns in March
1972 of Hunt's activities, and postburglary rushing of his case
agent to DC by auto, without traceable use of credit cards. The
essence of the Baker report was that Martinez and his chief had
been concerned of illegal activities involving Hunt, but the arti-

---

32   Ibid.

cle, again, made the tableau sound very bland. Here is the way Stern describes this section:

> *The section of the report dealing with Eugenio Martinez asserts that Martinez, a CIA operative, alerted his CIA superiors that Hunt was in Miami in early 1972. The response from the CIA to Martinez's superiors, according to the report, was that Hunt was involved in domestic White House business and to "cool it."*[33]

In fact, was Martinez merely alerting his superiors that Hunt was in Miami? Of course not. This is a false rendition of what the report said. This paragraph is such a dishonest rendering of the report that if it were within the jurisdiction of the SEC, Stern would and should be a good candidate for indictment.

Now, let us quote the paragraph treating Pennington:

> *Baker did unearth the case of Lee R. Pennington Jr., a $250-a-month CIA contract employee who acknowledged that he witnessed the destruction of Watergate burglar James W. McCord Jr.'s records by his wife at their home after McCord's arrest in Watergate.*
>
> *CIA's then-Director of Security Howard Osborn, no longer with the agency, fed files on a different Pennington to the FBI when agents made inquiries about the incident—presumably to throw the bureau off the track. Columnist Jack Anderson reported the incident several months ago.*[34]

---

33   Ibid.
34   Ibid.

Of course, left out of this is the notion that Pennington him-self helped burn those documents, most importantly to hide any evidence of McCord's *ongoing* link to the CIA. That should have been the big headline, but the item was omitted in material part by Stern. Now, at least the page A10 article names Pennington. If the reader only read the page A1 article, following it to its con-tinuation on page A8, the Pennington affair is even more air-brushed, not even naming him, instead calling him a "former federal investigator," not a CIA contractor:

> *The Osborn material, as presented by Baker, sug-gests that the former CIA security director provided misleading information to the FBI on the identity of a former federal investigator who helped Watergate burglar James W. McCord Jr.'s wife destroy CIA records at their home immediately after her hus-band's arrest in the Watergate break-in case.*[35]

By calling Pennington only a former federal investigator, Stern is clearly trying to dissociate the CIA from the burning of these documents. As we have described, the Baker report speaks of a massive agencywide effort to aid Hunt, notwithstanding Agency claims to have ended its help shortly before the Ellsberg burglary. The point of the Baker report regarding CIA aid to Hunt is quite specific: the Agency never terminated widespread support of Hunt. But Stern clearly, and quite dishonestly, says just the opposite:

> *The report asserts, and the CIA denies, that it was only when these photographs were developed that assistance to Hunt by the agency was terminated.*[36]

---

35   Stern, "Report Critical of CIA. Baker Hints Agency Knew of Break-In," *Washington Post,* July 3, 1974, A8.
36   Ibid.

This refers to the casing photos of the Ellsberg psychiatrist. So, Stern directly says, dishonestly, that the report claims that the Agency *stopped* the support of Hunt but not until after the casing photos were developed, implying falsely that at least by then the Agency withheld support, whereas the report details that support was never stopped, an incriminating fact.

Finally, Stern's report ignores altogether the CIA documentation showing Bennett's claims to have hushed up Woodward and the *Washington Post*, also minimizing Bennett's use of attorney Hobart Taylor to intercede with the Williams firm to cover up the Mullen/CIA role:

> The report asserts that Bennett "funneled" information to Edward Bennett Williams, then a lawyer for the Democratic National Committee and The Washington Post, through another Washington lawyer, Hobart Taylor.[37]

Note that there is nothing here about keeping Mullen's role out of the news, or Bennett's deal with Woodward, or his assignment to Taylor to lobby the Williams firm to hush any public reference to Mullen. In other words, he ignores the cover-up of Mullen's undercover status. Rather, his article claims only that Bennett "funneled" information to the law firm, which is entirely innocent activity.

We have provided key excerpts from the *Post*'s reporting on the Baker report. If any readers have the time or inclination, they can examine the Baker report online. Why is the *Post*'s rendition of it so significant? Because if the *Post* is brazen enough to lie about findings in black and white issued by a respected sena-

---

37   Ibid.

tor, then we can make inference about how the *Post* was treating other facts not so readily accessible.

When the paper covered up the CIA' s Watergate role, it was more broadly condoning an intelligence agency run amok. Its Watergate reporting, which should have refrained from hiding CIA criminality, should have also been concerned about a political culture in Washington tied closely to prostitution and the buying and selling of females. Yet because of *Post* journalism, our society was robbed of a meaningful discussion of these issues. Instead, in 1972, our society began the deification of the bread and circuses of scandal and "gotcha" journalism, no longer considered distasteful muckraking. Our political culture, as a result of deceitful *Washington Post* journalism, has become a scandal culture. And modern journalism would no longer be about truth but, rather, the political power of mass communication.

The *Post's* shameful treatment of an important public report, then available, if at all, to the wider public audience only through newspapers, can never be erased by the fog of memory. It remains solidly documented in our country's archives. This is the true legacy of Watergate.

Image of Russian President Vladimir Putin and United States President Donald Trump, Presidential Press and Information Office (ихаил Метцель, ТАС).

CHAPTER 30

WATERGATE JOURNALISM'S BITTER HARVEST

As WE COVERED IN THE past chapter, the *Post*'s Watergate journalism was the proof of concept of the modern project of investigative journalism. It is our thesis here that even though society and certainly the world of journalism did not consider this reporting to be fraudulent, it nonetheless gave rise to a form of journalism that is not only partisan but is also as a necessary result thereof deceitful. How so? As I explained earlier, once an investigative journalist gets a target, the idea is not to tell both sides. A willful omission of a material fact is fraud, a concept lost on most modern journalists pushing their predetermined narratives.

Investigative journalism is more properly termed "prosecutorial journalism." If a prosecutor can put on his evidence without defense counsel, how fair a trial would ensue? Of course, it would not only be unfair, but also in the sense we have discussed, fraudulent. One must always be careful about any one-sided presentation because fraud, especially without an opposing party to fill in the blanks, occurs whenever a truthful, full treatment of a subject requires more facts than are told. For this reason, whenever a company offers securities for sale to the public, the SEC makes sure that the offeror discloses all facts, not only positive and hopeful, but also negative and cautionary, to the public on pain of criminal guilt.

It is the burden of this chapter to show how in fact modern investigative journalism now regularly reports major stories deceitfully, largely as a result of Watergate journalism's stunning success. In this chapter, we will examine some important, highly publicized scandals to determine whether substantial deceit by the major media defrauded the public of the true narrative, or at least of the true narrative as one possibility to be considered.

Let us start with an odd subject: Mark Felt. In the wake of Watergate, understandably, every politician wished to get in on the reformist wave sweeping a shellshocked nation. One of the most impactful public investigations in the wake of Watergate was the Church Committee, an exploration of intelligence agency abuses, named after Idaho Senator Frank Church. What was odd about this investigation was that during Watergate, the CIA had been pictured as an innocent target of President Nixon, and the FBI had, on the whole, performed in exemplary fashion. To be sure, the FBI's interim Director L. Patrick Gray had permitted the White House, through John Dean's office, to sit in on FBI witness interviews. Later, Gray was forced to admit he had, at the behest of Dean, destroyed sensitive documents found in Howard Hunt's safe. But outside of misconduct of this politicized hack, really an acolyte of a seemingly corrupt White House, the FBI had been incorruptible, performing in exemplary fashion.

During the Church Committee hearings, there were presented some past examples of FBI abuses, mainly those of William Sullivan, the bête noire of Mark Felt and the man behind the infamous COINTELPRO. This was a legitimate intelligence program directed to infiltrating terrorist groups to gain antiterrorist intelligence, but which unfortunately introduced or subverted agents provocateurs too readily into these groups.

In the course of the investigation, it was determined that the FBI had conducted warrantless, covert searches of both Palestinian Liberation Organization (PLO) targets and, more concerning, the residences and offices of "above ground" supporters of the Weather Underground Organization, or WUO, wanted by the FBI for the bombing of over fifty government facilities. Although these were mainstream FBI intelligence operations not connected to COINTELPRO, they were inevitably discovered as a result of the probe. One hundred forty lower-level FBI agents as a result were investigated by the Civil Rights Division of the Department of Justice, its lawyers in the early nineteen seventies mostly red-hot, righteous young prosecutors seeking FBI and police scalps.

Mark Felt threw a monkey wrench into these prosecutions by publicly admitting he approved the searches, claiming that they were proper national security incursions. Felt told that not only to the grand jury, but to television's *Face the Nation* in August 1976, angering the young Civil Rights Division prosecutors, because it negated the criminal intent of the lower-level agents. As a result, the attorney general ultimately determined as a result of Felt's approvals to dismiss these cases. After much debate, the prosecutors persuaded the grand jury to indict Felt for violation of the civil rights of the Weather Underground supporters.

What does this have to do with journalism? Well, the *Washington Post* wrote editorials urging the Justice Department to indict Felt and was its biggest public cheerleader for Felt's conviction. Notwithstanding that attorney Griffin Bell was not excited about indicting Felt, the *Post* advocacy carried the day with the Carter administration, and the Civil Rights Division prosecutors prevailed. Ignorantly on the part of the court in that case, and reprehensibly on the part of the prosecutors, the judge was persuaded by the prosecutors to instruct the jury to *presume Felt guilty*. Why? Because he did not have a written note from the attorney general giving him permission, never a requirement in 1972, a mandate put in place in 1977 by President Ford's former attorney general, Edward Levi. The paper ignored this heinous deprivation of Felt's civil rights.

The *Post*'s cheerleading was both ignorant and partisan. How can we be sure? As we explained in an earlier chapter, national security trumps the Bill of Rights, such that a Fourth Amendment warrant is not required if true national security is at issue. In 1940, we could shoot Adolf Hitler if the president said so, even if we were not yet at war with Germany. And George Washington could put down the Whiskey Rebellion without obtaining warrants. But what is our proof that this is so? The passage of FISA, which clearly approved of what Felt did.

FISA searches are not probable cause Fourth Amendment incursions. FISA does not *require* that the FBI obtain prior approval of a warrantless search by the foreign intelligence surveillance court, but such approval immunizes and protects agents from unfair prosecutions, such as occurred with Felt. The whole purpose of FISA was to protect against cases like Felt's, which was based on an ignorant understanding of our Constitution. But, as we will see, it introduced a new maze of bureaucracy, hampering emergency action while immunizing abusive action that can be pushed past a FISA court.

The *Post* suppressed the true nature of the case made by Felt, ironically its iconic Watergate source, on whom it depended for truthful analysis during Watergate. But even if the *Post* was partisan and was wrong about Felt's Weather Underground searches, how did that harm society?

First, the societal ignorance that the *Post* reporting engendered led to extreme, unnecessary remedies. Today, we all know that 9/11 was caused in part by the "wall" artificially constructed between criminal investigations and national security intelligence surveillance. Never the twain could meet, it was decreed. After all, a government agent could pretextually begin a FISA intelligence investigation to try to snare a criminal conviction, it was thought.

In addition to this wall, FISA also added a layer of bureaucracy that the FBI had never been forced to endure. Indeed, a court and the FBI had been dithering for a month as to whether to allow the FBI to examine the computer of Zacarias Moussaoui at the time that airplanes hit the Twin Towers on 9/11, while the investigators had been deprived of information on the other side of the wall. This is all to some extent the result of the dishonest reporting by the *Washington Post* as to Felt's guilt in the Weather Underground searches. In fact, everything he did was constitutional and legal, but partisan reporting caused awkward bureaucratic remedies for problems that did not exist. The FBI had the situation under control, but the *Post* railed against a problem that was only a problem because inexperienced young lawyers thought so, whereupon the Post took up the cause, with harmful unintended consequences.

Mark Felt had warned in 1980 that society could not put its fingers in its ears, pending the next terrorist explosion, which he thought would be the result of his prosecution. But that is exactly what happened on our way to two long wars. Felt was right and the *Washington Post* was wrong, and as a result, the paper's ignorant partisan journalism caused many deaths. But there was yet more harm and unintended consequences from this media suppression of one side of an important debate. FISA was passed to protect agents as a result of the unnecessary prosecution of Felt, but it also immunized them when they pushed a politicized warrant through the FISA court. To be sure, agents apply under penalty of perjury, but perjury is difficult to prove. This FISA protection directly led to the horrid Russiagate fiasco, which caused our society years of turmoil.

So, what exactly did the *Post* miss? Its gold-plated source, Mark Felt, proclaimed loudly that a national security exception to the Bill of Rights existed, but the *Post* concealed and suppressed this defense, of which most members of the public would be ignorant. Most citizens know that a probable cause warrant is needed for a normal search, and national security searches were not even taught in law school when I graduated in 1972. But Felt made the rationale known to anyone who asked. When the paper could enlighten the public, it kept the matter shrouded in darkness for its own partisan, political purposes. After all, the FBI was "conservative" and therefore retrograde in the post-Watergate catharsis. The White House was now controlled by the Carter administration and the Weather Underground supporters were nice liberals. How about, we would suggest, telling both sides of this debate?

Where else has partisan concealment caused large scale society ignorance and harm? In 2003, in the wake of the Iraq invasion resulting from 9/11, the Left in America sought to discredit the basis for this war. After an anti-Iraq War *New York Times* op-ed by former ambassador Joseph Wilson, syndicated columnist Robert Novak mentioned that Wilson's wife Valerie Plame worked for the CIA in its research into Iraq weapons of mass destruction. Plame and the CIA then screamed that releasing her name and her identity as a CIA agent was prohibited by the Foreign Agents Identification Act, which seeks to prevent foreign agents that are or were recently undercover from getting killed or harmed. Accordingly, the identities of these agents cannot be "outed."

The *Washington Post* immediately echoed the CIA, as did the *New York Times*, and demanded prosecution of the leaker. Acting Attorney General James Comey named a special prosecutor, Patrick Fitzgerald, to investigate. Eventually as a result, the chief deputy to Vice President Dick Cheney, Lewis "Scooter" Libby, was indicted by the grand jury for falsely denying leaking Plame's name to another reporter, not to Novak. This prosecution now consumed all the air in the room of public discussion, as part of a narrative that Libby was helping Cheney hide the Bush administration's supposed lies about the basis for the war. This narrative was made into a hit movie with Sean Penn and Naomi Watts. It was a good movie. However, it simply lacked basis in fact, not disclosing the full story about what happened.

So, what was the problem with this reporting? Well, the *Post* and *Times* suppressed the fact that, first, Plame's name was relevant to show that Wilson's account was less than honest. In other words, it was helpful to full and fair reporting. More importantly, leaking Plame's name was not a crime, since she was not an agent protected by the Act, as Special Prosecutor Patrick Fitzgerald later admitted, an admission drowned out by his sensational indictment of Libby, for lying regarding an unrelated leak. Yes, when our society reasonably should have been examining the basis for the Iraq War and America's unnecessary postinvasion nation building, we concentrated on the political bread and circuses of the Libby prosecution which, of course, built *Post* circulation. But was this brouhaha good for society? Obviously not.

Now, let us proceed to Russiagate, where the FBI surveilled the Trump campaign and the Trump presidency, using the protection of FISA to hide a false and politically motivated narrative put forth by the FBI, again through Comey, to the FISA court.

The absurd narrative, of course, was this: the Trump campaign was conspiring with Vladimir Putin to subvert the 2016 election. Of course, the *Washington Post* deliberately championed this cartoonishly false narrative, to the great harm of our country.

But how was the *Post* to know enough to report the other side of the story, that maybe, just maybe, this may be an absurd tale with no foundation other than a campaign smear by the Clinton campaign? The *Post*'s willful failure to tell both sides to the public is obvious to anyone reflecting on this and was obvious at the time to anyone who knew just a smidgen more than the public.

How did the *Post* falsely report on this? The so-called Steele dossier was the basis for the FBI's obtaining the FISA warrants, allowing it to investigate Trump. In early 2017, BuzzFeed printed one version of the full dossier, which immediately led to the identification of one Sergei Millian as a key witness to the alleged Trump-Russia conspiracy. How did the *Post* treat Millian? Highly uncritically, highly respectfully, and highly deceptively.

On March 29, 2017, before the Mueller Russiagate investigation began, but nine months after Comey's FBI had opened the Crossfire Hurricane investigation, the *Washington Post* blared a front-page story that had uncovered Millian as "Source D" of the dossier, who related the salacious peeing prostitute tale, that is, that Trump had prostitutes pee on a Moscow hotel bed. Deep in the article, the *Post* casually mentioned that Millian was also "Source E," seemingly Steele's alternative nomenclature for Millian. But not disclosed in the article, Source D, the supposed Trump loyalist, had a far different alleged source of knowledge than Source E, the Kremlin insider. That Sources D and E were the same person should have been a stunning revelation, showing both Steele's deception and the absurdity that one source could know both sides of an explosive international conspiracy, while he would eagerly risk his life by blabbing it.

Rather than concluding that the narrative was a likely canard, the *Post* observed in this article that Trump "was unable to shake the Russia story," while portraying Millian as either a "shrewd businessman" or "a bystander unwittingly caught up" in the scandal, and likely "a little of both." Think of James Stewart in *The Man Who Knew Too Much.*

How else did the *Post* deceive in this piece, either by omission or affirmative misrepresentation? If the paper had pursued a superficial look into Millian, it would have yielded the strong probability that Millian was a low-level Russian intelligence asset, or perhaps an asset of Western intelligence, but in any case, not an individual who had access to the inner circle of either Trump of Vladimir Putin.

Moreover, Christopher Steele was reported by the *Post* as being a respected former British spy, but any slight investigative digging would have shown that his main client through his company Orbis was none other than Oleg Deripaska, a Russian aluminum oligarch very close to Putin and for whom Steele wrote over one hundred reports to various U.S. government agencies in a way that helped Deripaska. Was it likely that Deripaska's main U.S. representative would betray Putin's conspiracy? Not if Deripaska wanted to avoid his face falling into his Cheerios. These treatments of Millian and Steele are just two examples of deceitful *Post* reporting which suppressed the truth.

After Trump's election, the *Washington Post* actively assisted the FBI's efforts to trap Trump insiders. In late 2016, around December 28, incoming National Security Adviser Michael Flynn talked to Russian Ambassador Sergei Kislyak to calm any Russian reaction stemming from President Obama's sanctioning of a number of Russian representatives in the wake of so-called Russian electoral interference. Soon after this perfectly proper conversation, David Ignatius of the *Washington Post* leaked that the holdover Obama Justice Department officials were considering prosecuting Flynn for violation of the Logan Act, a two-hundred-year-old act, never successfully prosecuted, forbidding a private citizen from conducting foreign affairs.

By this clever gambit, the *Post* intentionally made Flynn wary. Soon, however, the *Post* published that the Justice Department was now not inclined to prosecute Flynn for this act. So, Flynn's guard was down, but not so much that he would be forthcoming about potential criminal liability under the Logan Act. Then, as FBI Director James Comey admitted, he sent two agents to the White House in Trump's first days, knowing that it was not yet organized and had not yet set up a system of curating and managing FBI queries of officials. The two agents, acting relaxed, casually dropped in on Flynn and innocently asked Flynn if he spoke to Kislyak about sanctions. Flynn said he didn't remember; he didn't think so. Then the *Post* leaked that Flynn had lied, and, more significantly, as well lied to Vice President Mike Pence, who had previously supported Flynn publicly. Quickly, Flynn was forced to resign while the Russiagate narrative was now supported by this sordid trickery.

Trump thus lost his key national security adviser based on a trapping plot helped by the active involvement of the *Washington Post*. So, we ask, is our country helped when the president's key national security adviser, whom he trusts, is removed? How many Kurds might still be alive today had Flynn not been drummed out of his office by the *Post*? And how helpful is it that a president would feel boxed in if he wished to be accommodating to Russia, if he thought that would help America's interests? Did all of this keep Trump from making a deal with Putin to protect Ukraine's sovereignty? Clearly for the *Post*, politics did not end at the water's edge.

In the spring of 2019, in an upset, Ukraine president Petro Poroshenko was defeated by challenger Volodymyr Zelensky. Ukraine at the time was a strategically important "jump ball" between Russia and NATO influence. Clearly, it was in our best interest to fight corrupt Russian influence in a highly corrupt country. Foreign aid for anti-Russian weaponry had been allocated to Ukraine, with Trump's approval, on the condition that the State Department certify that Ukraine had corruption under control. The State Department so certified but did so a month before the newly elected Zelensky was to take office. Clearly, there was now a corruption issue, because Zelensky was sponsored by the most corrupt and violent of all Ukrainian oligarchs, Ihor Kolomoisky. Kolomoisky had pilfered $5.6 billion in foreign aid through his PrivatBank, leaving a $5.6 billion hole for the U.S. to fill. During the time of this pilfering, before 2016, Vice President Joe Biden was America's Ukraine point man for the purpose of fighting corruption.

But Kolomoisky was represented by Biden's son Hunter Biden, while Kolomoisky stole the $5.6 billion under the vice president's nose. Do you get this picture? In 2016, as VP Biden was sure to leave office no matter who won the election, Kolomoisky fled Ukraine. He reappeared after Zelensky won the election, seeking, incredibly, to get back his bank, which had been seized.

Before Zelensky took office but after his election, Trump lawyer Rudy Giuliani learned much about apparent Biden-centric corruption in Ukraine, especially through Hunter Biden. After the election of a new president, the prior State Department certification of noncorruption was now seemingly inapplicable. Trump, clearly not a fan of Biden's, asked Zelensky on one phone call to investigate Biden corruption, while seemingly delaying foreign aid for weapons, a discretionary action within the national security and executive powers of the commander in chief. Now, because of this one phone call, with great *Post* support, Trump was impeached. But nothing about Zelensky's connection to Kolomoisky and Biden's to the corrupt Kolomoisky was ever revealed by the *Post*.

With Trump now under fire, Zelensky was not pressured to break with Kolomoisky. Meanwhile, Kolomoisky not only brazenly sought return of his bank, but also casually mentioned that Ukraine had no choice but to return to Russian influence. We ask, did *Washington Post* suppression of these facts help America, or did it hurt America? How much did Trump's impeachment help Vladimir Putin? If it helped defeat Trump and his policies, and then helped get the more accommodating Biden elected, quite a bit. Ukraine is suffering as we speak.

Finally, in the fall of 2020, the *Post* suppressed the Hunter Biden laptop story, calling it, absurdly, Russian disinformation, even though the foundation was solid that this was Hunter Biden's laptop put forth by a repairman. The laptop showed that, contrary to Joe Biden's previous adamant denials, he actively helped his son with a Ukrainian client connected to Kolomoisky and his venture Burisma. The laptop also revealed Hunter's candid written remark to his daughter that he shared half his fees with his father. Since Hunter was also involved with our key adversary China, this admission is of great concern. Nine percent or more of Biden voters say they would have reconsidered their vote for Biden had they known about this laptop story.

Meanwhile, after Biden was elected, while Russia was massing on Ukraine's borders, Biden paused a large package of lethal military aid approved by Congress for defense against Russian aggression. While the paper had excoriated Trump for delaying aid by a few weeks, it emitted not a peep about this troubling action of Biden, a message to Putin akin to an engraved invitation to invade.

These are just a few examples of American foreign policy issues which have all been adversely affected by deceitful *Washington Post* reporting. It is one thing for a paper to publish partisan op-eds about favoring the paper's party or candidate. That is fair play. But deceit as to the reporting of important facts for the American public is not acceptable. How does this *darkness*, this suppression of key facts, affect our democracy? The *Washington Post* answers that question on its masthead with each of its issues, "Democracy dies in darkness." The *Post* is absolutely correct in this expression.

Since Watergate, the *Post* has kept America in the dark about important issues for partisan purposes. Other papers have reported in similar fashion, proud to be on the "right" side of history, as they see it. This is the bitter harvest of the *Post's* Watergate journalism. On this note, we end our own reporting on *Washington Post* fraud and deceit in its journalism, all begun as it bamboozled the public so successfully in its Watergate reporting. How this can be remedied, we leave to democratic discussion and debate, assuming that such discussion will not be discouraged by major media.

As we conclude this work, we can safely say that the *Post's* Watergate journalism legacy of partisanship and inevitable deceit by omission has harmed America greatly, but we hope not irreparably.

At the very least, we should understand that our history has been falsely reported—by a paper that won a Pulitzer Prize—to our great societal harm. We hope our divided country will heal as we struggle to remedy this serious deficiency.

POSTSCRIPT

WE HAVE DISCUSSED THE PARTISAN and thoughtless cheerleading to which the *Washington Post* resorted to indict W. Mark Felt, known to the paper secretly as a man of honor, Deep Throat.

Felt refused a misdemeanor no-jail plea deal because he would not admit that the FBI had done anything wrong.

On the first day of trial, Felt introduced his nervous, proper wife Audrey to the prosecutor, who was appropriately cordial. Then, Audrey heard the zealous youngster rip into her husband as a criminal, depriving upstanding citizens of their civil rights. As she left the courthouse that day, her daughter Joan told the press that her mother would not be returning to court.

During trial, five former attorneys general, former president Nixon, and former deputy director Felt all testified that, contrary to the prosecution's contention, national security can trump the Bill of Rights to permit warrantless searches, Felt's alleged crimes.

With this testimony, Felt seemed a shoo-in for an acquittal. But the red-hot prosecutor convinced the clueless court to instruct the jury *to presume the defendant guilty* if he did not have a signed approval by the attorney general, not a requirement in 1972-73, only enacted in 1977, after Felt's searches came to light, and only then to protect agents like Felt who acted in good faith.

Felt was furious and continued with his appeal after President Ronald Reagan pardoned him. But Audrey had been hit hard, and the beautiful, high-strung woman, raised as an orphan and fixated on respectability, never recovered. According to her close friends, she spiraled downward, especially after her husband was convicted.

In 1984, when Felt was on an errand, Audrey pulled out his service revolver and shot and killed herself. Felt and his son Mark Jr. did not tell anyone, including Joan, of this suicide until we announced Felt's identity years later. This stoic man refused to induce his daughter's pain.

Felt lived out his final years happily seated beneath a beautiful oil painting of his beloved spouse of over forty years. Meanwhile, the *Washington Post*, as a result of Felt's astute guidance, had vaulted from its second-tier, local-rag status to preeminence, profit, and Pulitzers, becoming one of America's top two dailies along with the *New York Times*.

Each reader is left to decide whether the *Washington Post*'s Watergate reporting, which profoundly shaped today's "investigative" (read: partisan) journalism, has been a net benefit or a net detriment to our democracy.

ACKNOWLEDGMENTS

ALL WHO EXPLORE THE UNTOLD stories of Watergate stand on the shoulders of a true giant, Jim Hougan, author of *Secret Agenda*. Another great researcher to whom all owe a great debt is the late Len Colodny, who, together with co-author Robert Gettlin, wrote the stunning work *Silent Coup*. Other noteworthy contributors to this ever-expanding research are authors Geoff Shepard, Ray Locker, and Phil Stanford. I owe much to them.

My efforts would not have been possible without the highly competent, Swiss Army Knife of an assistant, Allison Baltzersen, who researches, proofreads, processes and accounts for all of my work. Loyal librarian Will Rehling and brilliant associate Ben Pekarek deserve special mention.

Thank you all.

ABOUT THE AUTHOR

JOHN O'CONNOR IS A HIGHLY accomplished, complex-case trial lawyer, who has represented both plaintiffs and defendants before juries and courts, state and federal, throughout the country for over fifty years. He has won numerous professional accolades, including consistent selection by his peers as a "Super Lawyer." He is a former federal prosecutor who wrote key government "brainwashing" and psychiatric defense briefs in *United States v. Patricia Hearst*. As a private practice lawyer, he represented government regulatory agencies in the savings and loan crisis; a major tobacco company in smoking and health litigation; and NBA coach Don Nelson.

Perhaps his most well-known client was Mark Felt, a.k.a. Watergate's "Deep Throat," whom John had so identified in the 1970s and represented in his explosive revelatory article in *Vanity Fair* magazine.

John is a 1968 graduate of Notre Dame University, *magna cum laude*, and a 1972 graduate of the University of Michigan Law School, where he earned numerous honors, was an associate editor of the *Michigan Law Review*, and was selected to the Order of the Coif for graduating in the top 10 percent of his class.

He lives in Marin County, California, with his wife Jan, a sports marketing executive, and has three children: John W., president of a San Francisco investment fund; Christine, a senior federal criminal defense trial lawyer in Los Angeles; and Caroline, a vice president of a Fortune 500 company in San Francisco.

INDEX

F

G

H

Manufactured by Amazon.ca
Bolton, ON

29685519R00234